FROM TRIBE TO NATION IN AFRICA

Studies in Incorporation Processes

THE CONTRIBUTORS

R. G. ABRAHAMS (Ph.D. Cambridge) has done field work among the Nyamwezi of central Tanzania, and has published *The Political Organization of Unyamwezi* (1967) and *The Peoples of Greater Unyamwezi, Tanzania* (1967). He is at present Lecturer in Anthropology at the University of Cambridge.

RONALD COHEN, Professor of Anthropology and Political Science at Northwestern University, has done field work in Africa and the Canadian Arctic. His publications include *The Kanuri of Bornu* (1967) (co-editor), *Comparative Political Systems* (1967), and *Handbook of Method in Cultural Anthropology* (1969) as well as numerous articles on Africa, the Arctic, and method and theory in the social sciences.

ELIZABETH COLSON (Ph.D. Radcliffe) has been Research Officer and Director, Rhodes-Livingstone Institute, Zambia; Senior Lecturer in Social Anthropology at the University of Manchester; and is currently Professor of Anthropology at the University of California at Berkeley. She has done field research on the Makah Reservation, the Colorado River War Relocation Camp, and, over a period of twenty years, among the Plateau and Gwembe Tonga of Zambia. Among her many writings are *The Makah* (1953), *Marriage and the Family among the Plateau Tonga* (1958), *Social Organization of the Gwembe Tonga* (1960), and *The Plateau Tonga* (1962); she was co-editor of *Seven Tribes of British Central Africa* (1951).

JACK GOODY (Ph.D. Cambridge) is a Fellow of St. John's College, Cambridge, Lecturer in Anthropology and Director of the African Studies Centre, Cambridge University. His field work has been among the Lodagaa and Gonja of northern Ghana. Among his many writings are *The Social Organization of the LoWiili* (1956), *Death, Property and the Ancestors* (1962), and *Studies in Kinship* (1969, a collection of his essays including the one in this volume); he has edited *The Developmental Cycle in Domestic Groups* (1958), and David Tait's *The Konkomba of Northern Ghana* (1961), and *Literacy in Traditional Society* (1968).

DAVID HAMMOND-TOOKE (Ph.D. Cape Town) has been Government Anthropologist for Transkei and Ciskei, Senior Lecturer in Social Anthropology at Rhodes University, and is at present Professor of Social Anthropology and Head of the Department of African Studies at Rhodes University. His field research has been among the Bhaca, Thembu, Xhosa, Mfengu, and Mpondomise of South Africa, on whom he has published many papers and *Bhaca Society* (1962).

JACQUES MAQUET (Ll.D. Louvain; D.Phil. Louvain; Ph.D. London) has done field research in Rwanda, Congo (Léopoldville), Tanzania, and Uganda.

Among his numerous writings are *The Sociology of Knowledge* (1951), *Aide-mémoire d'ethnologie africaine* (1954), *Ruanda* (1957), *The Premise of Inequality in Ruanda* (1961), *Afrique, les civilisations noires* (1962), and *Africanité traditionalle et moderne* (1967); he has been co-author of *Elections en Société féodale* (1959) and co-editor of *Dictionnaire des civilisations africaines* (1968). His academic positions have included Head of the Scientific Research Centre for Ruanda-Urundi, Professor of Anthropology at the State University of the Congo, (Elisabethville), Directeur d'Etudes, Ecole Pratique des Hautes Etudes, University of Paris; he is at present Professor of Anthropology at Case Western Reserve University.

JOHN MIDDLETON (D.Phil. Oxford) has done field research among the Lugbara of Uganda, the Shirazi of Zanzibar, and the Ibo of Lagos, Nigeria. He has been Lecturer in Anthropology at the University of London, Senior Lecturer in Social Anthropology at the University of Cape Town, Professor of Anthropology at Northwestern University, and is at present Professor of Anthropology and Head of the Department of Anthropology at New York University. His writings include *The Kikuyu and Kamba of Kenya* (1953), *Lugbara Religion* (1960), *Land Tenure in Zanzibar* (1961), *The Lugbara of Uganda* (1965), (co-author) *Zanzibar: Its Society and Its Politics* (1965), *The Effects of Economic Development upon Political Systems in Africa* (1966). He has been editor or co-editor of *Tribes without Rulers* (1958), *Witchcraft and Sorcery in East Africa* (1963), *Spirit Mediumship in Africa* (1969), and *The International Bibliography of Anthropology* (1956-1963).

JOHN N. PADEN (Ph.D. Harvard) is Assistant Professor of Political Science at Northwestern University. He has carried out field research in Kano, Northern Nigeria, and in Cameroun.

ELLIOTT P. SKINNER (Ph.D. Columbia) has done field research among the Mossi of the Upper Volta and also in Guyana. He has written many papers on the Mossi, and two books, *The Mossi of Upper Volta* (1964) and *A Glorious Age in Africa* (1965). He has been on the faculty of both New York University and Columbia University, where he is Professor of Anthropology. At present he is the United States Ambassador to the Upper Volta.

AIDAN SOUTHALL (Ph.D. London) has been Professor of Sociology and Social Anthropology, Makerere University College; Chairman, East African Institute of Social Research; Professor of Anthropology at Syracuse University; and is at present Professor of Anthropology at the University of Wisconsin. His field research has been among the Luo of Kenya, the Alur of Uganda and the Congo, the Ganda of Kampala, and the Betsileo of Madagascar. Among his numerous publications are *Lineage Formation among the Luo* (1952), *Alur Society* (1956), (co-author) *Townsmen in the Making* (1957), and he has been editor of *Social Change in Modern Africa* (1961).

iii

Chandler Publications in ANTHROPOLOGY AND SOCIOLOGY
Leonard Broom, *General Editor*

ANTHROPOLOGY
L. L. Langness, *Editor*

FROM TRIBE TO NATION IN AFRICA

Studies in Incorporation Processes

Edited by

Ronald Cohen
Northwestern University

.

John Middleton
New York University

CHANDLER PUBLISHING COMPANY

An Intext Publisher   Scranton, Pennsylvania 18515

CONTENTS

vii

MAPS

TABLES

ACKNOWLEDGMENTS

The editors would like to express their appreciation to The Council for Intersocietal Studies and the Program of African Studies at Northwestern University for providing aid and encouragement in the preparation of this manuscript. Mrs. Joanne Schipp assisted in the typing and preparation of this book in its final form, and to her persistence and forbearance we owe a personal debt of gratitude.

INTRODUCTION

Ronald Cohen and John Middleton

INTRODUCTORY REMARKS

This book is an attempt to analyze the growth of political entities wider in scale than those which their members at a given historical period regard as "traditional." For various reasons, it has become the custom that both social anthropologists and political scientists, but almost always in isolation from one another, study this process of historical change as it occurs today. The traditionally comparative viewpoint of anthropologists has led them to disregard analysis of larger nation-states in favor of smaller, mainly non-Western societies; the traditionally ethnocentric viewpoint of political scientists sees these small-scale systems as of little interest, being aberrations or undeveloped variants of "proper" or "normal" societies. Yet both have been concerned with the same basic data, the various changing political systems of the modern world.

The authors of this book, with one exception, are anthropologists, and their subject matter is in a penumbral or boundary sphere between what are traditional topics of concern to anthropology and to political science. This focus of interest, at its simplest, is concerned with the development of and the relationships among the concepts of "tribe," "nation," and "state." All of these terms are used frequently without having been clearly defined, and the first two, at least, have developed highly evaluative and emotional connotations. Nevertheless, these concepts do refer to actual or delimitable social systems and as such merit objective and dispassionate study, both theoretically and from the viewpoint of the historian of twentieth-century Africa.

Among the most difficult to analyze and yet fundamentally important consequences of recent events in Africa have been both the emergence and at the same time the submergence of tribes or ethnic groups as viable entities of sociocultural reality. Their emergence has come primarily from problems of national integration, which are often said to be rooted in tribal as opposed to national loyalties or identification. Analysts often attempt to demonstrate that as politically active groups develop and compete with one another in a nation, they appeal to ethnic or tribal constituencies. This situation exacerbates older differences, creating obstacles to the development of pantribal groupings on the basis of a national framework rather than the constituent traditional or prenational sociocultural entities and loyalties. Such a theoretical approach focuses attention on tribes since they provide understanding of many of the problems of national unity. Students of these matters are concerned with the nature of such tribal units, differences among them, and the ways in which these phenomena produce varying types of problems in national development.

In another sense, however, thése same developments have submerged or blurred the tribe so that it lacks clarity as a unit of analysis. In urban areas, in the new bureaucracies, in the schools, and in the countryside, people are becoming more aware that there are no neatly homogeneous ethnic or tribal areas. Instead, ethnic-group identification is simply one feature among many which differentiate a local population. To characterize these local areas under one ethnic rubric thus may be a distortion of the nature of social interaction in the countryside. Even in areas of relative ethnic homogeneity, close attention to this particular point may turn up memories of heterogeneity that are often quite recent in the oral traditions of the people. Thus, as the ethnic variable becomes important at one level of analysis, that of the new nation-state, it becomes more difficult to maintain as a means of identifying local groups within the state.

A major reason for this difficulty lies in the history of the term "tribe" and its use by administrators and others in Africa, as well as by anthropologists who have adopted the tribe or ethnic group as a focus of analysis. It would seem that the popular notions of tribe and tribalism only emerged in Europe and America after the development of fairly clear-cut racist stereotypes concerning Africa. Earlier travelers, missionaries, and explorers spoke of "peoples," "kingdoms," "sultanates," and "customs," but only rarely of tribes. However, by the early twentieth century, colonial administrators and those reporting on Africa territories were using the term to describe what they believed to be clear-cut and stable groups, each having distinct cultural traditions.[1]

We may note that the rigidity of the conception determines the heightened drama of its change. If there is a clear-cut, empirically real and, therefore, identifiable entity called a tribe or if there is a real person whom we can label the "tribal" African, then of course there must be a sharp change or loss when the African man or woman does not manifest tribal qualities—hence "detribalization" became a problem for research in social policy. And there has been in recent years a spate of writing on the "detribalized" African.

In commenting on this point, Max Gluckman indicates some of the difficulties facing the anthropologist who is attempting to understand African societies and their change:

> [the] African is always tribalized, both in towns and in rural areas; but he is tribalized in two quite different ways. As we see it, in the rural areas he lives and is controlled in every activity in an organized system of tribal relations; in the urban areas tribal attachments work within a setting of urban association. Hence the African in rural areas and in town is two different men; for the social system of tribal home and urban employment determine his actions and associations, within the major politico-economic system covering both areas. (Gluckman 1966: 263)

Here Gluckman is trying to move beyond the oversimplified view of social change embedded in the concept of detribalization to an approach that can provide a framework for analysis based on the varying situations being observed. In this sense, both the traditional (rural) and the modern (urban) can be understood on their own terms. But to arrive at this perspective, Gluckman envisages the actor as "two different men," which he obviously is not, although he may well play the roles of two different "persons." This approach can and does aid in the understanding of the individual playing roles in two separate or semiseparate settings. But it is, we submit, still making assumptions (albeit for different reasons) about the nature of traditional society in Africa that are analogous to those made by the layman when considering these same ethnic units.

Gluckman's main point is the important one that detribalization refers to the process of individual adaptation to a nontraditional milieu, whereas the subject matter of the anthropologist (and others) should rather be the changing social system as such. It is the confusion between individual and societal change that has confused the issue of detribalization for so long. (see also Mitchell 1960)

The phrase "organized sytems of tribal relations" in the passage above merits some discussion. From the early twentieth century onward, anthropology has based its progress as a discipline on field research. Much of the early research dealt with isolated or semi-isolated peoples who could be identified by name and whose name often served as a part of the title of books and monographs written on their ways of life. Sometimes the anthropologist attempted to describe the aptness of the label, the difficulties of finding a boundary that clearly demarcated a tribe, and so on. Well-known examples are those studies by Nadel on the Nupe, Evans-Pritchard on the Nuer, and Fortes on the Tallensi. (Nadel 1942; Evans-Pritchard 1940; Fortes 1945) But since anthropologists were describing groups which did actually exist in semi-isolation, they were talking about something that was real, at least for the people concerned. In describing and analyzing the interrelations among component parts of these entities, anthropologists also built up and documented a case for an "organized system," which helped to make sense of these data and which is one of the major contributions of anthropology to social science in general.

The focus of attention was some identifiable culture and its concomitant social system. If there were significant numbers of other persons who identified themselves as belonging to other culturally dissimilar ethnic groups, they might be mentioned, but they were left to be the focus of another worker's research task. Given the difficulties of learning about one African cultural tradition through field work which necessitates learning the local language, it is not surprising that precious field time was not spent in trying to learn several of these cultures at once. However, no matter what the reasons, the result has become the traditional unit of study in anthropology and has achieved an assumed stability symbolized by the use of the ethnographic present, which is often a conveniently fiction-like way to describe customs, some of which have long since fallen out of view: but in order to achieve a functionalist purity of analysis, it must still be assumed that they are in active existence.

The epistemological basis for ethnic stability in anthropology has not been the political conservatism of its practitioners, nor the myopia of its field workers, both of which are accusations that have frequently been made by non-anthropologists. Ethnic units, or tribes, have come to be regarded as more stable entities than they in fact are because of the logical operations necessary for comparative analysis and theory building within the discipline. In order to establish a variance among societies and then to explain the variations, anthropologists often compare societies as if they were cases or examples of systems that do not exist in time at all. As cases, they are also units or entities that can be counted among a set of similar units. All are assumed, for purposes of analysis, to be systems of the same type; that is, they are assumed to have boundaries—however conceived—and to have some degree of maintenance through time of their component parts and interrelations. But there is in fact no clear agreement about what constituents make up these units nor are there very decided notions about what the boundaries are. Furthermore, even where these criteria are established they cannot be shown to apply universally to all cases, which means that for comparative purposes groups of societies must be reduced to subgroups that share common elements. In other words, anthropologists have always been aware that their methodological isolation of the tribal or ethnic group is in large degree an abstraction, useful for both the gathering of field data and the comparative analysis of ethnographic material.

However, the actual nature of African society is usually more complex, and is increasingly more obvious as the pace of social change quickens across the continent. We visualize it in terms of a set of widely varying social settings in which groups and individuals identified with one or more kinds of cultural traditions are, and always have been, interacting and creating among themselves the bases for new types of groupings that are or will be institutionalized within new or altered forms of social structures as well as new or altered cultural expressions of these relationships. Whether interaction takes place between individuals or groups, and whether there are barriers to the interaction, are the questions that allow us to explore the major variables affecting processes of group formation and change involved in this conceptualization of the social setting and its cultural concomitants.

This conceptualization of social life is not new; indeed, it goes back at least as far as Ibn Khaldun. In contemporary social science it is best seen in the writings on integration theory in political science, in assimilation theory in sociology, and in discussions of the plural society in anthropology. However, these theoretical viewpoints do not easily encompass the kinds of materials which are reported on in the case studies that follow.

THEORIES OF INTER-ETHNIC RELATIONS

Within political science, integration is a concept that usually refers to the processes by which groups interact to form some kind of viable political system. The broadness of the term has, however, led to a feeling that it may not be an overly useful notion. Thus Zolberg suggests that the only reasonable way to salvage the concept of integration is to use it in an open-ended way, that is, to refer to the process of attempting to achieve political order. (Zolberg 1966: 2; also Jacob and Teune 1964)

The problem in discussing integration is two-fold: there is the need to analyze the ways in which existing political systems function, which is not, as such, the concern of this particular book. And there is the need to analyze the ways in which existing political systems change in scale and/or take on new functions as a consequence of economic and other developments; the latter is the concern of this collection of essays.

Discussion of the processes of integration goes back a long way in both anthropology and political science. As far as anthropology is concerned, it goes back at least to the works of Emile Durkheim; but here we may start with the analysis made of integration in Central Africa by Godfrey and Monica Wilson. They based their analysis on the concept of scale in social and political relations. Scale is measured by the intensity of cooperation and communication, both of material objects, of services, and of intellectual and emotional values; and the interaction thus measured may be in contemporary, territorial, and intergenerational as well as historical terms. (Wilson and Wilson 1945, Chapter 2 and *passim*)

The Wilsons' ideas have been built on by many later writers. In general, there are three interlinked criteria relevant to the measurement of the processes and degree of integration in changing political systems. These include what are often called "transaction flow," an essentially geographical concept; functional interdependency; and congruence of values.

Transaction flow refers to the amount and nature of interaction between various segments of a population within or between political systems. The units of analysis are generally such things as goods, persons, or messages (for example, mail, telephone calls, labor mobility, legislative meetings, and the like). By measuring such indicators, one can discover the relative importance and intensity of various kinds of transactions. (See, for example, Soja 1967.) The assumption underlying this research is that the more the interaction between units, the greater is the likelihood of integration. (See Deutsch 1964; Paden 1968:2.) This is by no means an undisputed assertion. For example, Almond and Coleman claim that greater numbers of transactions may simply indicate greater economic development, but because this development is associated with uneven distribution of wealth, it can also be associated with increased tensions or conflicts that produce and aggravate divisions within the society. (Almond and Coleman 1960: 537)

Functional interdependency is a concept well known to anthropologists, and originates with Durkheim's work on the division of labor. In its most simple terms it refers to the fact that differentiation has as one of its possible outcomes the notion of specialization, so that all parts of the system require contributions from other parts in order to satisfy their own requirements and the on-goingness of the system as a whole (Durkheim's organic solidarity). Most anthropological work on the process of integration has skirted this factor. There is a great deal of semispeculative work by evolutionist writers, but it has had curiously little relevance to problems associated with the growth of interdependency in present-day social systems. Apart from the Wilsons' pioneer work mentioned above, it has escaped much anthropological attention.

Congruency of values refers to a sense of common identity that binds people together, clearly a necessary condition for the formation of new nations or states. However, anthropologists have had little to say about what kinds of common value orientations bring people and groups together to produce new ones, and about what adjustments must be made by subgroups which form part of a larger sytem, namely that of a nation-state.

This criticism can also be leveled at integration theory in general. Whether they deal with transaction, functional interdependency, or values, almost all of the efforts have been devoted to a special case—that of the nation-state— and often to a specific set of instances within that type—namely the new nations that are at present experiencing the most difficulties with integration. However, among the anthropological materials that follow in this book there are cases of non-state integration, that of societies that voluntarily or involuntarily find themselves to be parts of larger congeries of peoples. And there are of course well-known cases in the anthropological literature of societies whose constituent parts divide and form coherent polities but whose members still feel some form of ethnic identity and congruence of values with other self-sufficient and similar units. (Middleton and Tait 1958)

In sociology, especially in the United States, the concept of assimilation has been used, at least since the late nineteenth century, to refer to the absorption of immigrants into American society. Park, borrowing a concept from physiology that refers to the incorporation of food into the organic system, conceived of alien people as being absorbed into the community and state "silently" and "unconsciously" until they were ideally, at least, full-fledged members indistinguishable from the majority of the population. (Park 1950: 209)

Just as integration theory is directed most forcefully at the nation-state, especially the developing nation, and is therefore less useful when applied to other situations, so too assimilation theory is traditionally a conceptualization that originates with American social experience. This has involved basically a dominant ethnic group and one or more that have minority status. The assumed goal has been one in which the minority eventually should, or must, or will be absorbed.[2] There is indeed an unwritten assertion that only if such absorption is complete or well under way can the minority group obtain full rights of participation in their new society. But this assumption may not apply at all to situations in which the minority group is able to conquer the majority by force of superior military strength and organization, and then change its own cultural practices to a greater (for example, Fulani over Hausa) or lesser (for example, Tutsi over Hutu) degree. Again, it may not apply to the creation of new ethnic strata from a former captive or slave population that adapts to the culture of its captors, but creates a new named ethnic enclave in the receiving society (Bela among the Tuareg or Kamadja among the Tubu, both of the Sahara). These situations and others given in the cases to follow are not at all comparable on a simple structural level to the assimilation experience of minority groups in America. In other words, the underlying assumption of a goal of eventual absorption of the minority by the majority does not underly all situations in which individuals or groups of different ethnic backgrounds come together to form one society.

Within anthropology perhaps the most useful conceptualization of intertribal or interethnic relationships has been subsumed under the concept of the plural society. It is obviously important to distinguish this concept from the idea of pluralism used in political science. In this case, there is the connotation of groups, rather than individuals, in competition with one another with equal or nearly equal authority and power or potential access to it in the society at large. (See Apter 1965: 33-34.) It is assumed that a common set of political institutions pervades all units within the plurality and that a rule of law supersedes all of them, including government. In such a conception, ethnic pluralism may or may not be involved since it is "groups in competition" (Apter 1965: 33) that form the basic components of the situation. These may be ethnic groups, or industrial corporations, or labor unions, whether or not ethnic groups are meaningful units in the society.

In anthropology the concept goes back to an original conception of a society that involves a "medley" of peoples and cultures which was introduced by Furnivall (1948) to describe southeast Asian societies in which ethnic groups interact only in their economic lives, but who for all other purposes remain separate, each participating in different cultural traditions. M. G. Smith (1960a) has attempted to refine the concept by making it refer to a specific condition "in which there is formal diversity in the basic system of compulsory institutions." He attempts to distinguish plural societies from others by creating a scale of differentiation running from homogeneous in which no serious differentiation of subparts exists, through heterogeneous in which "members share a common system of compulsory institutions (e.g. under a system of social stratification)," to one in which the members of society are participating in subunits that have differing and incompatible institutions in the spheres of "kinship, education, religion, property and economy, recreation, and certain sodalities." Finally, he further restricts his conception of pluralism by adding the qualification that a minority within the society is able to dominate it politically. (Smith 1960a: 767-769)

Like Kuper (1965), we see the concept of the plural society as a useful and stimulating one that can be applied to African societies in both precolonial as well as colonial and postcolonial times. However, we would apply it to all situations in which individuals and groups from differing cultural backgrounds interact in some continuing fashion. We do not see the utility in Smith's distinction between heterogeneous societies on the one hand and plural on the other. Indeed we should like to recast the conceptualization of ethnicity itself through the understanding of processes which are involved in its emergence and change. To do this we have tried to indicate that ethnic units as clear-cut entities are sociological abstractions from situations that very often, especially in Africa, involve multi-ethnicity both traditionally and in the contemporary setting. If such is the case, we then need some concept to describe situations or groupings that are not homogeneous ethnically; and to such situations we would apply the term "plural." Whether there is low or high interaction among groups and individuals from differing ethnic backgrounds, whether there are incompatible institutions or just how much or why they are incompatible we would relegate to research.[3]

The concept of pluralism, however, refers only to the situation itself in which people from differing ethnic backgrounds are interacting to a greater or lesser degree. To complete the idea of an emergent ethnicity we must have some way of referring to the unity of each subpart in the plural society and the developing unity or lack of it in the total plural society. To these processes of change that are embedded in such a situation we apply the term incorporation. We may define the term as the process of absorption ranging from low to high in which two or more groups are interacting. (See Cohen 1965.) The more each group changes toward reduction of boundary maintenance with respect to the other, the greater is the degree of incorporation. Boundary here is defined as any sociocultural, political, economic, or sociological feature that is observedly distinctive for constituent groups in a plural society. Total absence of, or completion of, incorporation is in all likelihood an "ideal" in the sense that no human group is or probably ever was so isolated as to not incorporate others or not be incorporated into some group, at least to some small extent. Nor can we envisage a society where the process is fully completed. This situation results from social stratification, differentiation, and human migration which are constantly producing variations in the ethnic components within a plural society. Nevertheless we find it useful to think of plural societies as more or less plural, which we would explain in terms of the degree of incorporation that has taken place within such a society. The degree of incorporation is the combined function of the number and intensity of social and cultural boundaries within the plural society. To put it another way, we can view the plural society as having some degree of identity and meaning for all its members while subparts have theirs as well. The entire system of parts is in process such that each part and the whole are constantly adjusting and changing their cohesiveness and degree of importance with respect to one another as groups, and for the individual actors who must live out their lives in this complex situation.

In order to provide some comparative scope and intellectual background, our use of the incorporation concept can be compared with its original use in legal and political parlance. In legal terms, a corporation is a group of persons who are entitled to act as a unit. Its use is now well established within anthropology to reflect corporate activities among societies having unilineal descent groups. (Middleton and Tait 1958: 3-4) Using the same logic and frame of reference, incorporation refers to the process and the product of becoming corporate.[4] Polities may incorporate others (usually surrounding or neighboring ones) thus enlarging their jurisdiction, such as a town incorporating a nearby hamlet.

Our use of the term "incorporation" is meant to connote all of these ideas, especially that of becoming corporate. In other words, we wish to isolate the processes by which groups merge, amalgamate, and develop into new collectivities with new and/or emergent identities. We feel that such a process is central to an understanding of contemporary Africa, but we are also of the conviction that such a process is as old as man himself.

THE INCORPORATION PROCESS IN A PLURAL SOCIETY

In order to obtain some inductive basis for developing this multi-ethnic view of society, we have assumed a rough amount of agreement among our authors on the constituent properties of single ethnic groups. In all cases there is a wide set of shared, learned, and at least partially transmitted modes of feeling, thinking, believing, and acting, along with a common set of environmental exigencies that provide a base line at any point in time for ethnic distinctiveness among peoples in all parts of the world. This indeed is the basis for the "culture" construct which has allowed anthropologists to carry out their work and has proven of such great utility within social sciences in general. We also assume, however, that for a variety of reasons inter-ethnic relations are a very widespread quality of all human situations.

To obtain our material we have asked authors who have worked in Africa to shift their focus from the ethnic group to that of inter-ethnic relations and to discuss the most significant aspects of such interaction. Because field work on which these reports are based was carried out using the ethnic focus, much of what follows is still ethnic-oriented, so that interactions are described from the point of view of the original ethnic unit that was isolated for study. From this point of view it is quite clear that the major criteria for distinguishing classes of events that are significant is that of sociopolitical structure. Thus, inter-ethnic relations are first and foremost a function of the authority structure of the societies concerned.

Using such a framework, we have isolated in the case material five different situations. First, there are the acephalous societies (Tonga and Lugbara) whose interactions and participation in a plural society are affected by their lack of centralized organization. Second, there are chieftain societies (Alur and Nyamwezi) in which no centralized bureaucracy exists traditionally, but whose ideology of leadership goes beyond that of local settlements and affects relations with surrounding peoples. Third, there are traditionally centralized states (Gonja, Bornu, Rwanda, Mossi). Fourth, there are traditionally ethnic entities which instead of becoming parts of larger new nation-states have themselves entered the modern international arena as new states (Rwanda, and perhaps in the long run, the Transkei). Fifth, there is the multi-ethnic urban situation (Kano).

Possibly the most fundamental reason for multi-ethnicity is ecological adaptation. Africa in general is not highly overpopulated and there have always been environmental niches within which multiple adaptation develops. Thus, open savannah country can support both sedentary agriculture and nomadic or seminomadic pastoralism; lakes and rivers can support fisherfolk. Such multiple adaptations are utilized unequally by groups within the same area so that differential ecology supports different or differentiating ethnic units. Once present, such differentiation often attracts newcomers into an area where their particular ecology is feasible and symbiotic relationships often develop between the groups. The specialized productivity of each group is then distributed throughout the area as a whole by means of exchange procedures, the most common of which are regular market places to which the different groups bring their specialized products. However, especially among acephalous peoples, blood-brotherhood relations (as between, for example, Amba and Konjo in Western Uganda), or patron-client relations (as between Kagoro and Tacherak iron workers in Nigeria or between Nandi and Dorobo in Kenya), or grandparent-grandchild joking relations (as between Fulani herdsmen and Kanuri butchers in Bornu), or intertribal joking relationships (as between the Nyamwezi and their neighbors in Tanzania) are also additional nonmarket means of attaining trading relations between economically interdependent people.

The result of such multiple adaptations is pluralism in traditional Africa. Peoples of different cultural traditions and ecological adaptations have utilized natural resources in the same geographic region to maintain cultural distinctions between them. One may wonder why diversity in ecological adaptation is not present in greater frequency so that at least some ethnic groups would have been able to develop a wide range of extractive techniques in relation to their environment. Obviously the relationship between ecology and sociocultural differentiation is so strong that even under the aegis of centralized governments, like those of Bornu or Rwanda, different ecological patterns are associated with divergent ethnicity. Conversely, when ecological adaptation is very similar, as among the nomadic peoples of the Maghreb, then no matter what the historical or sociopolitical distinctions among segmentary units, there is a striking ethnic similarity that is very widespread. (E. Gellner: *personal communication*) At the modern nation-state level this relationship also means that since there are generally goals of economic development involving "diversification" of the economy, such policies tend to strengthen or create ethnic divisions within the society and must be cross-cut with other types of activities (for example, a common and universal education system) if such differentiation is to be offset.

All of our cases, no matter what their level of complexity, have some concept of territoriality, but such ideas vary in scale with respect to ethnic groups, which is simply another way of expressing the concept of "situation" since there are many ways to use a common territory, as when groups of differing cultural identities share the same centralized state. At the acephalous level, territoriality is expressed, traditionally, in its most clear-cut manifestation at the sub-ethnic level. Thus Tonga vicinages or local communities consider themselves to be the owners of the land in their local area and this sense of ownership is expressed in the right of local people to be buried there. At the chiefly level, effective territoriality is defined by the jural community which may or may not include only one ethnic group, while centralized states utilize political power to distinguish (a) sovereignty—involving adjudication, taxation, and military levies— from (b) hegemony—a sphere of influence involving subject people who are autonomous with respect to internal affairs. Neither of these groupings is necessarily coincident with ethnic homogeneity, and in general the territory includes more than one ethnic group. Indeed, in some cases at the state level, ethnic groups traditionally overlap into neighboring states; thus Tutsi are found in Burundi and Rwanda, Kanuri in Bornu, but also in Zinder, Baghirmi, and the Hausa states. Only at the more complex levels of organization, as in Bornu or Rwanda, do we find a special place name commonly used for the land in which the polity operates. At other levels if such a name is required, it is constructed from an ethnic label.

An obvious characteristic of the territorial situation is that of being more or less indigenous. By this term we mean that any group which has occupied a territory longer is "indigenous" with respect to the other one. If three groups —A, B, and C—occupy a territory and have arrived there in alphabetical order, then A is indigenous with respect to B and C; while B is not indigenous with respect to A, but is indigenous relative to C; while C is not indigenous with regard to both A and B. All of them may be indigenous with respect to X, a group of newcomers.[5] Although Western aristocratic cultural traditions often tend to favor indigenous inhabitants over newcomers, our data indicates that whether or not a group or population is indigenous to a territory seems to have little systematic effect upon the outcome of intergroup relations. Thus in some cases, latecomers enter as conquerors and set up a kingdom while in others they are aliens or even slaves with varying status in relation to the indigenous population. In other words, other variables may determine the effect of indigenousness or varying degrees of it in the new situation. For example, conquest seems to set a base line in cultural time for indigenousness. The incoming conquerors usually attain a higher status position from that point on, which means that earlier inhabitants, or more indigenous ones, have lower status. However, in general, given roughly equal political power, higher status accrues to indigenousness. What this means is that if there are no other differentials, such as wealth or power, that corrolate to ethnicity, then indigenousness is available as the variable around which there can develop some consensus about differences among the groups. However, as a determinant of inter-ethnic relations, it is fragile in its effect and can be superseded by other factors which interfere with its impact.

A second set of characteristics of such plural societies are those having to do with the demographic features of the component groups. The most usual incorporating situation occurs when the indigenous society is very much larger than the nonindigenous. In such a situation, the most probable result is for the larger to absorb the smaller, all other things being equal. Thus Goody notes that in northern Ghana there have been instances of small groups of Muslim farmers from centralized states settling among pagan segmentary lineage societies. In such instances, many of the Muslims eventually adapted non-Islamic religions and took on the social organizational form of the segmentary lineage society. Such imbalances also refer to cases of individual migrants and/or slaves who are brought into the new society and must, in order to interact, learn the language and customs of the territory they have entered.

The opposite situation is less common, although often more dramatic and visible. Here the indigenous group is small relative to the nonindigenous one. Again, all other things being equal, the culture of the larger group will tend to persist. In Africa such situations are to be found in mining centers and earlier perhaps in the Bantu migrations of east and central Africa. As the mining example suggests, however, all other things are rarely equal, and therefore the direction of cultural change cannot easily be predicted from population statistics alone. On the other hand, in the postcolonial era, as in Nigeria in 1960-61, given a multiparty system and some form of ethnic-based polity, relative size can become crucial in deciding which group will obtain a dominant position in the new nation. At such times the national census becomes a politically charged issue in the country at large and the size of different groups within the nation determines which party will win the election.

The sex ratio can produce a situation that provides the conditions for each group to maintain itself as an endogamous unit, thus helping to perpetuate ethnic differences. If each subgroup within the society has a sex ratio that provides enough women for its males, then inter-ethnic unions are not necessary. The only alternative is to send back to the "home" area for wives to join husbands in the new territory. Yoruba follow this practice in northern Ghana, as did colonial officials who could not find European women in the colony.

One complicating feature here is polygyny. Many African societies are highly polygynous, so that the ratio of married women to men approaches to 1.5 to 1 or even higher, whereas census data suggest on the other hand that the numerical proportions are nearer 1 to 1. It has been suggested that this situation can be explained by the fact that women marry earlier than men, producing proportionally higher numbers of marriage years for women compared to men. However, in many such societies, especially those with high rates of divorce, women pass out of marriage into unmarried old age while men do not, thereby undoing the "balance" created theoretically by earlier marriages for women and leaving unexplained the source of polygynous unions. Using the tribal focus of analysis, such a problem is impossible to solve. On the other hand, if we see a territory as a situation in which more than one ethnic group live and interact, then we may hypothesize that extra women are being brought into one group from other groups in the area. To secure these women, the importing group must have a dominant position. Therefore, high polygyny rates are associated with intergroup marriage and political domination in inter-ethnic relations. Adjacent or subordinate groups who supply such women will have lower polygyny rates, thus creating a balanced situation equal to the actual sex ratio in the region as a whole.

Related to this same point is the fact noted by Goody that women are more open to marrying outside their own ethnic group as they become older, the result of a weakening of kin ties with age, as well as a lessening of desirability which makes the women more open to spouses who are further afield socially and ethnically. Thus where divorce and widowhood are frequent enough to permit a significant number of remarriages, such women may provide a group receptive to inter-ethnic marriage.

THE BOUNDARY PROBLEM AND POLITICAL ORGANIZATION

So far we have simply referred to the fact that people from different cultural traditions have always been in constant contact and interaction within a territory. Now we must ask whether any sense of clear-cut identification keeps people out of or in such territories or the ethnic groups within them. The overall generalization to be made here is that territorial boundedness increases in size and specificity as political control becomes more centralized and differentiated from social relations in general. A corollary of this proposition is the tendency for citizenship to develop as a specific cultural concept along with this same differentiation and growth of territoriality.

Among the Tonga, territoriality is defined not on an ethnic basis, but by the breadth of marriage alliances beyond a local neighborhood where disputes are expected to be settled into an area which Colson calls the vicinage. Outside such an area people are conceived of as aliens whether they share Tonga cultural practices and language or not. Aliens are then divided into Tonga speakers and non-Tonga speakers and the latter are thought of as foreigners. In other words, there is a scale of outsiderness. In Bornu, on the other hand, there are many ethnic groups within the sovereign state, all of whom are subjects of the monarch. Beyond the state are those who are not subject to the administrative and judicial rule of the state and they are divided into types of subordinate or tributary peoples within Bornu's sphere of influence. The several ethnic groups within Bornu all share in their subordination to the state and the administrative mechanisms that connect them to it. Among the Tonga, the people of the same neighborhood, or at most the same vicinage, are joined to one another by multiple links, only one of which is subordination to common political authority. For this reason many acephalous societies do not have clear-cut boundaries, but rather a penumbral or a fading quality to their boundary concept. As multiple links increase in number between an individual or group and surrounding groups, then sociopolitical distance decreases. Conversely, as they decrease in number, social distance increases. Because boundedness is not specific to a single or clearly defined set of criteria, there occurs this "fading" or scalar quality in which in extreme cases groups may have no clear-cut boundaries across wide spaces of terrain involving many localized cultural differences. It should be noted that this is not simply a restatement of the segmentary lineage principles of sociopolitical structure. Peters (1967) has shown that genealogical distance is only one among a number of factors by which acephalous groups unite, although they may believe and therefore report their lineage system to be the most important determinant of their intergroup relations. He suggests that all links between groups be used as a system of indicators for an acephalous society. Such a set would include marriage, political alliance, economic cooperation, ecological symbiosis, conflict-resolution mechanisms, memberships in cult groups, clan or lineage proximity, and possibly others. If all variables are a function of lineage proximity, then classical segmentary theory could predict the behavior of the system; if not, then a more complex intergroup situation is operating, as Peters suggests. Whatever the case, the intensity of intergroup relations is a function of the multiplicity of functional interrelations, and boundaries are defined by significant decreases in these relations.[6]

On the other hand, among centralized groups, boundary specificity becomes closely allied to the political sphere even though it is not uncommon for the culture to lap over such boundaries. The classical account of this situation is that given by Nadel (1942) for Nupe; in this volume, the Kanuri exemplify this same condition. The Kanuri live on both sides of their state boundaries and always have; within the state there are very significant cultural differences between the Kanuri, Shuwa, or Fulani. However, all of these latter groups share citizenship in the state. Although it has a Kanuri-dominated government, the state itself, with its own name, is a societal entity that has primary importance for those living within its borders. These borders can be defined territorially, especially if natural geographic features such as mountains, lakes, or rivers are available as markers. If not, then sovereignty is the specific feature that defines membership, and citizenship unites all members despite cultural differences.

To speak of citizenship for acephalous societies is to do some damage to the term unless it is limited to a subsection of the ethnic group—namely the jural community. However, even at that level, the idea of sovereignty is embedded into a welter of other social, cultural, economic, and political features that relate members of the jural community to one another.

Occupying an intermediate position between the acephalous societies and the centralized ones are groups like Alur and Nyamwezi. One of the most important types of links among the Nyamwezi is their common subordination to a chief. However, such links are embellished by common language, kinship, secret society membership, domestic groups, common territoriality, all of which are viewed not as lumped or diffused interactions in cultural dimensions, but as somewhat separate spheres. Thus, although links to a territorial unit are multiple and overlapping, some differentiation has occurred so that the multiple linkages themselves are becoming separate or semiseparate from one another. Among the Alur, as among the Nyamwezi, links are multiple and chiefship itself is valued for religious (rainmaking) purposes as well as leadership in war, defense, and some degree of conflict resolution. However, the links that bind people together in a territory are ranked so that subordination to an Alur chief, whether ego is Alur or not, is a superior value ranking above others, such as language, differentiated ethnic background, and indigenousness. Thus, for the Alur, not only are the social and cultural links that may bind people together in a territory shown to be differentiated, but their ranking creates a basis for citizenship, since political subordination to a chief is more highly valued than, for instance, a linkage such as ethnic origin.

In summary, the development of citizenship as a specific feature of territorial membership is correlated with the growth of centralized authority and the growth of ethnic pluralism. At the lowest levels of complexity the polity is characteristically sub-ethnic and the bonds that link members are multiple. As authority begins to coalesce towards chiefship and, finally, centralized state organization, the bonds that tie people together begin to differentiate and are at the same time ranked. This ranking places the authority system itself very high, so that the legitimate set of offices in the society becomes more important than other sociocultural features. Often this situation is further elaborated by tying the political to the religious sphere in order to heighten or symbolize the primacy of the authority system. Once coalescence has occurred, or while it is occurring, it becomes possible for members to come from and even maintain a variety of ethnic backgrounds if all accept the primary values of membership in a common polity. Clear examples of this development can be seen among the Mandari (Buxton 1963) and the Madi (Middleton 1955).

Looking at this development the other way round, we can generalize about incorporation. Only if citizenship has developed, can an organized society cope with a large group of foreigners and incorporate them within its system of social relations. Acephalous societies can take in small groups, slaves, clients, and affines, and over time incorporate them into local membership groups. However, to do more, that is, to cope with a large group, endangers the constitutional and cultural foundation of the society. Such societies are based on kinship, common residence in a localized or nomadic group, membership in common cult groups, and common ecological adaptation. When groups arrive that are considered different, they are either kept separate, as with the Ndu blacksmiths among the Lugbara, or absorbed, as is the case with small groups of Hausa in the acephalous villages of northern Ghana. Since there is no immediate structural device for incorporating such groups, such as citizenship, they must be absorbed culturally and socially into the larger group or remain as separate people living in the same territory. Cultural exchange and leveling will take place over time depending upon the degree of social isolation maintained. Within acephalous groups, lineage is more ascriptive and, therefore, boundary-maintaining than residence. Therefore, when stranger groups enter into contact with an acephalous society, the greater the emphasis on common residence as a criterion for membership, the greater its absorptive capacity in receiving and incorporating newcomers. Conversely, the greater the emphasis on lineage and clans, the lower the absorptive or incorporative capacity.

MARRIAGE AND THE INCORPORATION PROCESS

A major indicator for the existence of boundaries between groups occupying the same territory is the presence of intermarriage. In statistical terms, such a boundary is measured by the intermarriage rate which is significantly different from that expected when boundaries do not exist. Thus, the intragroup marriage rate equals the proportion of each subgroup to the total population when there is no boundary and rises to 100 percent when there is a condition of total boundedness.

Except for Goody's paper on northern Ghana, no detailed picture of intermarriage arises from the various areas described in the papers to follow. Nevertheless, some general patterns and their consequences seem clear. Given the fact that most subgroups range between totally free and totally bounded degrees of intermarriage, we can describe the situations that are associated with differing kinds of intergroup relations and which, in turn, help produce differing results. When there is intermarriage between local ethnic groups we can use Goody's term and call it a system of "open connubium." We can also, however, subdivide the concept such that a system can be symmetrical or assymmetrical. A symmetrical system is one in which women from both groups are free to move in either direction. This situation occurs in the relations between Nyamwezi and Sumbwa, who are described by Abrahams as ethnically close, sharing a language and even secret societies, so that a man can continue his cult-group membership even when he moves from one of these groups to another. Thus, not surprisingly, symmetrical exchanges of marriage partners between different ethnic groups is a function of cultural similarities that have developed over time.

On the other hand, open connubium can be asymmetrical, in that women move primarily in one direction but not the other. Such systems are associated with differential status relations between the groups and/or individuals involved, such that we can speak of the marriage as dominantly upward or downward in status direction, dependent upon which direction the women are moving. Both Alur and Gonja reflect the dominantly upward variety of unions in which the politically dominant group has men who marry women from subject groups, but who will not allow their own women to marry outside of the ethnic group. Such an imbalance is obviously also associated with a high value placed on women, either as sources of household labor and/or as producers of offspring. It is also suggested that a shortage of females among the higher-status group could cause such a system to develop. Furthermore, as we have already discussed above, such a system is hypothesized to be correlated with uneven rates of polygyny such that the higher polygyny rates are associated with political dominance.

Whatever the original causes, once an upwardly asymmetrical system develops, a number of likely effects can follow. Goody points out that in such a situation the primary arena of incorporation becomes the domestic group. Furthermore, there is some likelihood that a man's mother will come from another ethnic group depending upon the rate of upward asymmetry. This factor is associated with a man's tendency to learn his mother's language as well as to obtain meaningful and potentially profitable relations with his matrilateral kin, which in turn creates tendencies toward bilateral kinship such that he has rights to land, membership, and mutual obligations to both his matri- and patri-kin. The greater the number of wives thus drawn into the dominant group, the greater the possibility that the language of the dominant one will not prevail in the area over time. In some cases, religious beliefs have been noted to move into the dominant group in this same way. Tubiana (1964) suggests that among the Zaghawa, many aspects of ancestor worship and rainmaking ceremonial carried out by female relatives of chiefs express the historical development of the society. Local non-Zaghawa women were brought into the society because this group invaded from the east and practiced clan exogamy. This latter point plus the political dominance of the Zaghawa led to marriage with women of the conquered peoples who then brought their religious beliefs into Zaghawa society and carried out ceremonies for the welfare of their husbands' clans. As already noted above in the discussion of demographic factors, political dominance is associated with high polygyny rates. In brief, the greater the rate of upward asymmetry between one dominant group and its less powerful neighbor(s), the greater is the tendency for the dominant or higher-ranked group to have more married women in relation to married men. Conversely, this means that less powerful or subject groups are depleted so that there are fewer married women per married men, or in other words only a few men can maintain high polygyny rates and/or men must wait even longer in life to get married in these weaker societies.

The opposite type, or downward asymmetry, occurs when women from a higher-ranked or dominant group marry individuals from lower-ranked or

The "search for security" (Field 1960) in a network of social relations has been one of the factors contributing to the importance of kinship in African societies as well as an explanation for divination cults and other magico-religious beliefs and practices. But the violence of feuds and wars, the unpredictability of misfortune, the constant intermingling of peoples, and economic specialization of craft production and trade as well as the ambitions of individuals to create and maintain large numbers of personal dependents has produced tendencies in Africa for the development of clientage.[7] This is a bond of personal loyalty between a subordinate and a superior often described in kinlike terms. The patron supplies economic values plus status and protection to the subordinate client in return for service, loyalty, obedience, respect, and support in the community. As in the case of women and cattle, the value placed on such security, and its expression in a protective superior-subordinate bond, can transcend ethnic loyalties. This relationship leads in turn to relationships across ethnic boundaries and in some cases to the creation of a new ethnicity. Another value that cuts across ethnic groups within a territory is that stemming from membership in a common religion, such as Islam, or wide belief in the need for and efficacy of rainmaking ceremonials. Other values include common acceptance of the superiority of a particular language or culture within a region such as Kanuri in the Chad basin, Amhara in many parts of Ethiopia, or Swahili and Ganda in certain parts of eastern Africa. This factor is associated with political dominance as is the common value placed on chiefship and monarchy in which the politically dominant group spreads such values to surrounding peoples.

In some cases, the force of common values cutting across ethnic groups seems to be the major reason for their interaction. This is true for Rwanda and Alur societies. For the former, Maquet does not have data on the pre-Rwanda period. It seems plausible to suggest, however, that only a common value placed upon cattle could create or maintain the lord-vassal relations between Tutsi and Hutu. In the Alur material the data are clear. Both Alur and non-Alur placed high value on chieftaincy for purposes of rainmaking, conflict resolution between feuding groups, and leadership in war and defense against surrounding peoples, thus permitting the Alur to expand and incorporate non-Alur in their midst as well as neighboring groups, and creating a tendency for Alurization in the area. In the Mossi case, as we have seen, there is the interesting example of Mossi chiefs using women as if they were a capital pool to provide wives for their non-Mossi clients who were being absorbed into Mossi political hegemony and eventually into its society and culture. From a functional point of view then, cattle and women are serving the same purpose among Tutsi and Mossi respectively.

Other values center around language, culture, religion, and for acephalous societies the values associated with lineage ideology. There seems to be no simple generalization to be made concerning language when groups from different linguistic backgrounds merge, except possibly in the case of the acephalous societies in which only individuals or small groups are being absorbed and the language of the incorporating group predominates. However, as soon as the situation is more complex, it becomes difficult to establish patterns. Kanuri dominates in the Chad basin and yet was brought into the area by a minority who conquered the original inhabitants. Nearby, the Fulani are losing their language as a result of having conquered and settled among the Hausa. Further west in the Ivory Coast, Dyula, the language of a small group of traders, is spreading and becoming dominant in some areas. Trade languages are politically important in parts of the Congo—for example, Swahili, Lingala, Kongo—and although the spread of language dominance throughout a region (especially in its relationship to the extremely widespread African quality of multilingualism) is a matter of specialized sociolinguistic research, a number of variables seem crucial. As we have seen, acephalous societies tend to absorb individuals and small groups and, thus, in such cases the language of a host society predominates. Sex-ratio imbalances creating fewer women mean that wives from other groups tend to perpetuate their own language in child training. Specific uses for the language, as in trade or religion, create conditions for its continuity and possible dominance. There also seems to be a variation in the value of language to the self-image or identity of a people. In groups such as the Kanuri, the Arabs, or the French, the essence and highest expression of their cultural and social worthiness is embodied in a language, while for other societies languages per se seem to be valued less intensely along this same dimension.

It is clear that multilingualism is a widespread aspect of African social life. Wolff (1967) has pointed out that inter-ethnic relations are never blocked by linguistic barriers in Africa. However, he notes that languages, indeed even dialect differences, are ranked so that people tend to increase or decrease the reported intelligibility of languages and dialects as a function of this ranking system. Relating this point to language dominance, we can say that in multilingual or dialect situations, ranking of differences will tend to stratify language differences in value terms. An all other things being equal, this stratification will then lead to language dominance.

This same quality seems to hold across ethnic groups in their ranking of each culture in an area or territory. Anthropologists have made much use of the term "ethnocentrism," but by concentrating on the tribe, they have tended to see ethnocentrism as a product of the cultural group they were studying concerning its evaluation of itself as having a valuable and superior way of life. We do not dispute this point, but would suggest a counterforce in multi-ethnic situations, so that among a set of interacting ethnic groups within a territory there is a tendency for consensus to develop about the relative value of each constituent cultural tradition. This tendency is a function of the power and authority differentiation between cultures and, thus, approaches to zero when such differences are either not present or not accepted.

THE CONTEMPORARY SCENE

In modern Africa all of the processes we have isolated are both traditional and modern. They have been going on at local levels prior to the colonial period and continue to operate today, although some of them are altered by the new social and political organizations accompanying the inception of new states. This recent development has provided a number of common features which have, in turn, affected the nature of inter-ethnic relations.

No matter what the previous situation, today all inter-ethnic relations take place within the context of a centralized state so that all subgroups within the nation must have some relationship to the central government and its bureaucratic agencies. Furthermore, these governments are not only dedicated to the perpetuation of their political order, but to the goals of change. Thus measures must be adapted and carried out that are presumed to institutionalize growth and change in order to make change itself the characteristic feature of local and national life. And both of these features take place within an international arena that makes demands and sets limits upon the degrees of freedom of each of the nations concerned. Thus, Mali tried at first to create an independent currency, but found that for purposes of international trade it is essential for her to return to the franc zone, and Chad has had to maintain forced cotton growing even though it is now African rather than French officials who enforce the policy.

Within such developments, infrastructures, such as transport and communications, marketing procedures and their organization, as well as hierarchical networks of administrative organization, have been devised for using national units as the basic focus for coordinating change. However, the exact path or trajectory of development is dependent upon a plethora of factors (see Adelman and Morris 1967) which in turn affects the basis of inter-ethnic relations within a nation.

One of the most important features affecting intergroup relations is urban life in the new state. Thus Middleton reports that Lugbara lose interest in their segmentary organization and become simply members of a wider Lugbara ethnic group once they are in the city, and Paden suggests that the city itself can become an ethnic-like identification for persons who live there or are from the same city living elsewhere, no matter what their original ethnic identifications happen to be.

Urbanization rates and proportions, that is, the numbers of people in cities over a certain size and changes in these proportions, indicate the rate of change from rural to urban residence. And in a gross manner, such figures tell us something about the effects of urban life on the population. However, the primacy index is probably more indicative of the effects of urban life on inter-ethnic relations. This measure reflects the way in which urban centers are related to one another in size. Thus, a very high primacy index usually means that the majority of the urban dwellers live in one large capital city, while a low index indicates that urban dwellers live in a number of urban centers. In other words, two countries each with twenty percent of the population in cities over 10,000 may in fact be quite different. The first may have only one large city while the second has five. Although their gross urbanization is similar, its distribution is very different. (Zipf 1941; Berry 1961)

Given ethnic heterogeneity to begin with, then the higher the primacy, the greater the tendency for the major city to be associated with an emergent urbanism having a cultural identity of its own. In other words, if there is only one large capital, it takes on a life style of its own semiseparate from that of the rest of the country. On the other hand, when the primacy is low and larger urban centers are spread throughout the country, each one tends to be associated with a developing regionalism even though tendencies for urban cultural identification still exist.

Within urban centers themselves, however, there is a large literature which documents the fact that ethnic differences are very much a part of urban life in Africa, governing residence patterns, intermarriage, and political participation. Indeed, the very nature of traditional society may affect the nature of the urban adaptation. Thus, Southall (1965) has suggested that the number and complexity of voluntary societies in the urban areas is inversely related to the sociopolitical complexity of traditional rural society, and Clignet (1968) has shown how traditional cultural differences create differential changes in the ideology and practice of polygyny in the city. However, much less has been done to understand the way in which city life acts as a leveler of cultural differences among Africans and thus helps to create the urban-based ethnicity reported on by Paden. In this regard, Clignet has shown that in the city, sociocultural distinctions based on traditional ethnic differences tend to decrease as social rank increases, which is explained by a further proposition in which he claims that increased social rank "facilitates access to amenities which have universal value and are uniformly demanded by distinctive sub-groupings" of the urban population. (Clignet 1968) More tentatively, Gutkind (1967) suggests that unemployed men, whose numbers vary from 20 percent to 40 percent of total adult male urban population in African cities, go through a cycle of regarding first their kin, then fellow ethnic-group members, then other unemployed, or anyone else as their primary associates. Although unorganized, he wonders whether these men, who after a while have more in common with one another than not, are not in fact an incipient class whose widespread standards of living and style of life are bonding them together as an urban proletariat. Underlying such developments in the cities are the effects of common kinds of western schooling, common memberships in voluntary organizations (when this occurs), the use and development of a common language, inter-ethnic marriages or other forms of unions, and a host of other interactive situations. Some of these circumstances have been studied, but little is known as yet about the overall effect of such activities on restraining or facilitating the growth of new forms of ethnic identification for people from multi-ethnic backgrounds.

Finally, there is urban feedback. It occurs generally at the acephalous or chiefly levels of sociopolitical complexity when urban practices are transported back to the rural areas to create wider organizations and associations than existed heretofore. For example, Middleton points out that Lugbara ethnic identification as a whole and the crosscutting of the segmentary lineage units by voluntary associations are direct results of returned urbanites. These men have brought "new" experiences and ideas to the rural areas from the cities and are using them to create new organizational forms based on that common experience, a more modern outlook on life, and Lugbara ethnic identification as a whole. This also seems to be one of the factors operating in the Transkeian area.

Cutting across the effects of urbanism stimulated by the growth of national politics is the adaptation of ethnic groups to their incorporation as parts of nation-states and the concomitant growth of ethnic constituencies. In the Transkei, Hammond-Tooke shows that under certain circumstances ethnic politics do not arise and the people move directly from the traditional identification to "national" ones. He explains this process by describing an increase in transport facilities that has produced increased social scale, increased population density, and overstocking of cattle which in turn have produced population movements and migratory labor during which people outside the territory have been defined as Transkeian, not by their local ethnic labels. Furthermore, within the country there has been a growth of national associations, a common language, and no concept of representative bureaucracy in the civil service. Thus civil servants were not recruited on any quota basis nor were they allocated to local agencies on any basis of local representation. Add to this the constant problem of being a subarea within the Union of South Africa as well as the structural fact of being a unified administrative unit, and the result has been a lack of ethnic politics within the Transkei.[8]

On the other hand, Colson describes the growth of Tonga consciousness and ethnic solidarity where no such political awareness existed traditionally. This development seems to have been a function of political-party competition at the national level which made a direct appeal to Tongans as "northerners," of growing antagonism to outside administrators who executed national government policy in Tongaland and treated the Tonga as an administrative unit. The latter was correlated with the inception of a new idea concerning the stranger. From this point on, he was not simply looked upon as a potential ally and addition to the strength of the local group. Instead, a new idea crept into the local culture which suggested that the stranger might be a bad person who could conceivably be trying to take over the country or take it away from the Tonga. As the national political unit developed a pluralist content in Zambia, the Tonga as an ethnic group seem to be taking shape as a solidary group to be appealed to in a special Tongaland home area. However, neither of these units is traditional in any sense of the word. This situation is reminiscent of Fried's thesis (1967) concerning the nature of tribal units: he suggests that ethnicity as a distinct group identification does not develop on its own but in reaction to a wider political membership. We can thus hypothesize that the greater the pressure on a group from a surrounding hegemony (or hegemonies) then the greater is the possibility that such a group, no matter what its own multi-ethnic history, will form into a newly emergent ethnic unit in reaction to such pressure. On the other hand, the fact that all units are now parts of centralized governmental administrations of new nations assures minorities of some measure of security and personal safety. Goody notes that such groups would have been conquered and absorbed into Gonja in precolonial times, but under the Gold Coast and later the Ghanaian administrations they have been protected, which has led to a perpetuation of their cultural distinctiveness. He further notes that their lack of access to local political offices may cause tensions in the future. Thus the inception of centralized governments not only tends to create ethnic politics, it may also slow down the previous absorption of minority groups into locally dominant ones, thus fostering greater pluralism locally than would otherwise have been the case.

Incorporation of local units and the emergence of ethnic constituencies are also dependent upon the sociopolitical structuring of traditional authority systems. At present in the literature there is a conflict in theory on this point, since some would argue that societies organized as centralized states tend to incorporate and adjust to membership in a new nation more readily than acephalous societies (Fallers 1956), while others claim exactly the reverse. (Apthorpe 1959) Since both of these statements are made on the basis of actual cases, it is doubtful that either position is totally wrong. Although the following case studies cannot resolve this contradiction, they do lead the way to a theoretical solution that would allow for a synthesis rather than a denial of one position in favor of the other.

The key to such a solution is to expand incorporation into a time dimension so that we can speak of an early period of absorption (T_1) and a later period (T_2). At first centralized states are brought into new nations as already organized units. Local administration may be tinkered with, but its framework and personnel are already available, making the job of administrative incorporation easy. However, the unit is also able to organize as a pressure group within the new nation almost from the very beginning, thus creating a very early base for ethnic politics. It should also be noted, however, that since administration is in the hands of local people, they are more interested in promoting local rather than national interests. During this same time (T_1), the acephalous society has no means of articulating a traditional administrative heirarchy into that of the nation. Such articulating mechanisms have to be created, either by sending in African personnel from other areas, or by raising local chiefs to a higher rank, making them middlemen between national and local administrative agencies, or by the use of expatriate colonial officials—or a combination of all three. (see the essays in Richards 1960) At this time level (T_1) there is little sense of identity as a corporate unit or ethnic constituency among the acephalous groups, since the older subethnic structural segments are still meaningful. As the Lugbara material shows, such segments can even be used for adapting to migratory farm labor in other parts of the country. Given the fact that not all groups within the new country are centralized states, rivalries and competition between ethnic groups will be lessened when incorporation first begins (T_1) as a function of the number of acephalous groups and their proportions in the population as a whole. On the other hand, the greater the number of centralized states being absorbed, the greater the competition at (T_1). Thus at (T_1) the Fallers interpretation seems to apply.

At a later period (T_2) in the incorporation process, things change probably as a result of westernization and education, cash-cropping, party politics, and urbanization in the country at large. This is less true for the centralized states which still use locally recruited personnel, but who now agitate for significant proportions of bureaucratic and political posts in the central government based on their own claims to be ethnic constituencies. Thus ethnic politics which started early in such societies continues into the later period. Among acephalous societies the later period (T_2) witnesses the development of a pan-ethnic identity and solidarity, which is accompanied by demands that local administration be given over entirely to members of their own groups. The Tonga want Tonga officials, the Amba want to replace Toro officials with Amba ones; the Kagoro want a paramount chief or leader who is one of their own Kagoro people. (Smith 1960b) But all of this has taken place in Africa only after 20 or 30 years of colonial rule and in the mood of nationalist and independence political struggles.

From the national point of view, acephalous societies at this later period (T_2) are more clearly visible as interest groups. Whereas they were administered heretofore by outsiders whose loyalties were clearly with the regional, national, or colonial government, now local officials are representatives of local interests while being executives who must administer policies of the national government. At this time (T_2), the local acephalous society is more clearly an ethnic unit and sees itself as a whole in relation to the nation. Thus at this later period (T_2) ethnic rivalries begin to reach a peak, since both the acephalous and the centralized states are capable of being appealed to as unified interest groups. However, the growth of local bureaucracy among acephalous societies is dependent upon the institutional framework of the nation—its schools, civil-service recruitment practices, modern political patronage, and so on. On the other hand, the basis for recruitment to bureaucratic and leadership positions in the centralized state is still traditional (and so in general is considered "reactionary") or is partly traditional and partly modern. Thus, at the later level (T_2) it appears to outside observers that the acephalous society has managed more easily or "better" and the Apthorpe interpretation seems more applicable. In fact both types of societies are simply following different adaptation trajectories based on conditions of their immediate past.

The ultimate in ethnic rivalry is revolution and secession, both of which have already occurred and will certainly be repeated, especially in southern Africa. Where the intergroup relationships are characterized by caste features and a dominant minority, then in the modern new-nation context conflict is inevitable. This situation occurred in Rwanda and is occurring in southern Africa. When inter-ethnic relations produce a lack of security for the members of one group, or when they feel their status can be raised by either independence or incorporation into a neighboring state in which their group is dominant, there is a tendency for a secession movement and more intense conflict in the new nation at large.

CONCLUSION

In effect, all of the statements made in this introduction have been an attempt to synthesize and draw conclusions from the papers presented in this volume. Obviously, these generalizations are not meant to be "hard" or fully validated. It is in the nature of such a symposium that it be exploratory—looking to map out the shape of a new terrain. Our sample is small and possibly less representative than it might be. However, we have tried to look at a wide range of inter-ethnic relations using societal type as a criterion for such coverage. Hopefully, we and others can now go on to test, refine, and expand these ideas on other cases and with a larger sample of incorporative situations.

On the other hand, even though our generalizations are tentative, we hope that our approach may have pointed the way to more fruitful kinds of field research within anthropology and dispelled the idea that the tribe or ethnic unit is an immutable entity upon whose reification scholarship depends.

NOTES

----

1. The word comes from the Latin *tribus*, originally a third part of the Roman people and used later for the "poor" or the "masses." It has been used by historians to refer to peoples living on the peripheries of stable empires—the Germans at the time of the Roman Empire, the Scots and Welsh in early Britain, and so on. Today the only widespread use of this term outside popular speech would seem to be in the same tradition: Americans refer to Indian tribes, and in India the word is used for non-Hindu aboriginal groups. See the discussion in Fried (1967 and 1968) and in Anderson, Mehden and Young (1967: 29).

2. The theoretical expansion of this view then involves finding variables

that enhance or inhibit its movement through time. Thus Lieberson (1963: 7) suggests that the lower the intergenerational occupational mobility, the greater the maintenance of ethnic distinction, and Shibutani and Kwan (1965) have devoted themselves to working out many more of the relationships between social stratification and the assimilation of ethnic minorities.

3. Another reason for such an open-ended approach, in addition to our desire to refocus observations so that ethnicity becomes a variable rather than a unit of analysis, is the epistemological problem associated with the term society. Society is ultimately defined by the researcher as his way of establishing useful boundaries around a set or sets of interacting roles. However, when it is realized that households are connected to villages, which are connected to regions, which in turn are connected to countries, which are in turn connected to international networks, then boundaries are heuristic devices and in no sense impermeable or even stable.

4. In English law, groups may incorporate in three ways: (1) by statute of Parliament, (2) by royal charter or letters patent, for example, by petition to the Crown as in the case of universities asking for a "charter," and (3) by registration under a company's act. Politically a village may "incorporate," that is, receive a charter recognizing its corporate status in the larger political system.

5. This pattern is found even when there are in fact no true or autochthonous people at all. A case is that of Zanzibar, where the Shirazi "tribes," that themselves entered the islands from the mainland and elsewhere, were "indigenous" with regard to Arab and Bajun immigrants, who were "indigenous" in their turn to European, Indian, Comorian, and recent Arab groups. (Middleton 1961)

6. We should mention that for analytic purposes specified boundary constructions are possible; for example, for politics one can use the jural system at the acephalous level for the boundary of the polity. Other boundaries in kinship, economics, religion, and so on can be devised and applied analytically for subsystem characteristics.

7. See Mair (1962) for a discussion of the political significance of clientage, and Cohen (1966) for the relationship between insecurity and the development and maintenance of superior-subordinate relations.

8. Whether the Transkei is part of a larger unit, mainly that of South Africa or an independent country, is of course the most important issue in this area. If they are part of the Union, then they are an ethnic group as a whole; if not, they are a national grouping. However, the point remains the same for our present purposes because the traditional subparts which had some ethnic identity in the past are now not significant aspects of contemporary politics and cultural distinctions.

REFERENCES

Adelman, A., and C. T. Morris. 1967. "An economic model of socioeconomic and political change in underdeveloped countries." Paper prepared for the Comparative Economic Association Meetings, December 1967, Washington D.C.

Almond, G. A., and J. S. Coleman (eds.). 1960. *The politics of developing areas.* Princeton, Princeton University Press.

Anderson, C. W., F. R. von der Mehden, and C. Young. 1967. *Issues in political development.* Englewood Cliffs, Prentice-Hall.

Apter, D. E. 1965. *The politics of modernization.* Chicago, University of Chicago Press.

Apthorpe, R. 1959. Introduction. In R. Apthorpe (ed.). *From tribal rule to modern government.* Lusaka, Rhodes Livingstone Institute.

Berry, B. J. L. 1961. "City size distributions and economic development." *Economic development and cultural change* 9, 4: 573-588.

Buxton, J. C. 1966. *Chiefs and strangers.* Oxford, Clarendon Press.

Clignet, R. 1968. "The concept of social rank and the processes of nation building." Paper delivered at faculty seminar, Program of African Studies, February, 1968, Northwestern University.

Cohen, R. 1965. "Political anthropology: the future of a pioneer." *Anthropological Quarterly* 38, 3: 117-131. Northwestern University, Program of African Studies, reprint number 4.

1966. "The dynamics of feudalism in Bornu," in J. Butler (ed.). *Boston University Publications in African History.* vol. 2. Boston, Boston University Press.

Deutsch, K. 1964. "Communication theory and political integration," in P. E. Jacob, and J. V. Toscano (eds.). *The integration of political communities.* Philadelphia, Lippincott.

Evans-Pritchard, E. E. 1940. *The Nuer.* Oxford, Clarendon Press.

Fallers, L. A. 1956. *Bantu bureaucracy.* Cambridge, Heffers and Sons.

Field, M. J. 1960. *The search for security.* Evanston, Northwestern University Press.

Fortes, M. 1945. *The dynamics of clanship among the Tallensi.* London, Oxford University Press.

Fried, M. H. 1966. "On the concept of 'tribe' and 'tribal society.' " *Transactions of the New York Academy of Sciences,* Ser. II, 28, 4: 527-540.

Fried, M. H. (ed.). 1968. "Essays on the problem of tribe." *Proceedings of the 1967 annual spring meeting of the American Ethnological Society.* Seattle, University of Washington Press.

Furnivall, J. S. 1948. *Colonial policy and practice.* Cambridge, Cambridge University Press.

Gluckman, M. 1960. "Tribalism in modern British Central Africa." *Cahiers d'Etudes Africaines* 1: 55-70.

Gutkind, P. 1967. "The urban unemployed." Address delivered at Northwestern University, November, 1967.

Jacob, P. E., and H. Teune. 1964. "The integrative process: guidelines for analysis of the bases of political community," in P. E. Jacob, and J. V. Toscano (eds.). *The integration of political communities.* Philadelphia, Lippincott.

Kuper, L. 1965. "Some aspects of urban plural societies," in R. Lystad (ed.). *The African World.* pp. 107-130. New York, Praeger.

Lieberson, S. 1963. *Ethnic patterns in American cities.* New York, The Free Press.

Mair, L. 1962. *Primitive government.* London, Pelican.

Middleton, J. 1955. "The political system of the Madi of Uganda." *African Studies* 14: 29-36.

———, and D. Tait (eds.). 1958. *Tribes without rulers.* London, Routledge and Kegan Paul.

Mitchell, J. C. 1960. *Tribalism and the plural society.* London, Oxford University Press.

Nadel, S. F. 1942. *A black Byzantium.* London, Oxford University Press.

Paden, J. N. 1968. "Conceptual dimensions of national integration theory, with special reference to inter-ethnic (horizontal) integration." Internal working paper 2, Instability/integration project. Council for Intersocietal Studies, Northwestern University.

Park, R. E. 1950. *Race and culture.* Glencoe, The Free Press.

Peters, E. 1967. "Some structural aspects of the feud among the camel-herding Bedouin of Cyrenaica." *Africa* 37: 260-282.

Richards, A. I. (ed.). 1960. *East African chiefs: a study of political development in some Uganda and Tanganyika tribes.* London, Faber and Faber.

Shibutani, T., and J. M. Kwan. 1965. *Ethnic stratification: a comparative approach.* New York, Macmillan.

Smith, M. G. 1960a. "Social and cultural pluralism in the Caribbean." *Annals of the New York Academy of Science* 83, 5: 768-774.

Soja, E. 1967. "Transaction flow analysis and political integration in East Africa." Paper delivered at the Association of American Geographers meetings, April, 1967, St. Louis.

Southall, A. W. 1965. "Voluntary societies in Kampala." Paper delivered at the African Studies Association meetings.

Wallerstein, I. 1963. "Ethnicity and national integration," in H. Eckstein and D. Apter. *Comparative politics.* New York, The Free Press.

Wilson, G., and M. Wilson. 1945. *The analysis of social change.* Cambridge, Cambridge University Press.

Wolff, H. 1967. "Linguistic pluralism in modern Nigeria," in O. Olakanpo, R. Cohen, J. Paden (eds.), *Problems of integration and disintegration in Nigeria.* Proceedings of a conference held at Northwestern University, April 1967, (mimeographed).

Zipf, G. K. 1941. *National unity and disunity.* Bloomington, University of Indiana Press.

Zolberg, A. 1966. *Creating political order: the party-states of West Africa.* Chicago, Rand McNally.

2

THE ASSIMILATION OF ALIENS AMONG ZAMBIAN TONGA

Elizabeth Colson

INTRODUCTION

This article deals with the methods used by Zambian Tonga to create an ethnically homogeneous society in which immigrants lose their foreign identity and it considers also the implications of their growing hostility to aliens in a number of social contexts. It raises the question of what factors encourage people to deal with aliens as potential recruits to their own order rather than as representatives of opposing interests or bearers of a unique and different heritage who must receive a special status.

TONGA SOCIETY AND THE ALIEN

Today something like 300,000 Tonga-speakers occupy the larger part of the Southern Province of Zambia.[1] They represent the largest linguistic group in the country. Another 50,000 to 60,000 live across the border in Rhodesia. Until the beginnings of the colonial period, approximately seventy years ago, the largest named territorial unit found among the Tonga was the small neighborhood community. These neighborhoods still form the basis of much of daily life and have considerable importance in the thinking of people though more and more the central government, first of Northern Rhodesia and then of Zambia, has imposed its authority over local affairs. Each neighborhood was once a ritual community united in service to a shrine or a set of shrines, and some still have this character. Within a neighborhood men are expected to settle their disputes with one another though no formal authority existed until this century to force them to this conclusion. Ritual offices existed within the neighborhood, but political office was embryonic or nonexistent until the central government recognized headmen and chiefs and later developed a local council with an appointed civil service. Leadership was highly situational in the past and is still likely to conform to this pattern. The

Tonga have had little respect for authority, and a good deal of respect for the man able to manage his own affairs without interference. In the past men with wealth, personality, and luck could attract followers from within their neighborhoods and also from a distance, but they had influence rather than authority. On occasion they wielded power because they controlled a following which could be used to exert force. But as they grew old or other men succeeded in acquiring reputation and followers, the power was redistributed among the various contenders for position. It did not stabilize into offices. At the neighborhood level, this is still very much the situation.

Beyond the neighborhood extended a vaguely defined area which I have called a vicinage which represented the region within which the spread of kinship ties and marriage alliances provided safeguards to the visitor and encouraged the settlement of outstanding differences among those who were periodically drawn together by the obligations and rituals of kinship. Within this area men and women could move freely as *banyezi*, members of a familiar community, without the need to invoke special precautions. Once outside his vicinage and a man became an alien who travelled at his own risk or guaranteed by formal ties of bond friendship (*bulongwe*) forged with influential men who agreed to offer protection in return for such advantages as the traveller could offer. It did not matter whether he was a fellow Tonga-speaker or a man of another linguistic group; in either case he was an alien. It was outsiders who first grouped Tonga-speakers together under a common term which only in this country has been generally adopted by the people it designates.

Aliens who speak other languages can be distinguished from aliens in general (who may be Tonga-speakers or of foreign speech). They can be referred to as *Makalanga*, "the babblers." Henceforth I shall use the term "foreigner" to refer to such people, while "alien" will include both stranger Tonga and "foreigners." Only recently has this distinction been important to the Tonga. In the past, for all practical purposes, all aliens were equally strange and equally acceptable. Any alien might settle and rise to full membership in a new community if he found acceptance among its people. The man or woman who built a house and cultivated for one year in a new neighborhood thereby established effective residence as witness the old rule that such a person had the same right as the native-born to die and be buried in its soil without pollution to the earth.

During the colonial period the amorphous political system was transformed to provide an administrative hierarchy more appropriate to the needs of the central government, and this government assumed the responsibility of guaranteeing the safety of person and property of all those within the coun-

try. District offices staffed with European administrators and African subordinates were the local representatives of the central administration. Anyone
could appeal to the district office for protection or for redress. The colonial
government also sponsored the development of another hierarchy of authority directly responsible for the well-being of the local people. Neighborhoods
were first consolidated into chieftaincies, each headed by an official chief
advised by a council and with a court to hear cases arising among his people.
Later these chieftaincies were grouped into three divisions, each treated as a
separate polity, and an attempt was made to develop a governmental appara-
tus for each to administer local affairs. In the early 1960s these were termed
the Valley Tonga Local Government, the Plateau Tonga Local Government,
and the Toka-Leya Local Government. More recently with the transformation
of colonial Northern Rhodesia into independent Zambia, they have become
rural councils.

While this political evolution was taking place, the Tonga were also becoming consolidated as a self-conscious ethnic group in contrast to the other
peoples of Zambia and Rhodesia as they had never been when neighborhood
and vicinage reflected their parochial universe. Their new sense of Tongahood
has clashed on occasion with the existence of the three political divisions
created by the administration: Plateau Tonga, Valley Tonga, and Toka-Leya
then view one another as threatening aliens representative of different politics
though in the past the same network of alliances, kinship, and friendship knit
people together from one end of the country to another without any abrupt
points of differentiation.

During the colonial era, Tonga neighborhoods received and absorbed a
large number of aliens. In a sense, as I have already pointed out, every Tonga
is an alien beyond his vicinage, yet this has not hindered wholesale migrations
from one part of the country to another. Valley Tonga moved in large numbers to the Plateau until the 1940s; on the Plateau there was a general drift
from east to west at the same time. Moves from one neighborhood to another
were common. There has also been an influx of foreigners from other parts of
Central Africa. Many who came to work on farms and in townships of the
railway line which crosses the Plateau later moved into Tonga villages to take
up cash-crop farming. Western Zambians, some of whom originated in Angola, began to appear in the late 1930s and early 1940s as they pressed eastward
to the railway and the greater economic opportunities created by the transportation system. Africans from Rhodesia or from further south either followed the railway north or moved from the highlands of Rhodesia down to
the Zambezi River and across into Zambia to find refuge from higher taxation
or from hunger in periods of shortage or for other reasons of their own.[2]

In the Tonga villages they found ready acceptance. Plateau Tonga in the 1940s identified only two categories of foreigners—other than Europeans and Indians—as outsiders who had no rights in the country. A small number of Ndebele who had been servants of early missionaries settled in a Tonga neighborhood where they succeeded in maintaining their identity for some thirty years despite Tonga attempts to absorb them. Those born in the country still considered themselves to be Ndebele and were referred to as such. Over the years they had sought repeatedly to be removed from the jurisdiction of the local Tonga chief and placed directly under the district office staffed by Europeans. Since they insisted on their separate status and sought to deal with others on the basis of Ndebele custom or European law, the Tonga found relationships with them difficult. Intermarriage was rare. Friendships were few. Tonga referred to the Ndebele as outsiders with no rights in the country and sought to have them forced out. The Ndebele refusal to be absorbed reflected their sense of superiority to the Tonga, whom they had raided and enslaved in the past. It also reflected their awareness of the dominant position of the administration which if necessary could intervene to defend them against Tonga aggression and which made it unnecessary for them to conciliate Tonga opinion. In the Zambezi Valley, remote from district offices, where appeal to the administration was more difficult, the few Ndebele villages founded at the end of the nineteenth century rather quickly lost their distinctive character and assumed a Tonga identity.

The Tonga also found it difficult to absorb the so-called Balovale who had arrived from the west in the 1930s and 1940s. These settled in distinct hamlets, tended to associate among themselves, and sent their children back to the west for initiation. They stood out against assimilation and dealt with Tonga neighbors for economic reasons or through political channels. The Tonga consistently treated them as a body of aliens and imputed to them knowledge of sorcery. Their arrival had been too recent for me to judge their long-term effectiveness in maintaining a separate ethnic grouping within Tonga country, but like the Ndebele of the Plateau they depended upon district office and central government rather than upon courting the good will of Tonga neighbors to secure them good treatment.

Other foreigners who were living in Tonga villages were treated as neighbors rather than as aliens. Several chiefs' courts had Lozi members when they were first established without arousing anxieties about foreign domination. Foreigners were to be found among court messengers in the 1940s. In any post, people seemed as willing to accept foreigners as those born locally. Foreign settlers were encouraged to join villages along with Tonga settlers so long as land was available for their use.

All foreigners, with the exception of the Ndebele, were first generation immigrants, a fact which might indicate that it was the colonial era which encouraged the intrusion of strangers into a formerly homogeneous region. Yet travellers in the 1870s and 1880s report the presence of large bands of Chikunda and Lozi settled in different parts of Tonga country. By the mid 1940s these had disappeared as identifiable minorities. Genealogical data collected from residents of Tonga villages scattered through the Plateau and the Zambezi Valley provide the answer to their disappearance.

Tonga have short memories for historical incidents or genealogical detail and very early immigrants or distant ancestors are forgotten. But many typical Tonga elders, including some headmen, of the 1940s and 1950s were children and grandchildren of immigrant foreigners: Chikunda from Mozambique, Shona from Rhodesia, Lozi from the west, Soli and Lenje from the north. These arrived before the colonial period and settled either in their own villages or in Tonga villages. Though they themselves were remembered as foreigners, their children were absorbed into the Tonga population with which, in turn, they identified themselves. This is not surprising in the case of children of foreigners by Tonga wives; for, given the matrilineal organization of the society, they would in any event be identified with their mothers and their mothers' kin. But children of foreign women who came with the immigrants were as much at home and as fully Tonga as the others. Even in the bitterest quarrels, opponents did not raise the question of ethnic origin though they might hurl accusations of former slave status. All were regarded as equally Tonga by birth, as are the children of the more recent immigrants now settled in Tonga villages.

THE ABSORPTION OF ALIENS

In their introduction to *African Political Systems*, Fortes and Evans-Pritchard deal briefly with the ease with which aliens are absorbed into the general population in differing types of political systems. They comment: "Centralized authority and an administrative organization seem to be necessary to accommodate culturally diverse groups within a single political system, especially if they have different modes of livelihood." (Fortes and Evans-Pritchard 1940: 9-10) In the so-called stateless societies, on the other hand, aliens quickly lose their foreign identities and become one with their hosts or conquerors. Centralized governments can therefore be expected to be associated with ethnic heterogeneity; those lacking differentiated authority systems show a homogeneity which belies the actual history of their recruitment.

The observation of Fortes and Evans-Pritchard is borne out by more recent studies of state and stateless societies in various parts of Africa. In Zambia the two areas with the most highly developed indigenous political systems are also the two areas with the most consciously heterogeneous populations. These continue to stress their alien origins even when linguistic and other cultural features distinguishing them from their fellows have largely disappeared. In the Luapula kingdom of Kazembe, which lay astride the Zambian-Congo border, men identified themselves in the 1950s first as followers of Kazembe and then as Lunda, Shila, Bemba, Shinga, Bwile, or any one of a number of other groupings though their ancestors might have lived for several generations as members of a common polity in neighboring villages or even in the same village. They intermarried. They spoke the same language. They worked and played together. Still they boasted of their different origins. (Cunnison 1959: 30-61) In the equally strong Lozi kingdom of the upper Zambezi, men also stressed their different origins while they claimed membership in the same political unit. (Gluckman 1965a: 27-30)

The crucial factor lying behind this maintenance of ethnic diversity appears to be the fact that in the kingdoms men could regard themselves as subjects of a king who would guarantee them against injury in return for loyalty and service. They stressed the primacy of their ties to the political hierarchy of the kingdom over their neighborly ties to fellow citizens. They based their political loyalties on common allegiance rather than on participation in a common culture. The obverse of the coin may lie in the willingness of a ruler to admit to diversity among his subjects, for this underlined his success as a conqueror or his ability to attract followers from beyond his realm. Either redounded to his credit and reknown. He and his immediate allies also had a motive in stressing their own separation from the rest of the population and their exclusive right to office and rank based on their particular origin, which provided a model for ethnic claims to others in the kingdom.

In noncentralized societies men had to secure themselves by other means than allegiance to a ruler if they wished to venture among strangers. When they settled, they sought to entrench their position by an appeal to the common values of kinship and neighborhood. In societies such as the Tonga, the newcomer was safe only if he merged with the rest of the community and sought to develop with its people the same kind of ties as those which bound them to one another. All members of a neighborhood were subject to the same disciplines and met the same misfortunes; there was little or no advantage and some disadvantage to be found in seeking to remind one's neighbors of countervailing allegiances to other areas and possible enemies.

Though the Tonga have long been part of the centralized state of Zambia, the methods by which aliens have been absorbed are still fully available to investigation. When Tonga move to a new area they employ the same devices for grafting themselves on to the new community as they use in absorbing the foreigner or alien who settles among them and indicates his willingness to be treated as a recruit.

The newcomer in a Tonga neighborhood is fair game to the first comer, and the first comer arrives rather promptly. He views the stranger as a treasure trove, as an asset to be used in advancing his own interests; for a stranger has property, or he can give service, or he has links to the rest of the world which can be exploited. In the distant past, the stranger's vulnerability to manipulation depended greatly on whether he came alone or with a following. In the first instance he was liable to enslavement on some pretext. In the latter it was reasonable to enter into an alliance with him. Today since no one may be enslaved, alliance is the common tool for subjugating the stranger, but the stranger may be viewed as patron, equal, or client depending upon his strength and status. The poor man is given accommodation and food for a limited period and is then expected to begin working for his host, who in turn, sponsors him before the rest of the community. The wealthy man or the man who holds a government or other post is an equal or superior who is expected to repay his sponsor's attentions with favors and gifts. It is the wealthy man of status who is most likely to be referred to by his sponsor as *mwenzu wangu*, which may be variously translated as "my alien," "my stranger," "my guest." Innumerable Tonga proverbs play upon the desirability of being visited by strangers and the good treatment which should be extended to the stranger/guest. Between host/sponsor and stranger there is a finely balanced reciprocal relationship, with the host quick to remind his stranger of his debt of gratitude and his obligation to be generous. Even a man with little local prestige may serve as a host-sponsor, but a stranger is likely to transfer his chief alliance to some more powerful man as he learns the local scene. Men of power compete with one another to attract stranger-guests just as they compete with one another for local followers.

The stranger who is only a short-term visitor may go no further and depart again, though he may create a permanent bond friendship with his host to provide for future visits. Bond friendships may exist between men in the same neighborhood and vicinage but they are most common either between those who live at a distance or between an alien temporarily employed in an area and some local man.

If the stranger stays, the initial arrangement is only the preliminary move in a game which has as its end the transformation of the stranger into a member of the community. It is carried out by providing him with a variety of roles which permit him to interact in differentiated personal terms with the maximum number of local people and which obviates any further use of the host/sponsor as a mediating link with others in the community. In effect the newcomer is assigned a place within the ongoing structure of social life on the same terms as others in the neighborhood. This is done by his cooption as clansman and kinsman. A number of devices exist for creating what we can regard as quasi-kinship where no kinship is known to exist. The most far reaching in its effects is the placing of a person within the clan system.

The Tonga have some twelve clans whose members are spread throughout the country on a nonlocalized basis. These clans are in fact conceptual models rather than actual groupings of people. They provide the permanent framework of the Tonga social order though some Tonga are sceptical of their real existence.[3] Each clan is associated with a number of natural species. For convenience I shall call these totems, though clans have no rituals relating to their totems and do not regard them as sacred. Only rarely does the name of a clan coincide with the name of one of its totems, but clan praise names do play upon the totemic associations and men may call themselves "people of the totem" as well as by the clan name. Clans are linked together in a joking-relationship which has broad implications; here again the joking plays upon the characteristics of the totem species and their alleged enmity or fellowship. In the past men were expected to shout out their clan names as they entered a foreign village alerting fellow clansmen or joking-clansmen that here was someone in need of hospitality. Today this is not done, but any stranger who can boast a clan can find those upon whom he has a claim for hospitality.

The system restricts the number of clans that may be recognized in any one vicinage. New clans do not emerge through segmentation and immigrants do not introduce new clans to those known in the vicinage. Anyone who belongs to a clan must therefore belong to a clan already present which is thought to have come into existence with the beginning of things. The Tonga themselves have no trouble in associating themselves with an appropriate clan when they move from one vicinage to another though clan names and clan totems may be very different in different parts of the country. In the upland area around Mpwe, the Bantanga clan claims leopard as its major totem; elsewhere leopard is associated with the Bansaka. Throughout much of Tonga country Bakuli, Batenda, and Baaunga are alternative names for the same clan which has elephant as its major totem. People of Mwemba claim these as three different clans, and the Bakuli here have dog as their totem. The Tonga who seeks his clan in some other area apparently first attempts to follow up his clan name and then accepts whatever totems are attached to it in the new area. If he can find no clan of the same name, then he uses a major totem as grounds for attaching himself to some clan in the new area.

Foreigners are more difficult to incorporate into the local system, though many who reach Tonga country come from areas which have clans as important institutions. Nevertheless equation between one clan and another is not always easy. In northern Zambia the local systems contain forty or more clans; elsewhere both clan names and totemic species are different from those found among the Tonga. Ndebele and some others do not have totemic clans. Lozi lack both totemic clans and unilineal descent groups.

Willynilly those who settle among the Tonga find themselves forced into the Tonga system. Perhaps the stranger has a totem which links up with a minor totem of some Tonga clan and so he finds his place. Some attribute may be seized upon as indication of totemic identification and this is then extrapolated to create clanship. When all else fails the foreigner can be given his patron's clan, just as slaves in the past received the clan of their owner. Tonga are well aware that their clans have been recruited by adoption as well as by birth, and though the clan dogma is one of friendship and mutual aid based on common descent this is only a dogma. No matter how different the system is from which the foreigner stems, he can be absorbed. Those from patrilineal areas discover that their clans have become matrilineal by definition as they are equated with local clans. I do not know if Chikunda have clans in Mozambique or other parts of Zambia where they settled. All I could trace among the Tonga are said to have come as elephant hunters and dealers in ivory, and all are reported as having belonged to Elephant clan.

Each person should know his father's clan, which has special rights and obligations in respect of him as well as his personal clan; this multiplies the number of definable roles he may fill in the local society. Children of European fathers belong to their mothers' clans as does any Tonga child. They are not cheated of a paternal clan by their father's origin. Various people have told the Tonga that Europeans, especially the English, are Lion clan. Their children are therefore children of the Lion clan.

The Tonga are well aware that in using clanship in this way they are condoning a fiction of common descent. They are cynical about the possibility of knowing another's real clan if he comes from another area and say that a stranger always reports his clan as that of some powerful man of the locality. They are sceptics about the clan associations of various foreigners settled among them. They doubt that the difference in clan names and clan totems in different parts of the country are variants on an underlying unity, and suspect that they are due to real differences in origin. Still when it is convenient they prefer to behave as though clanship created a universally reorganized primary relationship and through it to extend the range of classificatory kinship. By playing upon the fiction of clan identity they can deal with any alien in kinship terms—as children, parents, grandparents, grand-children, siblings, spouses, affines—and thereby justify claims upon him. As a rule they play fair. If the stranger accepts his clan assignment and abides by the rules, he too can appeal to his neighbors in kinship terms and remind them that he deserves a hearing. Thus clanship gives entree into a form of quasi-kinship exchange with many people in the neighborhood, and the jok-ing-relationships which exist between clans extend the realm of known rela-tionships to encompass almost all one may encounter.

It is the fixed number of clans which associates the stranger as a social being with other residents of the vicinage and prevents him from maintaining a separate status. The small number of clans maximizes the efficiency of the system in promoting this end. It is notable that in parts of Zambia where kingship or chieftainship existed and men associated themselves as king's men or chief's men rather than as neighbors, either clans do not exist, as among the Lozi, or the number of clans proliferate with strangers introducing new clans to the local system.[4] Only among the Tonga who emphasized the spread of kinship ties, a general lack of authority and office, and full egalitarian manipulation of the social network does the limitation on clan number occur. With only twelve clans in existence, and with the rule of exogamy compelling mixed descent and mixed marriage, the probability is very great indeed that anyone who has a clan can deal with the great majority of others in his vicinage on the basis of "kinship" expectations.

Clanship, however, is not true kinship, and on occasion kinsmen of one's lineage are carefully distinguished from clansmen. Clanship does create an immediate known bond to other people who can be called upon to fill kin-ship roles when true kin are lacking. It regulates relationships by the use of terms of address and reference which emphasize the values of the world of kinship.

A more personal kind of fictional kinship also provides for the placement of an outsider within a local kinship network. Here entrance upon the fiction-al kinship is a matter of choice. Any newcomer may be invited to name a newborn child. A midwife has the option of naming a baby she delivers. Friends give their names to one another's children. Those who bear the same name, especially if one is named for the other, are thought to have a special relationship and may assume one another's kinship usages. The donor of a name is called "child" by his namesake's parents, and other kin may also speak of and to him as though he were the child. The giving of the name thus sets up a reciprocal relationship of mutual responsibility both between the namesake and between the namegiver and the parents of the child. This last is the important immediate aspect of the custom and has somewhat of the same effect as the creation of a compadre-commadre relationship in Latin America. (See Mintz and Wolf 1950)

Clanship and namesaking permit the newcomer to take advantage of the local situation since they allow him to enter into and play upon the network of social ties within which other inhabitants are already enmeshed. But they deal with fictional, not real, relationships, and this is recognized by the various parties involved in playing the situation. The newcomer makes a different commitment to the system when he marries locally, as he then substitutes legal relationships for fictional ones. In the past Tonga have been as prepared to marry their women to resident foreigners as to Tonga in the neighborhood and more willing than if marriage to Tonga in distant neighborhoods were involved. The exchange of kinswomen as wives commonly reinforced alliances between strong men in the precolonial period—a patron gave a wife to his slave or adherent. Intermarriage with settled aliens, including foreigners, is still common. With marriage the newcomer enters upon highly specific roles where the standards to be met are the same for all affines whatever their origin.

In the past, absorption and obliteration of an alien status was the common fate for those who entered the Tonga ambit. Slaves, invaders, refugees have all been subject to the pressure of Tonga neighbors who first called them visitors or guests, then introduced them to the idea and responsibilities of clanship and ended by submitting them to the discipline of kinship. In the next generation it was clan and kin affiliation which was remembered rather than any association with alien group or alien home.

TONGA INTEGRATION IN NEW VICINAGES

The general Tonga preference for dealing with strangers in personal terms and as potential members of their own society rather than as representatives of some foreign community was apparent in recent years when large numbers of Valley Tonga were resettled in new vicinages as their old territory was flooded by Lake Kariba. Kariba Dam was finished in 1958 at which time the resettlement was provisionally completed. Research in 1962-1963, concentrated on four settled neighborhoods, gives some basis for assessing the speed with which new ties are created and the degree to which one device may be seen as more effective than another in particular situations where people are in contact with aliens.

Musulumba Village of Mpwe neighborhood, formerly in the Upland hills behind the Middle River region[5] had been moved 100 miles northeast to the Lusitu country downstream from Kariba dam. With them went 6,000 other

Upland and Middle River people with whom they had old established ties. Resettlement pushed them all together into a small area where close contact was almost inevitable. By 1962-63 intermarriages were common; kinsmen and clansmen exchanged frequent visits and attendance at funerals included people who formerly would have dropped away; half-forgotten ties were reactivated. Resettlement, however, also brought Mpwe villagers into close contact with two other kinds of people. They were settled close to villages of Shona-speakers who were long residents of Lusitu and also to a little settlement of alien traders and employees working for shops, school, dispensary, and a boat-building establishment. Many of the aliens were foreigners who were strangers both to the Lusitu and to one another. With the foreigners of the settlement, Mpwe people formed both bond friendships and name friendships; Mpwe people sought to remind the foreigners of clan ties and called them by kinship terms; two Mpwe women had already married foreign men. With the inhabitants of the Shona villages relationships were more formal, though it was notable that in seeking to come to terms with the Shona, the Mpwe people ignored the village headmen and the local chief. Instead they sought personal ties with individual Shona from whom they could then borrow fields, beg for food and use as intermediaries. In return they expected to help with gifts or assistance with ploughing. Some apparently first tried to develop friendly claims on the basis of clanship. They were successful in that they could equate their own clans with Shona clans with a little effort, but the Shona who were here on their own ground and in numbers were prepared to give no more than an amused nod to Tonga tracing of clan identities. Mpwe Tonga retaliated by doubting the genuineness of Shona clans—since Shona claimed to take their father's clan they could have no clans: a legitimate clan could only be based on matrilineal descent. In conversation with Shona they continued to play on clan identities even though they regarded the matter as a hoax. For real advantage they put their trust in bond friendship which involves a balancing of reciprocal gift and service between specified partners. Here the Shona were prepared to cooperate, for a bond friendship meant the acceptance of obligations to one particular Tonga friend rather than the diffuse network of obligation to many people created by clanship. In 1963 Mpwe had 51 men and 82 women over the age of twenty. These had entered into 35 bond friendships since resettlement. Five friendships were with fellow Tonga. Thirty were with foreigners, either Shona villagers or employees at the settlement. I do not have precise data for Mazulu village, a Middle River village resettled in Lusitu,[6] but its people also formed a large number of bond friendships after resettlement and the majority of these seem to be with Shona villagers. By 1963 neither Mpwe nor Mazulu had inter-married with Shona.

Chezia, a resettled Middle River community, though much larger in popu-lation than Mpwe, formed a few new bond friendships after resettlement. It moved some fifteen miles inland along the tributary river at whose juncture with the Zambezi it had formerly been settled. In its new vicinity it adjoined Tonga villages which were in a sense part of its old vicinage. The river was the route Chezia people had used for generations to reach kinsmen on the Pla-teau. More recently it had been their route to wage work. A few older Chezia men had bond friends in villages along the route. These friendships were strengthened after resettlement with renewed exchanges of gifts. Most people preferred to furbish up ties of kinship some of which had been on the point of slipping from memory. Lineage segments which had become almost inde-pendent drew together. People reminded one another of half-forgotten affinal links. Those who had no such ties through which to orient themselves to their new neighbors used instead the general framework of the clan system. Mar-riages between newcomers and old residents quickly took place to link the two groups more closely together. Chezia informants said there was no point in developing bond friendships with fellow clansmen, kinsmen or affines. Few foreigners had come to work in the vicinity. Chezia may have had some 360 adults in its population in 1963, but these had made only 10 new bond friendships in the period after resettlement.

Siameja, an Upper River community, was the only one of the four neigh-borhoods whose people dealt with their new neighbors as a corporate group rather than in personal terms. Siameja again had moved inland along its river and settled on its old route to the Plateau in an area occupied by other Tonga. Few foreigners reached the area after resettlement. In this Siameja's situation was comparable to that of Chezia. But Siameja is in the one Tonga area where people have some concept of chieftainship and office and some respect for rank and authority, and where there is at least a minimum devel-opment of historical interest. Siameja legitimated its corporate relationship to the people of the new area by explaining how in the distant past Siameja of the Zambezi and the leader of the people of the hill area had been kinsmen and allies. Siameja stayed to guard the river and warn of Ndebele attacks, while his henchman went to the hills to watch for Lozi raids stemming from the east. When Ndebele struck the river, Siameja took refuge in the hills; when the Lozi drove down through the hills, his henchman found haven with Siameja at the river. Both were of the same clan and therefore rightfully they worked together, but Siameja was the superior. After resettlement, Siameja villagers asserted their rights to the new area as followers of Siameja and did not immediately attempt to obtain individual advantages by forming special links with the older inhabitants as did Chezia and Mpwe people. It was the assistant headman of Siameja who married a local woman in the nearest village and used his affinal ties to strengthen his position as a channel of contact and negotiation. It was the assistant headman again who developed several bond friendships with the foreign traders who opened a shop in the village, and with one or two of the foreign technical assistants stationed in the area. These men secured their position in the neighborhood through him, and he in turn expected them to consult him and to give him gifts in cash and kind. Where Mpwe and Chezia people ignored headmen, their own and others, as channels of negotiation and entered freely into bond friendships and affinal relationships or stressed their own clan and kinship links to relate them to such strangers as promised advantage, Siameja viewed itself as a unit and used its formal leaders as mediating links for the rest of the population.

STRANGER GUESTS AND THREATENING FOREIGNERS

The Tonga still tend to be remarkably tolerant of the stranger amenable to local control even under circumstances where they might be expected to show a self-interest that would lead them to challenge the foreigner and his competition.

When Lake Kariba was formed, the then colonial government protected Valley Tonga interests by clauses incorporated in the Order in Council governing the use of the lake. Only Valley Tonga were permitted to fish commercially on the Zambian side of the lake. Europeans and other Africans, including Plateau Tonga and Toka-Leya, were excluded from its shores if they fished for profit. During the next several years numerous Valley Tonga, with government encouragement and assistance, invested in nets (and some also in boats and motors) and began to devote themselves to commercial fishing. A 1963 amendment to the Order in Council opened commercial fishing to other Africans. In 1965 fishing was largely in the hands of foreign Africans whose long experience in the Nyasa, Bangweulu, Mweru, Luapula, and Kafue fisheries gave them a competitive advantage. They were more efficient, they maintained nets and other equipment at a higher standard, they were more geared to regular delivery of fish for a commercial market. Many Tonga abandoned the fisheries to the foreigners. With this they abandoned a source of cash income in a time when they were very conscious of the difficulties of obtaining money to maintain their current standard of living. A shortage of work in Zambia and the closing of Rhodesia to Zambian workers made labor migration a doubtful resource and left people more dependent than in the past upon local sources of income. Foreigners prospering from local fishing still seemed to rouse little hostility. Most foreigners were scattered in small fishing camps along the lake, and had already acquired ties of friendship with the heads of nearby Tonga homesteads. The Tonga neighbor referred to them with pride as "my strangers" or "my visitors" and stood sponsor for them on the local scene. The fishermen bought meal and beer and other produce from local people, and thus some of their earnings went into local pockets. A sponsor who received supplies of fish, occasional gifts of cash, and a share in the beer purchased by his "visitors" may have felt that he reaped a profit from their fishing without risking his own funds on equipment or his own life on the lake. He also avoided some of the importunities from kin and friends which he would meet as an active fisherman whose gains could be computed. A sponsor may therefore have gained more than he lost from the presence of his foreigners, and his support ensured acceptance by others. His tolerance reflects Tonga approval of the foreigner who has something to give and can be induced to share. It does not matter if his gains are made locally if they are seen as assets to be tapped by people of the community through their personal claims upon him.

In the few large fishing camps where Tonga and foreign fishermen lived side by side, they were also said to be on good terms. A headman living near such a camp remarked of Lozi fishermen, "After all, we and the Lozi really are one people from long ago." Of the Bemba fishermen, he said with equal cordiality, "We and the Bemba can always laugh together."

This tolerance of foreigners on the local scene is the more striking as at this very time strong opposition to foreigners appeared in other contexts. Increasing hostility to the outsider developed with an increasing awareness of the national political scene, the growth of Zambian nationalism, and the organization of African political parties.

The majority of Tonga backed the African Nationalist Party (ANC), the first major African party, which was founded and headed by an Ila from a neighboring district within Southern Province. Ila and Tonga are dialects of the same language. In the context of towns and farm compounds, Ila and Tonga group themselves as one people in contrast to the Bemba and other peoples of Zambia and Central Africa whom they encounter. The formation of the United National Independence Party (UNIP) under a Bemba-speaking leader from the north did not shake Tonga allegiance to ANC and its leader. A few joined the new party, but the bulk of the rural people remained staunch adherents of ANC. They gave various reasons for preferring ANC over UNIP, some of which echoed the propaganda of party leaders. They said that since ANC was the first African party, its leader had created the post of national leader and this belonged to him just as a chief's position belonged to the chief who had first created it. The founder of a new party who attempted to usurp the old leader's following was comparable to the upstart clerk who tried to replace his chief. They also said that the ANC leader was their choice because he was one of them: he spoke the same language and in fact was a Tonga to all intents and purposes. Valley Tonga in 1962-1963 and again in 1965 usually voiced their solidarity with ANC and its leader in their terms, though in other contexts and on other occasions they showed the greatest apathy for chieftainship and considerable antipathy for their fellow Tonga of the Plateau whom they said were like the Ila.

This antipathy to the Plateau Tonga was in existence at least by the 1950s and little in recent years has undermined Valley opposition to Plateau Tonga claims to be more sophisticated, more advanced, and more truly Tonga. In 1957 elders of one Valley neighborhood wrote to the district office demanding the removal of a Plateau Tonga technical assistant stationed near them. They declared against having any other Plateau Tonga stationed in their country as teachers or technical assistants and said they preferred men from Eastern Province, Northern Province, or Barotseland for they had found such people to be good and able men who did not despise those among whom they worked. The one thing they could not abide, so they said, was a Plateau Tonga.

Their willingness to follow the ANC leader therefore did not signify their stand for ethnic solidarity and the south against the north on all occasions. In 1963 many complained of both Valley and Plateau teachers and technical assistants and said they preferred Bemba, Sala, Shona, or Ndebele workers whom they praised individually as friendly and considerate people. In contact with such foreigners, they tended to rate them highly as giving better treatment than expected, for a foreigner as such had no reason to serve them as well and still did. On the other hand they undervalued fellow Tonga who seemed never able to meet the expectations held of them because they were seen as kin and neighbors who should be bound by the values of kinship and neighborliness and only secondarily by the demands of their posts or by the values of the newly emerging elite.

The local foreigner was the good foreigner and by extension his people would be praised for producing good men whom one could deal with. When it came to national politics, this formulation no longer held. The most commonly voiced objection to UNIP was its domination by foreigners, especially Bemba. Some said they had no objection to UNIP governing in Bemba country. It was only right that it should rule its own people. The Southern Province, however, was not Bemba country but Tonga-Ila country and here it was right for ANC to rule. UNIP was foreign and could have no rights in the south. The fact that the chairman and several other national officers of UNIP were Plateau Tonga and that most of its local officials were Tonga did not affect this image—the party was foreign and it was evil. By extension, anything associated with UNIP was also seen as evil and threatening. Local foreigners, even those usually accepted, were threatened if they were suspected of being agents of UNIP or of being favorable to its cause. They were reminded that they were foreigners with no right in the country, and told they would be driven away.

On the Plateau the build-up of the struggle for independence through the 1950s and early 1960s combined with rivalry between African parties made the position of resident foreigners uneasy even if they attempted to stay out of politics. This was especially true if they held some official position which linked them to the outside. Some school teachers from other provinces were derided by their students, ostracized by their neighbors, and in a few instances forcibly expelled from their schools. "Tongaland for the Tonga" became a rallying cry for the first time.

For the first time, perhaps, the foreigner was being seen as a complete alien, though for the most part those foreigners who entered the local system and responded to neighborhood pressures continued to be the welcome strangers who graduated from alien to kinsmen to native. Public foreigners, i.e. those familiar only through press, wireless, and party propaganda, could not be thus assimilated. They could be identified, their foreignness noted, their continued attachment to their homes and people presumed. Increasingly they asked for local support and a control of local life as government expanded its services and demands. Given their established means of dealing with strangers, the local people could see no possible way that they could gain from tolerance of the remote foreigner who had neither bond friendships, acknowledged clan ties, nor kinship to channel his generosity and support in their direction. Advantage to such foreigners could only mean loss to the local people, a subjecting of them to outsiders who would drain their substance and their independence to build up the resources of their own people.

In the 1960s Tonga might at one moment speak of the good foreigners "with whom we always laugh" as admirable neighbors and good friends with whom one entered into relationships of clanship, namesakehood, marriage alliances and kinship. In the next breath they might denounce the evil foreigners who were attempting to take over the country and who were capable of any evil. Familiarity with the "good foreigner" had no affect upon this other stereotype, though sometimes the stereotype aroused suspicions against the "good foreigner." Increasingly the Tonga saw themselves as a people united against the challenge of other ethnic groups, and increasingly therefore terms referring to foreigners appeared in contexts which emphasized their strangeness and their differences from the Tonga.

In the past Tonga tended to view strangers as individuals to be manipulated and absorbed into the local community. In the precolonial period they feared foreign nations which raided them, but the foreigner who ventured into their country for any length of time was close at hand and could be dealt with on the basis of intimidating friendship. In a sense foreigners were either completely outside their system and no danger to it except for occasional forays, or they were within it and controllable. This is no longer true in the new world of rapid communication and ever increasing encroachment of the agencies and officials of central government. Publicity keeps before the people the names, faces, and histories of men from distant regions who thereby become a part of the local scene though they are never present in a fashion that makes them vulnerable to local pressure.

In this world known public foreigners retain their alien status inevitably since they are never part of the local system, and as yet many Tonga do not give allegiance to any larger national system that could encompass them both. At the same time these foreigners have real power to force their views upon the local scene and thus to threaten the old adjustments of the people. Resident foreigners are at times viewed as agents of the aliens. Today these have less reason to accept a pressure for conformity and attempts to assimilate them into Tonga society. Rapid communications make it possible for them to maintain contact with their old homes and old compatriots. More and more they are likely to be in the country on short-term jobs or for some temporary exploitation of local resources, rather than long-term settlers. They look to central government for protection and the police station is close at hand when they clash with local people. There is little advantage in assimilation. An emphasis on old ties and loyalties may even be an advantage, for it may allow an appeal not only to government but to particular officials who share the same language and the same home memories.

Absorption and assimilation are no longer the inevitable future for those who come to dwell in Tonga country. A diversified society marked by ethnic enclaves is now developing.

NOTES

1. I did research among the Plateau and Valley Tonga in 1946-1947, 1948-1950, 1956-1957, February 1960, 1962-1963, July, August 1965. All research, save that of 1965, was sponsored and financed by the Rhodes-Livingstone Institute, now the Institute for Social Research in the University of Zambia. Work in 1965 was financed by a grant from the Social Science Research Council, with the Institute loaning equipment and giving general assistance. I have also to thank my colleague, Dr. Thayer Scudder, for access to his field notes on the Valley Tonga (1956-1957 and 1962-1963), and Miss Leanne Hinton and Miss Caroline Hills for general assistance in organizing field data. Grants from the research funds of the University of California, Berkeley, and from the African Studies Program, University of California, Los Angeles, provided assistance in the writing of this analysis. The first draft of this paper was presented to the Anthropology Colloquium at the University of Oregon, March 1966.

Further information on Plateau and Valley Tonga will be found in Colson 1958, 1960, 1962, 1964, 1966a, 1967; and Scudder 1962.

2. Europeans and Indians also settled in the region either on farms or in the railway townships, and others were to be found at administrative and mission stations. I shall not discuss the way by which the Tonga sought to incorporate them into the local structure by adopting them as patrons. This is discussed in Colson 1967. Here I shall be concerned only with Tonga absorption of alien Africans.

3. This analysis owes a good deal to various discussions by Gluckman of the nature of Tonga clanship. See Gluckman 1965b: 94-97. In the northwest of Tonga country the clan system is very different and this analysis would not apply. In a few areas, fourteen clans are recognized.

4. See Richards 1937: 188 (Bemba); Stefaniszyn 1964: 3-7 (Ambo); Cunnisonn 1959: 62-63 (Kazembe's kingdom).

5. The terms "Middle River," "Upper River," "Uplands," are defined in Colson 1960: 4, 13-18.

6. Studied by Scudder whose analysis of the Mazulu census is not yet completed.

REFERENCES

Colson, E. 1958. *Marriage and the family among the plateau Tonga.* Manchester, Manchester University Press.

1960. *Social organization of the Gwembe Tonga.* Manchester, Manchester University Press.

1962. *The plateau Tonga.* Manchester, Manchester University Press.

1964. "Social change and the Gwembe Tonga." *Rhodes-Livingstone Journal* 36: 1-10.

1966a. "The alien diviner and local politics among the Tonga of Zambia," M. Swartz, V. W. Turner, and A. Tuden. *Political Anthropology.* pp. 221-228. Chicago, Aldine.

1967. "Competence and incompetence in the context of independence." *Current Anthropology* 8: 92-111.

Cunnison, I. 1959. *The Luapula peoples of Northern Rhodesia.* Manchester, Manchester University Press.

Fortes, M., and E. E. Evans-Pritchard (eds.) 1940. *African political systems.* London, Oxford University Press.

Gluckman, M. 1965a. *The ideas in Barotse jurisprudence.* New Haven, Yale University Press.

1965b. *Politics, law and ritual in tribal society.* Oxford, Basil Blackwell.

Mintz, S., and E. Wolf. 1950. "An analysis of ritual co-parenthood (Compradrazzo)." *Southwestern Journal of Anthropology* 6: 341-368.

Richards, A. I. 1937. "Reciprocal clan relationships among the Bemba of North East Rhodesia." *Man* 37: 188-193.

Scudder, T. 1962. *The human ecology of the Gwembe Tonga.* Manchester, Manchester University Press.

Stefaniszyn, B. 1964. *Social and ritual life of the Ambo of Northern Rhodesia.* London, Oxford University Press.

3

POLITICAL INCORPORATION
AMONG THE LUGBARA OF UGANDA

John Middleton

INCORPORATION IN TRADITIONAL LUGBARA SOCIETY

The Lugbara of Uganda have a traditional political organization that is small in scale and based upon a segmentary patrilineal lineage structure. Although their society has changed markedly in recent years, most Lugbara still conceive of it in traditional terms. However, they are today part of a wider economic and political system. In this paper I discuss both the process of "internal" incorporation in Lugbara, which is minimal when compared to many other African societies, and also the process of their incorporation into a political system greater than that of their traditionally bounded society. Two main interrelated problems are relevant in this context. One is that of the widening of the political scale of Lugbara society; the other is that of the development of forms of social stratification.[1]

The traditional Lugbara political system was based upon a series of some sixty jural communities,[2] which I call subtribes, each with an average population of some 5,000-6,000 people. Each has its own territory and its own rainmaker, the genealogically senior man of the senior descent line. There are also men of personal wealth and influence, known as *'ba rukuza* (men whose names are known). In the past both they and rainmakers could bring feuding to an end and so had rudimentary political authority, and both are generically known as *opi*, the word also used today for government chiefs. The subtribe is typically segmented into four or five levels of segmentation, each territorial segment being formed around a host patrilineage to which are attached a few accessory lineages. The head of the minimal lineage, the core of a family cluster, is the *'ba wara* (elder), who is the most senior political figure except for the rainmakers and "men whose names are known." Traditionally they had neither king, nor chiefs in any specialized political sense. Although in historical fact Lugbara society was presumably never static or unchanging, we may assume that it was stable over relatively long periods; at least Lugbara maintain that this was so and we have no evidence to the contrary. Therefore this account of the growth of forms of incorporation will begin with those "traditional" forms of the precolonial past which are still observable in operation today, despite many other changes.

Forms of incorporation have always been recognized by the Lugbara, but those accepted as "traditional" were, and still are, seen in terms of individual attachment to small local groups. Individuals of different lineage ancestry attach themselves as "strangers" to host groups. The strangers are either people who are accepted by their hosts as "mother's brother's people," or as "wife's brother's people," or as unrelated clients. They attach themselves for many reasons: shortage of available land in their natal settlements, quarrels with agnatic kin (especially if accused of persistent witchcraft), and famine or other disaster. Clients, in particular, may move long distances in times of trouble. These attached "strangers" are permitted to remain and to beget small lineages, which in time become "stranger" accessory lineages, with their own territories set within those of their hosts. The significant point is that traditionally Lugbara society has been able to permit considerable mobility and absorption of individuals (with their elementary families), but not of entire groups: despite the existence of these intergroup ties, the actual process of attachment has always been by individuals.

Another kind of incorporation in traditional Lugbara society has been that of non-Lugbara. The most common was, and is, that of Ndu blacksmiths. These come to settle in Lugbara areas, and in time there develop small lineages of Ndu scattered across the countryside. They differ from Lugbara clients in one significant respect: they do not intermarry with their hosts. They are Ndu, and remain Ndu, although their general social status and style of living are not noticeably different from those of ordinary Lugbara. However, they are feared for their reputed powers of cursing; this is due to their power of transforming metal, not to their non-Lugbara origins.

There are also numerous client families of non-Lugbara origin along most of the boundaries of Lugbara territory, especially of Madi to the east, Kakwa to the north, and Keliko to the west. Their position is similar to that of the Ndu, except that they are not feared for possessing mystical powers.

Traditionally, then, Lugbara society has been small in scale, comprising many small semi-autonomous political units, the jural communities or subtribes. Until recent years each has had minimal social stratification. In the past there were no wider political ties and incorporation has always been at a minimal and individual level only. Although this leads in time to the growth of accessory lineages, these are politically of the same order as host lineages. This process may be included under the rubric "incorporation," but it involves neither change in the political scale of Lugbara society (although it may have led to a continuous but slight increase in the population size), nor to political stratification.[3]

THE YAKAN CULT

We have no historical information about the relationship between the Lugbara and the outside world before about 1880, and ethnohistorical data provided by the Lugbara themselves tell only of feuds between Lugbara territorial groups and of small-scale wars between Lugbara living on the edge of Lugbaraland and their non-Lugbara neighbors. During the last fifteen years of the nineteenth century Lugbaraland came marginally into contact with the Arab slavers who destroyed so many of the indigenous societies of the southwestern Sudan, and in 1900 they entered the colonial world with the establishment of a Belgian post at Ofude, in north-central Lugbaraland. Chiefs were appointed by the Belgians, but their influence seems to have been small and certainly they cannot be said to have played any important part in widening the scale of Lugbara society as far as the setting-up of wider political entities is concerned. However, the fact that many of the first chiefs were kin of one kind or another is significant: at least the handful of chiefs and their immediate followers were aware of the possibilities of a wider network of social relations than the traditional ones being possible.

After the establishment of British colonial administration over the eastern and central parts of the country in 1914, a significant historical event took place. This was the attempt by the prophet Rembe to change the traditional political system and set up a wider-scale one controlled by himself in its place. He established an organization consisting of three ranks of people distinguished by their ritual status in the Yakan cult, of which he was the leader. The highest rank was that of *opi* (chief), the men who acted as Rembe's assistants in the cult; the second rank was that of the men who dispensed the "water of Yakan," which they received from the *opi*, to those of the lowest rank, the ordinary adherents. This last category included both men and women, and in northern Lugbara at least virtually the entire adult population joined the movement. Clan and lineage affiliation were considered irrelevant, and the traditional seniority of the aged was superseded by that in the system of ranks. Among the aims of the cult were the restoration of life to the dead and the immortality of the living. Thus the traditional principles of organization of Lugbara society—descent, sex, and age—were all disregarded and replaced by those of individual achievement; and in place of the narrowly bounded traditional units—clan, subtribe, and lineage—was substituted the wide-ranging class-like system of the cult-grades.

The attempt to change the traditional form of Lugbara society failed for two main reasons. One was that Rembe himself was hanged before he had gone very far in his plans, and that attempts to continue the cult were met by superior force on the part of the colonial administration. The other was that to substitute for the traditional lineage system a new organization based on differences in rank, though temporarily effective over a wide area of northern Lugbaraland, proved to be too difficult. Although meningitis and rinderpest had changed the former distribution of men and livestock, the basic economy was not affected, and the traditional economic basis for an unstratified and territorially small-scale system remained.[4]

THE CONSEQUENCES OF COLONIALISM

The period of the First World War, during which the Yakan cult flourished, marked the first stages of two other developments which were ultimately to lead to the effective political modernization of Lugbara society. These were simultaneous and interconnected, but it is convenient to describe them first independently. They were the development and increase in the power of government-appointed chiefs, mission officials, and the like; and the growth of labor migration. Between them these developments marked the increase in the scale of Lugbara society and the growth of forms of social stratification.

There is no need here to present a detailed account of the development of the colonial administration and of Christian missions: such accounts have been published elsewhere.[5] But the consequences merit discussion. Until the early 1920s chiefs were appointed by the district administration to represent traditional units: the higher chiefs were in charge of subtribes, with subchiefs below them. But since then there has been continual amalgamation, so that today, among the Uganda Lugbara, there are only five "county" chiefs. The traditional political units, the subtribes and their constituent segments, have lost most of their significance. County chiefs have authority over areas much larger than subtribes and are mobile members of a bureaucracy; they do not come from the areas which they administer. The lower chiefs, those of sub-counties and "parishes," are often still in charge of traditional units, but the subcounty chiefs, at any rate, come from groups other than the subtribes that they administer. In addition, the central district administration is concerned not only with Lugbara but also with those sections of neighboring peoples who inhabit the West Nile District of Uganda and the Chefferie of Aru in the Congo: the Alur, Madi, Kakwa, Kuku, Ndu, 'Bale, and Keliko.

Since the early days when the central administration used Ganda and Nubi "agents," and the missions occasionally used Ganda and Nyoro evangelists, members of peoples from outside West Nile District have been common in Lugbaraland. In addition, of course, the presence of Europeans, Indians, Arabs, Swahili, Congolese, Nubi, and other foreigners in the one or two small townships of the region has long been accepted. And the opening up of roads has enabled a fair proportion of ordinary Lugbara to move about more easily than before and to meet members of groups other than their own. The dispersal and intermingling of members of different tribal and ethnic origins is, of course, a commonplace in modern Africa, and need not be elaborated on further. But one point should be made: it has enabled the Lugbara—or, more accurately, a small proportion of them who came into contact with these various strangers—to realise more clearly than formerly the existence of a wider world.

The senior chiefs, those responsible for counties and subcounties, have for many years been educated men. So long as chiefs represented traditional political groupings, their main qualification was their ability to be accepted by those whom they represented and their educational standards were of little consequence. But once they ceased being representatives and instead came to hold impartial authority over units wider than any in the traditional system, their main qualification became bureaucratic skill, which meant that they had to be educated. Education in this region of Africa has always been in the hands of the two Christian missions and of small Islamic schools, although under the ultimate control of the government. For many years now education has been the road to power for Lugbara, whether in administration, mission activity, or trade other than petty retailing. And education has also enabled men to bypass the old, slow, traditional road of acquiring power by age and genealogical seniority.

There has developed in the last thirty years or so a class of people, recognized as such by the Lugbara, and known as *'ba odiru*, "the New People." This class consists of the senior chiefs, clerks, and other officials of the central and local governments, the more educated members of the missions, and various other people with a similar degree of education, power, or wealth. They tend to intermarry, to send their children for higher education outside Lugbaraland, to live in brick houses with modern-style furnishings, to eat and drink non-traditional food and liquor, to dress in Western-style clothing, and so on. Again, the development of this class has been occurring throughout

Africa for several decades, at least, and the cultural details need no elaboration here. What is significant is that this class is recognized to exist by all Lugbara, that its members so recognize themselves, that young men aspire to become members of it (although their efforts may well be blocked by those they wish to join if they are not related to them by kinship), and that its members comprise not only Lugbara, nor only inhabitants of West Nile District, but they see themselves as having common interests with people of similar status throughout Uganda, the Congo, and beyond. They are, of course, related by kinship to Lugbara who are not "New People," and so provide a link between the traditional, tribal system and the modern, wider one.[6]

A small group which merits mention here, and which has a very similar position to that of the New People, is that known as "Nubi." The Nubi are the Muslims of the small towns of Arua and Aringa, both in Lugbaraland, and of many other small towns throughout Uganda and neighboring countries. The men among them are either the few remaining ex-soldiers of the old Egyptian administration of the Sudan, who after the Mahdi revolt clustered at Wadelai under Emin Pasha, or their descendants; they marry Nubi women and also Lugbara women, who accept Islam and adopt the Nubi way of life. The Nubi of West Nile District number about 6,000, most of them living in Arua. They are petty traders and hawkers, concerned particularly with dealings in hides and skins, and in liquor.

The Nubi have ties of affinity with many Lugbara living in the vicinity of Arua and Aringa, and these Lugbara may also act as agents in petty trade for their Nubi affines. In addition, Nubi maintain strong "ethnic," religious, and kinship ties with other Nubi communities eisewhere in Uganda, the Congo, and the Sudan: there is much intervisiting and intermarriage, and they are very conscious of their separate identity in the wider Ugandan society.[7]

THE WIDENING SCALE OF SOCIAL RELATIONS

The New People and the Nubi are symptomatic of the widening of the scale of Lugbara society and of the growth of a fairly simple form of social stratification within it. Related to these developments and the process of modernization itself is the growth of forms of population movement.

Traditionally, that is, before the establishment of colonial rule in the early years of this century, there was always some movement of population in Lugbara. There was a slow drift from the northwest to the southeast, as part of the age-old process of intertribal movement and adjustment. Individuals seeking land or more agreeable personal relationships with neighbors and kin would move a few miles and attach themselves to their mothers' lineages; and men and women would attach themselves as clients to wealthier men in times of famine or other disaster. But in the past half-century there has been another kind of movement, that of men seeking employment as labor migrants and looking for unoccupied lands outside their own natal areas on which to grow cash and food crops. The most obvious way of acquiring money for taxes and consumer goods is by the sale of their labor.

The Lugbara supply several thousand labor migrants to the towns, factories, plantations, and farms of southern Uganda each year; they are one of the more important sources of unskilled and semiskilled labor in the country. Lugbaraland is unable to provide more than a small proportion of its cash needs. Its elevation is too high for growing cotton, and although a good deal of tobacco is grown in one or two areas, most of the country has no readily available cash crops, nor can it offer many opportunities for wage labor. The only way for most of the population to get money is to sell their labor outside the district. The nearest markets for labor are in southern Uganda, in areas of different ethnic, language, and traditional political affiliation. The Lugbara send their younger men, especially the unmarried ones, to be labor migrants. They go, of course, to earn money. But the return is slight: money and the value of trade goods brought back by returning men after a year is about $9.00, or some $2.75 per head of the total population, as against an average of $1.50 per head from all other sources. This total provides for taxes and some consumer goods. The distribution of these moneys is, of course, unequal, since the migration rate differs from one area to another. Men may go south more than once, the average number of journeys being about 1.7.

Further details of this labor migration need not be given here: some have been published elsewhere.[8] But the sociological causes and consequences of this phenomenon merit some discussion. The actual absentee rate is decided more by the factor of land shortage than by the need for money as such. The areas with the highest densities of population actually living on the land provide the highest migration rates, the highest being one of the central areas, with a density of population of well over 200 to the square mile and 27 percent of adult men absent at any one time. These areas, therefore, have the highest densities both of actual population and of what might be called "genealogical" population. The latter includes everyone of a particular area, whether present or temporarily away on migration, who is featured in genealogies as a living and effective member.

Migrants go south not haphazardly, but according to plans made by the elders of family groups, who decide how much money the group needs and how much spare land it has for its married men and their wives. The whole institution of labor migration is, therefore, an important part of the general system of land control, tenure, and allocation.

LABOR MIGRATION

The movement of labor migrants has had several consequences of significance in the modernization of Lugbara society. To demonstrate this, some account must be given of the organization of labor migrants, especially of those living outside their own country in southern Uganda.

There are four categories of migrants, although they overlap. There are the workers on Indian-owned sugar and timber plantations; workers on Ganda- and Nyoro-owned farms, who rent plots for cotton-growing on a share-cropping basis and who tend to live in large Lugbara settlements in Buganda and Bunyoro; daily- and monthly-wage laborers in petty urban occupations, who tend to live in small groups of Lugbara in the towns of southern Uganda; and those who open their own farms in the peripheral areas of their own country and the empty lands of northern Bunyoro, and who also live in large settlements of their own.

Workers on the Indian plantations are in the main temporary migrants, younger men who use the free transport offered them as a means of reaching southern Uganda. They either work for the contract nine months and then return home (often to sign on again later); or at the end of the contract period they move to Ganda farms or the towns; or they move to farms or towns by simply breaking their contracts. The sharecroppers on Ganda or Nyoro farms tend to be more stable, but most return home after one or two seasons.[9] The town laborers tend to stay even longer, since they are not bound so much by seasonal considerations. The final category usually includes a higher proportion of permanent migrants ("lost" migrants, the Lugbara say) than do the others.

The lands of southern Uganda are divided up, as far as the Lugbara themselves are concerned, into extensions of subclan areas in Lugbaraland, which are the main political units of their own society. And they are known colloquially to Lugbara by the corresponding Lugbara clan names. These settlements, both in the south and on the edges of Lugbaraland, are permanent and many have been in existence for thirty years or so. The smaller groups of Lugbara living in the towns (and this is probably the fastest-growing category of migrants) and among the larger and more permanent settlements are also stable but not so attached to particular areas: they are not given Lugbara clan names, except occasionally in a derisory fashion. In all cases there is a steady turnover in membership, but the settlements and places of residence are permanently occupied by Lugbara migrants.

Formal internal authority in the southern and peripheral farming settlements is usually held by men who are senior in the subclan from which the members come, and who have been in the south for several years. Many are closely related to the rainmakers and other influential men of the subclan and are said to act as their "Agents" in the south.[10] On the other hand, representation of the members of the settlements vis-à-vis the outside world, and especially to government officials and African landlords on whose land the members work as tenants, may be the responsibility of younger men, although their authority is much less formal.

Such a younger man is typically the local settlement leader of an association. Lugbara in southern Uganda enter into tribal associations, all fairly closely but informally linked, which provide welfare, recreational, and what might be called protection services. The Lugbara have no traditional form of age-set organization, nor initiation, and so have no traditional model on which to build. But in recent years in Lugbaraland many loosely organized associations have been formed: veterans' groups, ex-school and church groups, and associations, each comprising labor migrants of certain years. This latter type of association exists both in the south and also in the homeland among ex-migrants. Although the veterans' and school associations include people of many clans, the labor migrants' groups in the homeland are limited to members of particular subclans, following the settlement organization in the south.[11]

The Lugbara regard these associations, in both the south and homeland, and the "extensions" of fellow subclan members as being similar. All lack formal structure, a characteristic of Lugbara social organization. However, they differ in their means of recruitment. Briefly, what I have called associations consist of those men in a settlement (or often in a cluster of neighboring settlements where these include members of the same subclan group) of about the same age and of the same date of arrival in the south. The associations are thus the constituent segments of a settlement; however, due to the fact that most men stay only a year or so in a settlement, most of the members of a settlement may at a given time belong to the same association. A man may later return to the same settlement, but then he usually holds a somewhat peripheral position as a senior and more experienced leader. Membership in an association may often be merely a function of belonging to a settlement, but usually the organization is somewhat more formal than that. It may consist in merely accepting the authority of the association's leader; or it may be much more formal and include recognizing a name and paying some form of dues. The difference between the settlement and the association is mainly that between the situations in which they are called into operation. Both are segments in a wider system. The settlements, the groupings of fellow subclan members of different degrees of migration-experience, act as segments in the intratribal system of all Lugbara migrants over a wide area. They are not found in the homeland, where their members merge back into the traditional subclan groups. In the south, among the migrants, they are significant outside the situations of residence and residential authority mainly when migrant Lugbara meet for recreational and other social purposes: there is much visiting among Lugbara and much calling of meetings of all the Lugbara living in a given area. On the other hand, the associations are segments in the wider intertribal systems of Buganda and Bunyoro, of which the other segments are associations of other tribes, local landlords, police, government chiefs, and so on. Despite the differences in their forms, each represents a certain interest—that of immigrants of whatever tribal origin, and various local groups and offices.

These associations of the Lugbara in the south are sometimes formally organized enough to be known as "companies" and by other English terms. Leadership in them is by initiative and expertise in affairs of the local political organization and labor market. Thus genealogical status is usually not relevant. Members who return to the homeland first remain members, acting as informants and contacts in the home subclan area and district.

The associations found in the towns are rather different. They are not sections of settlements as such. They represent various categories of Lugbara, and are often overlapping in the sense that a man may belong—or at least have informal affiliation—to more than one. Criteria for membership in various Lugbara associations include age and migration experience, the longer the experience the less effective being membership in subclans and lineages in the homeland; attachment to homeland loyalties wider than those of the subclan, especially the county; the area of residence in the town where they are living; similarity of employment; and wealth and standards of education and living. These associations are important for welfare and recreation. I do not know enough about them to know whether they have significant occupational and employment functions. They are segments in a wider system of which the main elements are groupings of different tribes, which are arranged hierarchically according to economic skills, educational achievement, and political power: the Lugbara rank at the bottom of all three series throughout southern Uganda.[12]

After their return to Lugbaraland the ex-migrants continue these associations. They are obviously in some opposition to the traditional lineage groups under traditional lineage authority. The associations of ex-migrants are concerned mainly with such nontraditional matters as political elections, pro- or anti-government, and pro- or anti-mission activities,[13] and modern economic enterprises of many kinds. They are often financed by money received from their southern members, either the younger men who have not yet returned home or older ones who have gone south for a second or even a third time. Two points may be made here. One is that once back in Lugbaraland the formality of organization tends to increase, at least for a year or two; only at this time may members give themselves a collective name, which usually refers to the place and date of their stay in the south. Leaders of associations may regularly attend chiefs' courts in their "official" capacity when their members are on trial. After a year or two there tends to be attrition as the members either become more senior in the lineage system—and especially when they get married and set up their own homesteads—or return south again. If they do this, they may join a second association, often while retaining membership in the original one,[14] although if they are not given positions of leadership these second-stage migrants prefer to keep more to themselves and may opt out of associational activity. Secondly, since most of them are founded in the subclan extension settlements in southern Uganda, the associations of ex-migrants are limited to single subclan affiliation, at the widest. They see themselves as representing the younger men versus the older, the educated versus the uneducated, the ambitious versus the old-fashioned, and the possessors of modern wealth in money versus those of traditional wealth in livestock. But they do not represent all the junior men versus all the seniors over a wide area and so are limited in their possibility of expansion and future political importance.

I have been writing so far mainly about those Lugbara living in the southern farming settlements. The members of urban associations are in a rather different position, since, as I have mentioned, the concept of subclan "extension" is of minor significance in the southern towns. So far as I know, there are no widespread associations of ex-migrants, as such, irrespective of age or subclan membership, on the pattern of the veterans' associations, for example. The reason would seem to be that if widespread, the nature of the migratory experience does not mark men off from their fellow Lugbara to the extent that they feel themselves all that distinct; they see themselves, as I have mentioned, merely as junior men in opposition to senior men and the migration experience is not very relevant.

The consequences of labor migration may be summarized. First, it has enabled the traditional lineage organization to continue in the recent years of increasing land shortage and need for cash.[15] Next, it has led to changes in effective nonlineage leadership, both in Lugbaraland and outside it among the emigrant Lugbara. I say that it has "led to" changes, but it might be more accurate to say that it has provided the Lugbara with an answer to the problem of finding effective leadership among the younger men vis-à-vis their seniors. The need existed already, as it were, and with the setting up of migrant settlements in which there can be few old men, and with the opportunity for young men to acquire money-wealth outside the traditional economic system, labor migration has provided the opportunity for resolving it. Third, it has been part of the process of the increase in the scale of Lugbara society, both with regard to relations within Lugbaraland and to relations outside it; the latter in particular has involved ever-increasing contact between Lugbara and non-Lugbara, in which traditional genealogical status is largely irrelevant. The groupings that are significant in this situation are recruited on the basis of relative youth and junior status, or relative wealth and differences in its acquisition, and of experience of non-Lugbara cultures. As yet they do not include many women, since women go south comparatively rarely; but I know of young women, and particularly of young divorcees, who are permitted to join them.

It should be mentioned that senior and junior Lugbara view the total situation of change differently. The older Lugbara, who, as heads of families and lineages, to a large extent control the migration since they control the allocation of land, see their junior kin in the south as comprising extensions of their lineages and subclans, with authority in the hands of their deputies, the senior migrants; for these older men, the associations of migrants are ephemeral and unimportant. The junior men themselves accept this view to some extent, but also see the situation from another dimension, in which the more important groups are not lineage extensions but the associations founded for nonlineage ends, with authority in the hands of their own representatives both in the south and at home among ex-migrants.

CONCLUSION

There are several points to be made. The first is that during the last seventy years—and mainly during the last thirty—the Lugbara have changed from being a people little aware of or affected by the outside world to one very much aware of and affected by it. In economic, political, and also religious terms, Lugbara society is no longer isolated or autonomous, but is part of a wider polity of which the main center is the federal capital of Uganda, five hundred miles away in the south.[16]

This system, being wider in scale than the traditional one, involves mobility of persons and groups in its constituent parts. The mobility of Lugbara men and women within the traditional boundaries of their society has increased markedly. Attachment in most areas is still in the traditional forms of individual movement that I have described at the beginning of this paper. In some areas the attachment of unrelated clients has been far more important than that of kinsmen, especially in the colonial period when Congolese Lugbara moved in large numbers into Uganda to escape the harsher Belgian rule. However, the traditional values and sanctions in the relationship of host and attached person are still accepted.

The main development has been in economic terms, that of labor migrants who regard the entire system, including both Lugbaraland and the south, as available for their use according to their abilities, training, and experience. They have used this wider experience as a means to acquire new political authority. With this increase in scale new forms of authority and leadership have become necessary in the new social groupings that have come into existence, and to some extent replaced traditional groupings as being more effective in the new, wider system. Traditional groupings recognized only distinctions of status on the basis of sex, age, and genealogical position: the new ones are socially stratified, as yet to a minimal extent only, leadership being in terms of individual achievement.

It remains to ask why the process of modernization has been so slow in Lugbara. There are several obvious factors here. One has been the remoteness of Lugbaraland from economic and political centers that could have drawn the Lugbara into their orbit early in the colonial period. A second has been the nature of the traditional social organization, which has been geared to an ecology and productive economy that have not changed markedly; the exodus of labor migrants has in fact served to maintain both the traditional pattern of land tenure and the lineage system for longer than might have been the case had a cash-crop economy become important. A third has been the lack of traditional forms of social stratification. In the long run, however, the Lugbara are able easily to develop a system of markedly different statuses based on individual achievement, without the hindering forms of traditional differences in status based on ascription by birth or similar factors. Their experience of southern Uganda, with its hierarchical economic and traditional systems, and of the local colonial administrative machine, has provided new models. They can develop rapidly in the future, but it has taken them a long time to start the process.

NOTES

1. The field work on which this account is based was carried out between 1949 and 1953 with the help of the Worshipful Company of Goldsmiths and the Colonial Social Science Research Council, London. Initial writing was done at the University of Oxford with aid from the Wenner-Gren Foundation for Anthropological Research, New York. I am grateful to these bodies for their assistance. An early draft of this paper was presented at a conference of the African Studies Association in New York City in November 1967. I would like to thank Professors Ronald Cohen, Peter Gutkind, and Aidan Southall for their helpful comments.

2. See Middleton and Tait 1958: 9 for a definition of this term.

3. More detailed accounts of this traditional system are given in Middleton 1958 and 1965.

4. I have given a far more comprehensive account of the Yakan cult in Middleton 1963.

5. Middleton 1960 and 1965.

6. I have published a brief account of the "New People" in Middleton 1965. This incipient class organization is presumably found throughout Africa, but there seems to be little published data on it despite its obvious sociological and historical significance. Outside South Africa virtually all intensive work on elites has been on urban elites.

7. I do not know enough about the Nubis to be able to state definitely that much of their importance is that by becoming a Muslim, an ordinary man can both enter into a widespread mercantile network and also remove himself from customary social and legal obligations. This observation has been reported of the Arabisés of the eastern Congo. (see Abel 1960) The situation in Uganda is probably different in that the mercantile system has largely been controlled by Indians and Lugbara cannot enter it so easily by simply changing their religious faith.

8. See Middleton 1952, 1962. The figures given here for cash rewards of migrants are for the early 1950s; they may be considerably more now. Also, since that time communications between Lugbaraland and southern Uganda have been much improved, so that cash crops, especially tobacco, have increased in importance. Also, of course, the migration of laborers has become easier.

9. See Richards 1954 for an account of the Ganda sharecropping system as it has affected the labor migrants.

10. The term "agent" refers to the original Nubi and Ganda agents who controlled parts of Lugbaraland in the first years of British colonial administration. The word is used by Lugbara, therefore, to mean a representative in an alien country who exercises control on behalf of the "metropolitan" power, in this case the Lugbara subclan.

11. I am referring to the situation in the early 1950s. It is likely that I observed a phase in the development of these groupings and the position is likely to have changed since that time.

12. Parkin (1966) points out that Lugbara in Kampala, the largest urban area in Uganda, are extremely separated from other immigrant groups. This decreases the importance of "traditional" intra-Lugbara factors as criteria for membership of associations.

13. I am referring here to the colonial period; the situation may have changed radically since political independence.

14. Lugbara see no contradiction here, since the territorial basis for membership, the subclan at home, remains the same.

15. See Middleton 1952 and 1962 for evidence for this point.

16. According to the 1948 census (East African Statistical Department 1950) there were some 22,000 Lugbara living outside Lugbaraland, or 12 percent of the total Lugbara population. Of these, almost 11,000 were in Bunyoro, 7,000 were in Buganda, and 3,000 in Busoga. Of the tribes of the then Northern Province of Uganda, only the neighboring Alur had a higher proportion of absentees (24 percent). I do not have reliable total figures for the number of Lugbara living outside their homeland who were regarded as permanent settlers away with no intention of returning. These "lost" migrants are significant as an index of the degree of tribal admixture in this rapidly developing country.

REFERENCES

Abel, A. 1960. *Les Musulmans noirs du Maniéma*. Bruxelles, Centre pour l'Etude des Problèmes du Monde musulman contemporain.

East African Statistical Department. 1950. *African population of Uganda protectorate: geographical and tribal studies*. Nairobi.

Middleton, J. 1962. *Labour migration among the Lugbara*. London, Colonial Office.

1958. "The political system of the Lugbara of the Nile-Congo divide," in
J. Middleton and D. Tait (eds.). *Tribes without rulers.* pp. 203-229. London, Routledge and Kegan Paul.

1960. "The Lugbara." in A. I. Richards (ed.). *East African chiefs.* pp.
326-343. London, Faber and Faber.

1962. "Trade and markets among the Lugbara of Uganda." in P. Bohannan, and G. Dalton (eds.). *Markets in Africa.* pp. 561-578. Evanston,
Northwestern University Press.

1963. "The Yakan or Allah water cult among the Lugbara." *Journal of the
Royal Anthropological Institute* 93(1): 80-108.

1965. *The Lugbara of Uganda.* New York, Holt, Rinehart and Winston.

———, and D. Tait (eds.). 1958. *Tribes without rulers.* London, Routledge and
Kegan Paul.

Parkin, D. J. 1966. "Urban voluntary associations as institutions of adaptation." *Man* n.s. 1(1): 90-95.

Richards, A. I. (eds.) 1954. *Economic development and tribal change.* Cambridge, Heffers & Sons.

4

ETHNIC INCORPORATION AMONG THE ALUR

Aidan Southall

THE ETHNIC COMPOSITION OF ALUR SOCIETY

The Alur are a Nilotic-speaking people of the Lwoo group. (Southall 1956; Crazzolara 1950, 1951, 1954) Their tradition speaks of past migration from the northerly direction of what is now the southern Sudan. (Southall 1954a) They did not constitute a single polity, for they were divided among many more or less independent chiefdoms, some of which had various political and ritual relations with each other, but none of which was indisputably paramount over all the rest. They lived in segmentary patrilineages which were highly localized, but there were many links of common clanship between particular lineages in one chiefdom and another. Their country lies to the north and west of Lake Albert and the southern part of the Albert Nile which flows out of it. The Alur are divided roughly in half by the boundary between Uganda and the Congo.

To speak of incorporation it is necessary to be clear as to the entities which are incorporating and those which are being incorporated. The studies of the last few decades, in particular, have indicated that very many traditional societies are of a much more ambiguous nature than had been supposed from the earlier idea of the tribe as a simple and clearly bounded entity. In the case of the Alur this is not too grave a problem, for the identity Alur is a fairly clear self-cognizant entity, although it has a certain ambiguous periphery.

Incorporation is fundamental to Alur society, which could not have come into existence in anything like its present form without this process. Its origins are lost in the mists of time, so that any recent processes of incorporation which can be described with some empirical detail have occurred in the light of a preexisting pattern. I shall describe the unfolding of this pattern from the points of view of time, space, political structure, the means, the symbols, and the indices of incorporation.

Alur chiefs and the members of their patrilineages call themselves Lwoo. They form the most consistent and homogeneous core of the tribe. It is to them that the tradition of southward migration from the Sudan principally applies. The closer members of a chief's patrilineage had the position of nobles and many of the attributes of chiefship spilled over upon them. The more distant a patrilineage became genealogically from its point of origin in the son of a reigning chief, the more this aura faded and its members lapsed into the status of commoners, unless they had revivified their nobility through the establishment and maintenance of a new chiefship of their own. It was rarely possible for any noble other than the recognized son of a reigning chief to succeed in establishing a new chiefdom. On the other hand, an unsuccessful line of petty chiefs was sometimes replaced by another, so that the chiefship of the former lapsed, though they themselves might be reluctant to recognize this. But a chief is not a chief without subjects and the question arises as to who were the subjects of the early chiefs at the time of their migration and arrival into the present Alurland. This is part of the further question as to whether all Lwoo among the Alur are descended from chiefs and what such a claim would mean.

There are in most if not all chiefdoms certain ancient lineages which claim and are recognized to be Lwoo but do not claim chiefly descent. In the tradition they are the original close companions of the chiefs on their arrival in the country. They are also the original *lwak*, or "masses," the Lwoo commoner subjects of the chiefs. Such lineages often have special ritual duties in connection with the chiefs, their installation, burial, and general ritualization. Consequently they remain important even if, as in some cases, their numbers have dwindled and they are now quite small. Several of them belong to clans which are represented in this same capacity in a number of chiefdoms. (Southall 1956: 88-90)

So far we have an ordinary story of the wanderings of agnates with certain lines of descent claiming preeminence among them. But nearly all Alur traditions include non-Lwoo groups among the entourages of chiefs from the very beginning. The most important of these non-Lwoo ethnic groups in contemporary numerical terms are the Okebo (Ndu), Lendu (Bale), and Madi. (1956: 152ff., 170ff., 212-214, 348-351) All three exist today as quite large tribes with their own languages and cultures. Incorporation by the Alur affected only parts of these tribes, though in some cases large parts. The process of incorporation was sharply reversed and to a considerable extent unscrambled by colonial administration at the beginning of this century because it smacked of slavery. There are other non-Lwoo ethnic groups deeply embedded in Alur society, many of them small and obscure, though some consist of a number of separate but mutually recognized local sections scattered widely in Alurland and in different chiefdoms. Such a case is Abira. It has been suggested that they may have been connected with the Babira, a Bantu tribe to the southwest. This is no doubt possible, but the Abira do not claim it, there is no concrete evidence for it as yet and it may only be a phonetic confusion. Furthermore, some Abira communities are in fact Okebo, though others apparently are not. (1956: 23, 90, 115, 204, 213-214, 376, 383) The remote yet undefined origin of the Abira, as far as the Alur are concerned, is indicated by the widespread story among the latter that they found the Abira in caves on their arrival in the country, that they had tails like cows and that the Alur enticed them out of their caves with salt presented to them on the blade of a spear. The Alur cut off their tails and they became normal members of human Alur society.

The origin of such groups merges imperceptibly into that of the ancient Lwoo commoners. For example, Palei is one of the most respected of these Lwoo commoner groups found in several major chiefdoms. They trace their origin to Kwong'a, a legendary ruler whose daughter encountered a wandering hero, Ucak, who eventually seduced her and was killed by her brothers. She gave birth to twins who, as is usual in such stories, were condemned to death by Kwong'a but reared by foster parents. The younger of the twins replaced Kwong'a as ruler and from him major lines of Alur chiefs trace their descent. This myth integrates a large number of themes. It establishes an august origin for Palei, which no one cares to deny. But it is an origin which is nonetheless clearly distinct from the patrilines of Alur chiefs. Yet no one would suggest that Palei were not Alur. The setting of the story lies outside geographical space, at a point in time antecedent to the historical dimension of Alur settlement in their present territory. At this level, questions about differences in language or culture can have no specific meaning. It is a genuine origin myth, for *Kwong'a* means "beginning," *Ucak* means "the start," and his other name *Upodho* means "he fell," presumably from the sky. From his bones came the most powerful rainstones of Alur chiefs. Ba-Kwong'a are also an important clan in Bunyoro, the interlacustrine Bantu kingdom to the southeast across Lake Albert. Major Alur chiefs also claim common clanship with the Bunyoro kings. (cf. Beattie 1960) There is strong evidence for past interconnections between Alur and Bunyoro rulers and commoner groups, but it would be dangerous on present evidence to clothe it with too specific linguistic and cultural hypotheses. (Girling 1960: ch. 7; Southall, forthcoming [a] and [b])

The Palei myth, among many other things, charters dynastic change and ethnic pluralism at the very beginning of society. It is hardly distinctive in this, for perhaps most dynasties have this feature mythically expressed in some form or another, as is indeed the case in neighboring Bunyoro. The Abira myth correspondingly validates the dealings of the Alur as superiors with other ethnic groups. What is distinctive is that ethnic pluralism and incorporation remained such a characteristic and pervasive feature of Alur society until the present century. These processes were not simply the integration of conquered peoples into an expanding state. They reflect Alur social structure with its blend of segmentary lineages and incipient political chiefship whose very deficiencies in the effective mobilization of power demanded that the process of incorporation be a much more gradual and complex matter of complementary social and cultural integration. But probably the process of incorporation is similarly complex even in much more centralized states and is far from being a simple matter of conquest.

The many small groups of obscure but evidently non-Lwoo origin scattered about Alurland have no identification, either by themselves or others, with any other peoples outside Alur society. In this they differ radically from the Okebo, Lendu, and Madi. The members of these latter peoples who were to a greater or lesser extent incorporated in Alur society must always have had some awareness of their fellow tribesfolk who were not, and remained independent. In recent times the main growing edge of Alur incorporation was to the west and south, in areas which became part of the Belgian Congo just over half a century ago. It was here that the Belgians conscientiously endeavored to liberate and disentangle the non-Alur subjects from their superiors. This involved quite large-scale movement and resettlement of population as well as the actual rupture of political and social bonds. By the time of my fieldwork in the early 1950s it was becoming quite difficult to discover which groups had been subject to the Alur, and in what sense, and which had not. (Southall 1956: p. 17 map) However, it became clear that one of the simplest diagnostics was the question "Who made rain?" I was exploring this point in an assembly of Lendu and one elder after another gave the name of the Alur chief to whom they had gone for rain. Then one very old man, when asked the question, replied with a great sense of the inadequacy of the confession, "The rain fell on its own." I had similar experiences with the Madi.

If the Belgians decided that it was expedient to unscramble the Okebo and Lendu (the Madi were in Uganda) from the Alur as far as they could, why did they not do the same in other cases of domination by one ethnic group over another, as, for example, in the notorious case of Rwanda? The brief answer must be that this is an indicator of different types of African political systems and different types and degrees of incorporation.

It was the Germans who first gained control of Rwanda and the Belgians acquired it in the settlement after the First World War. But all the colonial regimes in this region, whether Belgian, German, or British, and irrespective of differences in their colonial policies, may be taken as good objective judges of political power.

They made no attempt to unscramble the Hutu from the Tutsi in Rwanda (until the eleventh hour in 1959) partly because they respected the political power of the Rwanda state and wished to deal with it delicately, using it for their own purposes, partly because the Hutu were not a distinct tribal or cultural entity. At any rate, by the nineteenth century they were not recognizably a subjected part of any other neighboring unsubjected people to whom they could be assimilated, although in fact the northern Hutu of Ndorwa were hardly at all distinct from their unsubjected Kiga neighbors in Uganda. The same considerations hold true of the dealings of the British with the Iru under the domination of the Hima in Ankole. The Belgians unscrambled the Okebo and Lendu because they were not politically incorporated into a recognizable state of respected power, and because there were still large numbers of unsubjected Okebo and Lendu with whom they could be administratively assimilated. In Alur society every degree of incorporation was represented, from groups whose ethnic origin was no longer known even to themselves, to groups of Okebo or Lendu no longer speaking their own language but only Alur, to groups still mainly speaking their own language yet under Alur rule, and finally the independent, unsubjected Okebo and Lendu in their traditional acephalous communities. The British did not attempt to unscramble the Okebo and Lendu from the Alur in Uganda because these particular groups were fairly highly incorporated, and because they were in any case cut off by the colonial boundary from the major territories of independent Okebo and Lendu in the Congo. Among the Madi in Uganda, who were adjacent to their independent fellow tribesfolk, those with the most tenuous links to Alur society and the most peripheral position were administratively separated, while those more deeply imbedded in Alur society and in a more central position remained under Alur chiefs.

THE PROCESSES OF INCORPORATION

The idea of incorporation echoes back to the myths through which the Alur express their view of the very origins of human society, and it also appears in the more particular traditions which charter each Alur polity. So it comes down to the incidents of incorporation which occurred within living memory and of which in one or two cases very old men still living were the central figures. (1956: 185) Such incidents could not occur overtly once colonial control had been imposed; therefore, the most recent occurrences

were still at least four decades before the time of field work and could only
be related to me by memory, even if in a few cases the chief actors were still
alive and available. There is a great continuity and homogeneity between the
accounts which such old men give of the events of their youth and the
traditions which record the foundations of the oldest Alur polities. Presumably the one reacts upon the other, and while people recount old traditions as
first instances of a type of event which they have even experienced and taken
part in themselves, so also they tell of such recent events as almost standard-
ized re-enactments of occurrences which have characterized Alur society from
its very beginning.

Alur incorporation of non-Alur has depended mainly upon the constant
proliferation of Alur chiefship and the gradual envelopment of new subjects
in its realm. Apart from this, there have been innumerable cases of the incorporation of strangers, foreigners, and captives through individual Alur households and families, but the overall significance of this was slight and, in any
case, such stray persons were the prerogative of chiefs and, in theory, at their
disposal.

To judge from their oral tradition (1954a), which there is no reason to
doubt on this point, the numerous Alur ruling lines varied greatly in their
opportunity, capacity, or desire to proliferate and spread their rule over other
peoples. This may also have depended upon economic and demographic factors. Probably all Alur chiefs ruled over ethnic groups of mixed descent and
saw themselves as having this special capacity, however small their realms
were, and some were very small. Sometimes they had remained fairly stable
or stagnant for many generations, with those groups of foreign descent who
were both geographically and socially central to their realms becoming highly
integrated, while those who were geographically peripheral remained also
socially marginal, retaining much of their independence. This seems to have
been true of several small Alur chiefdoms on the Albert Nile in their relations
with Madi groups to the north and inland to their west.

One particular descent line seems to have been more prone to proliferation
and incorporation than all the rest. More than a dozen of the ruling lines
extant at the end of the nineteenth century (1954a: figs. 2-7) have an agreed
upon common tradition which derives them all from a single line of chiefs
twelve generations ago. It is obviously of significance that no agreed upon
names of rulers are remembered before this point, which corresponds to the
epoch-making crossing of the Nile by this group and their first entry into the
country to the west of it. From this point in space and time proliferation into
new chiefdoms occurred in every generation. This closely linked group of

chiefdoms of the Atyak line constituted more than half of the whole complex of the Alur and their subjects. (Southall, 1956: 343, 352-354)

The process of incorporation depended not only on the proclivity of Alur ruling lines but on the advantages which it had to offer to the non-Alur peoples. The process depended upon complementary advantages in both social systems. It gave satisfactory expression to the Alur belief in their destiny and capacity to rule others, in the sense of bringing to them the benefits of rainmaking, general ritual well-being, and improved mechanisms of conflict resolution. It also permitted Alur chiefs to get rid of unruly and troublesome sons by sending them out to seek their own fortunes. The non-Alur subject peoples who thus became incorporated seem from their own account to have conceded these complementary advantages, at least to the extent of recognizing the need and convenience of a somewhat larger-scale social system and political order which was brought to them in this way.

In the postcolonial period, when most African peoples have just succeeded in freeing themselves from their former political masters, one cannot avoid asking whether it is realistic to represent the non-Alur subject peoples as welcoming subjection, even for its structural advantages and even by fellow Africans who, in global terms, were not so very far removed from the same general cultural level. At this stage we can only suggest that, in their situation, the interplay of self-interest among the Okebo, Lendu, and Madi led many marginal groups into gradual and hardly noticeable steps as a result of which they found themselves to be part of Alur society and subjects of Alur chiefs in much the same way that commoner Alur were themselves. The nature of this subjection and how it could occur surreptitiously or appear advantageous, we must endeavor to explain.

Oral tradition, ritual re-enactment, and the present spatial disposition of groups all lead us to envisage a gradual moving into Alurland by noble and commoner Lwoo together with some members of other ethnic groups some three or more centuries ago. The numerically preponderant Atyak group crossed the Nile north of Lake Albert, from the east, and moved gradually west, up into the fertile highlands of the Nile-Congo divide, planting settlements on the way as they went. Some Lwoo may already have been there when they arrived and a number of other Lwoo groups came after them to settle west of the Nile and Lake Albert, but no more Lwoo of importance seem to have arrived in the last eight generations and none increased, spread, and prospered quite on the scale of the Atyak Alur. The main opportunity for expansion, in the shape of suitably complementary social systems and relatively sparce occupation, always lay to the west, and it was on this frontier that the process of incorporation was still actively continuing up to the time when colonial administration brought it to a halt. (1954a: fig.7)

Chiefship was proliferated by the sons of chiefs going out to establish new realms for themselves, or being sent out by their fathers to do so, or by a combination or sequence of the two. Furthermore, they might go as adults with bands of followers, or they might go as children with their mothers, sent by the chief in direct response to an appeal by some group or groups to have a chief's son living with them. Sometimes a chief sent one of his commoners, a courtier, or even one of his wives with her household. Not surprisingly, cases are recounted in which neither a commoner nor a chief's wife proved adequate and a chief's son was subsequently sent. It seems likely that groups making such an appeal to an Alur chief would usually have been Alur commoners themselves, or at least partially incorporated non-Alur groups who were already dependent upon Alur chiefship and the services which it could provide for them. In fact such appeals seem often to have been made by groups of lineages and clan sections, some of whom were Alur and others not, but all of whom had been associated together under some form of Alur rule. 'When a new center and focus of Alur chiefship was thus established, it frequently came to be accepted or gained control over many new groups of outlying foreigners as well.

When chief's sons went out as adults to seek their fortunes, it was a political venture which later received ritual confirmation from the chief according to its success. When they went out as children with their mothers and followers, it was a largely ritual proceeding which later became confirmed with varying degrees of political fortune. It was described as kidnapping or carrying off, by analogy with the ritual kidnapping of the successful claimant to the stool of a deceased chief by the elders responsible for the succession, thereby dramatizing the ambivalent attitude towards succession to chiefship, which was, on the one hand, the seal of political ability and ambition as well as noble birth, while, on the other, it meant exposure to fearful ritual and supernatural dangers which lesser men could hope to avoid. The adult sons who were sent out were often said to have been in disgrace with their fathers for some unruly act, such as despoiling his hunting grounds, fornicating with his wives, or plundering his subjects of food, goats, or other property. (1956: Chapter 8)

As one example among very many, tradition relates that eleven generations ago Magwar, the eldest son of Chief Umier Dhyang' of Ukuru, accidentally burnt up one of his father's hunting preserves while smoking out bees to get honey. He had to go into hiding from his father's wrath. The Urabo Okebo found him and carried him off to be their chief. This marked the foundation of the new chiefdom of Paidha. But several other groups in Paidha claim the honor of having brought Magwar. The Avunu Okebo and the Pamitu Alur claim to have brought him from Umier. Perhaps the different accounts refer to successive incidents. The Amwonyo, of unknown ethnic ancestry, claim that Paratago was their chief at the time and had destroyed the crops of the Urabo Okebo, thus driving them to seek protection under the chiefly aura of Magwar. Paratago went off into the bush leaving Magwar as chief. Later on Magwar's father Umier called him back to be ready to succeed him, but Magwar refused, so his father gave him a drum, rain, and a grass slasher so that he could go among the Okebo and be revered as chief by them. When Umier died the elders again called Magwar to succeed him (according to the Paidha account) but Magwar again refused, saying "My own that I have is enough for me," so they made his younger brother Ng'ira chief of Ukuru in succession to Umier. In conferring the regalia of chiefship on Magwar, Umier had also instructed him to continue sending tribute to his father, but at the latter's death to eat the tribute himself, thus marking his effective indepen- dence of the chiefship of Ukuru.

Such instances echo through the generations of Alur rule, richly expressing the manner in which Alur and non-Alur, in varying stages of incorporation, view themselves in relation to the chiefs and to one another. One case of proliferation often reverberated upon another. In about 1880 the Abetse Lendu went to petition Chief Nziri of Ukuru for a chief's son to live among them and rule over them because the fighting among them was causing the people to scatter. Nziri sent his son Amatho, who went with three Alur of Pagei, one of Awura, and an Okebo of Avunu. Nziri later sent some Alur of Palei and Padwur to join him. These men, presumably the heads of extended families, went with their wives, sons, and cattle, but in any case it was a fairly small party which went out to plant this new center of chiefly rule. Amatho found not only the Abetse Lendu subclan, whose elder had called him, but some half-dozen or more other Lendu subclans which also recognized him. Later the Okebo Ngele complained to the chief of Ukuru that Amatho had been helping himself to their cattle. Amatho's younger brother Kubi was sent to live among them and protect them. Some of Amatho's Lendu switched their allegiance to Kubi, and Amatho moved further west and established himself over other Lendu subclans. At about this time a Pagei man got one of Amatho's sisters with child and then Amatho raided Pagei, who therefore complained to the Chief of Ukuru, as a result of which his son Aryem was sent to live with them and came to rule over a large assortment of Alur, Lendu, and Okebo groups. Here were three new potential chiefships founded in quite a short time. But their development was cut short by the coming of colonial administration and they never reached the stage of having their political independence ritually conferred and ratified by the Chief of Ukuru. Such new ruling lines were not always successful. They might either extend the frontiers, increasing the area and the population of Alur society and culture, or they might rather compete and tend to stagnate or to cancel one another out. In some areas tradition tells of three or four successive lines of chiefs' sons replacing one another over the generations as first one and then another had lost the confidence of his subjects. (1956: 205ff.)

Jukoth is the most striking case of a chiefdom which appears to have grown very rapidly and incorporated large numbers of non-Alur, in this case mainly Lendu, with some groups of Okebo, Abira, and Madi. Tradition tells of its founding eight generations ago by Uceng', a wanderer from Bunyoro, thus emphasizing the varied and tenuous identity of Alur. According to one version he was involved in a dynastic dispute near Mount Igisi in north Bunyoro. (1954a: fig. 4, 152, 154) This was almost certainly an area occupied by the Nilotic Palwo. They had rulers of their own but were under the suzerainty of the kings of Bunyoro with whom they had a very special connection that was related to the Nilotic ancestry of the latter. Uceng' fled west across the Nile into the territory of the Alur chief of Panyimur accompanied by a wife and a servant. His wife died and a quarrel arose over the question of her burial, so he went inland and was brought to the court of the Alur chief of Ang'al. There was famine and the Lendu were coming to beg the chief for rain. Eventually Uceng' made rain for them and they built a house for him to live amongst them and brought him goats to enable him to marry. He married a number of women and later sent one of his sons back to Igisi in Bunyoro to fetch his drum, regalia, and medicines. His line prospered exceedingly; each successive chief was a great polygynist, so that by 1952 there were over four thousand adult men who counted themselves in the patrilineage of Uceng'. (1956: 356-357) Many groups of Lendu were brought within the orbit of their realm, in addition to the various other Alur, Okebo, Abira, and Madi who joined them. The chief walked among the Lendu, selecting or confirming the heads of their local lineages and sometimes putting one of his sons among them to act as their local chief, to settle their disputes, receive their gifts and tribute, and gather them to cultivate the fields of the chief.

No traditionally representative instance of the initial acceptance of Alur chiefs by previously independent Lendu or Okebo can have occurred for well over half a century, so that in trying to discern the mechanism of the process we are unfortunately dependent solely on the recollections of old men. While this introduces an inevitable element of speculation, all available evidence seems fairly consistent. The fact that Lendu and other peoples went to beg

Alur chiefs for rain is quite plausible, because it is a particular instance of the prophet having greater honor in another country. The consultation of foreign prophets, diviners, witch doctors, and other ritual experts was almost ubiquitous in Africa. The important difference in the case of the Alur was that asking them for rain led imperceptibly to deeper and deeper political involvements. As we have seen, sometimes the foreign peoples took the initiative in asking for rain, or for the protection of a chief's son; sometimes chiefs' sons went out to found new settlements without any such invitation being mentioned; sometimes they were invited by peripheral Alur groups, and foreign peoples became involved when they found chiefship brought thus to their threshold.

The ritual, economic, and political advantages which the Alur could offer are always stressed. They made rain and, if necessary, drove it away, and by this token took responsibility for exercising a generally benign influence and control over the whole natural environment. (1956: 91-97, 376-379) They brought cattle with them, usually in large numbers and sometimes where there were none before. They fulfilled the requirements of a chief in providing meat, food, and drink to those who visited them: "They seduced us with food," the Lendu say. Through their very exploitation in calling the subject peoples to come and cultivate their fields, and to be fed in the process, they almost certainly raised the level of production and extended the cycle of economic exchange of goods and services. It may truly be said that, for better or worse, they introduced the subject peoples to a wider life. They introduced new techniques of peacemaking, arbitration, and conflict resolution and imposed a wider and more effective, even if still embryonic, system of law and order. But implicit in all these capacities was the courage, the self-confidence, and perhaps the arrogance to put them into effect. The successful chief's son felt himself superior, born to rule, and he commanded respect. This is all the more remarkable when it is remembered that Alur society was not rigidly stratified; the line between chief, noble, commoner, and serf was very faint, and in every generation a very large number of men were qualified by birth to play the role of chief if they had the ability to do so. The opportunity was almost always present. The hereditary successor to one of the greater chiefships may well be seen as slipping into an almost predestined role to which his upbringing had accustomed him, but the son who went out to become chief among the Lendu, to whom the role was foreign and perhaps but vaguely understood, took on a much more hazardous task to which only his own supreme self-confidence could assure success. Perhaps the structured oppositions of Okebo and Lendu segments demanded an arbitrating and even authoritarian role which their own cultures did not supply. When we have understood how among the Nuer the leopard-skin chief could almost be compelled by the combatants themselves to arbitrate between them (Evans-Pritchard 1940: 175-176), we can see how the Lendu or Okebo might welcome even a foreign chief among them. The initial impact of an Alur chief's son on first arrival among his new potential subjects must have depended to an important degree upon his personal bearing and the unmistakable presence of which tradition always speaks. But it depended also on some cross-cultural recognition of the awe-inspiring and commanding quality of ritual chiefship itself. They must have been prepared to believe as irrevocably as he did himself in the supernatural forces which he embodied. It is the cross-cultural transference of charisma which is somewhat unusual.

Once the initial impact was successfully made, the involvement deepened and spread. The adoption of Alur chiefs by one group tended to threaten their neighbors unless they followed suit and so the process snowballed. It is clear that many groups adopted one chief's son to defend them against the depredations of another and not just as an escape from their own internal conflicts. We have already remarked that these new ruling lines might prosper and acquire recognition as full scale chiefships, effectively autonomous politically, but ritually linked to their source, or they might ultimately fail and their lineage members lapse into the status of commoners. Even those which were effective were likely to remain for several generations as chieflets (Southall 1956: 181, 193ff.) recognized as subordinate ritually, politically, and economically to the chiefship from which they were derived. They were said to get their rain from it; they passed on part of their tribute to it, and were counted as part of it in cases of attack from outside. Although fighting occurred between local lineages and between Alur chiefs, large-scale or prolonged warfare was probably unheard of until firearms began to reach the country towards the end of the nineteenth century.

THE RESULTS OF INCORPORATION

As the initial charisma of a chieflet among his foreign subjects became routinized, it inevitably tended to take on the expected pattern of Alur chiefship, as its practices percolated from the small core of Alur commoners and kinsmen around the chieflet to the non-Alur subjects. As the chieflet's sons grew up they would themselves have Lendu or Okebo attached to their household, so that the link between chieflet and subjects became reinforced by many personal bonds. Everywhere the Alur, and especially their chiefs, married the daughters of the subject peoples and paid bridewealth for them. (1956: 88) But they tended to prohibit the marriage of non-Alur (and particularly Lendu) to Alur girls. Most chiefs forbade this, but it did occur in some peripheral areas, perhaps where the number of Alur was very small and exogamic limitations left them a very narrow choice of brides. The status difference remains and it is still difficult for an Alur of non-Lwoo descent such as Lendu, Okebo, or Madi to marry an Alur girl of Lwoo descent. This one-way system of intermarriage had the effect of concentrating marriageable women and polygyny among the Alur, causing their numbers to increase much faster than those of the non-Alur, but producing a new population of both noble and commoner Alur by descent, who were obviously, in fact, highly mixed both genetically and culturally. Incorporation was thus, to some extent, a two-way process.

As they became incorporated, the non-Alur had to take up the normal obligations of Alur towards their chiefs, as well as providing extra services of their own, such as ironworking in the case of the Okebo and general work as servants in that of the Lendu. They made their tributary contribution of foodstuffs either directly, by cultivating the chief's fields if they lived close by, or by cultivating for the chief through the organization of an Alur lineage head, or local Alur noble, or even through their own non-Alur subclan head if he had been recognized by the Alur chief. Those who brought tribute or came to cultivate were usually regaled by the chief with food or drink, but this was by grace not by obligation, though it was constantly emphasized as the mark of a true chief. Alur also had the obligation to cultivate for the chief as they also cultivated for one another when called on to do so in return for food or beer, so that the line of contractual and status distinction between Alur cultivating for chiefs or for one another, and non-Alur cultivating for chiefs, or for Alur, or for one another, is a fine one, though it was certainly felt by the Alur to be important. It would be difficult to detect any visible difference, but in theory cultivation for a chief, or by non-Alur for Alur, was compulsory, while cultivation by people for one another within the local community was voluntary. In the latter case there was a real element of choice on any particular occasion, though anyone who consistently refused would find his position untenable. Whereas anyone who failed to turn out when called by the chief was supposedly in trouble unless his excuse was a very good one. Furthermore, Alur who had Lendu attached to them, necessarily with the approbation of the chief, could presumably send their Lendu to cultivate for the chief in place of themselves. This is no longer possible, nor is it easy for the chief to get his fields dug today unless he gives beer for it like any commoner.

Chiefs did not attempt to eliminate fighting and feuding altogether. They generally permitted segments to fight for a day or two in prosecution of feud and vengeance, but would then send instructions for them to stop, or they might receive an appeal to do so from an elder of the fighting groups. The chief would send a courtier with his bow, or quiver, or in some areas just a wand of elephant grass. If fighting did not stop at this signal, the chief was insulted and would be apt to come with followers to plunder the property of the offenders, or even burn their huts in cases of extreme recalcitrance. It was in such situations that people liked to have a chief's son among them to restore order in a gentler fashion through his supernatural aura and personal presence. For homicide, in addition to the feuding involved, the killer and his group had to give a sheep to the chief, who poured its blood over his offended stool. Groups out of favor with the chief won back favor by sending him cattle or a girl whom he could marry or bestow on a favorite follower. In all these matters the status of the subject peoples was the same as that of the Alur, but the precision with which these procedures were fulfilled in each case depended upon the peoples' proximity to a chief and upon the magnitude of his power.

The responsibility and control of the chief over witchcraft was also of fundamental importance here. Not only was it often a crucial element in the incidence of violence, but it was central to the fears and anxieties of all, so that a chief's superiority over and immunity to witchcraft was the supreme demonstration of his personal and supernatural qualification to rule. Great chiefs had medicine which, when rubbed on their stool at night, brought the naked, red witches crawling before them. Like a police chief who could not afford to eliminate crime or criminals completely, the chief kept the activities of witches within tolerable bounds by identifying them and sometimes allowing one to be eliminated—but for this loss of a subject the witch's accusers had to compensate the chief. The general beliefs of the Alur and the subject peoples were sufficiently similar in this regard to permit fairly uniform action, presumably after centuries of trickling assimilation.

While in the older and larger Alur chiefdoms Alur was the dominant language and Okebo, Lendu, and Madi groups no longer spoke their own languages at all or were in some cases bilingual, speaking their own languages with many Alur words mixed in, the newer and more peripheral chiefdoms also tended to be more marginal in language and culture. In Jukoth the chiefs and most of the people spoke Lendu as well as Alur. The Mambisa Alur (1956: 220-224), who went furthest away among the Lendu, lost their Alur speech altogether and became highly integrated into Lendu culture, except for the crucial fact that they retained their political dominance together with most of the politically relevant aspects of Alur culture. Next to the Mambisa were the Hima (Hema) (1956: 16-17) rulers and cattlekeepers who had left their interlacustrine Bantu kingdoms and gone among the Lendu, becoming likewise highly acculturated except in the political sphere.

In the case of the Okebo there was a very special aspect to their complementary assimilation to the Alur since most of them were ironworkers, both smelting ore and forging tools and weapons. Tradition portrays the Alur as dependent on Okebo ironworkers since time immemorial. There seems to have been no time at which any Alur could either smelt or forge, so that the Okebo presence goes back in a real sense to the very beginnings of Alur society. Okebo ironwork, symbolized in the hoe which was an important article of exchange and payment as well as the technical foundation of agricultural production, gave them an immense pride and self-satisfaction which compensated for their political subordination. They never tired of repeating how helpless the Alur would be without them and how quickly they would starve. Strangely enough not all Okebo clans were smiths, but most of those in close association with the Alur certainly were, and the latter tend to speak of Okebo and ironwork in the same breath. Nonetheless the Okebo remained basically subsistence cultivators and keepers of domestic animals like everyone else.

None of the other ethnic groups had any complementary specialization comparable in importance to that of the Okebo nor any that was generally recognized. However, some chiefs seem to have had a corps of Madi followers who acted as a kind of bodyguard. (1956: 90, 231) Although the southern Madi with whom the Alur had dealings lacked any organization which could muster a strong fighting force, they were regarded individually as intrepid warriors. Although such a group of Madi were Alur subjects their position was an honorable one. The Alur had many affinal and consanguineal links with independent and semi-independent Madi resulting from intermarriage with them. Alur on the escarpment above the Nile valley went down to the lower country of the Madi for shea butternuts in season. They also obtained their solid wooden stools by exchange with the Madi whose country provided a better supply of suitable hardwood trees. The chief of the Ukuru Alur, whose own mother was a Madi, told me that their greatest diviners in the past (*julambila*) were always Madi who used the rubbing stick method similar to that of the neighboring Lugbara and the Zande.

In some chiefdoms where the Abira counted as aboriginals relative to the Alur, they performed a special rain dance as a part of the rainmaking ritual of the Alur chief. If the Lendu had any complementary specialization it lay in their abundant herbal medicine and magic, much of which was drawn upon by the Alur as their vocabulary in this field indicates. The Lendu, Okebo, and Madi, although each speaking quite distinct languages, particularly in the case of the Lendu, nonetheless belong to the Moru-Madi language group and in this sense and in a great deal of their culture stand together over against the Alur. The latter have certainly borrowed rituals, kin terms, and a great deal of material culture from them. Indeed Alur material culture is more Moru-Madi than Lwoo in tools, weapons, basketry, and often in house construction, reflecting a time in the past when the local Moru-Madi groups attached to Alur chiefs and noble families were required to produce these goods for them.

Although there were some radical differences between these Moru-Madi peoples and the Alur in such structural features as their patrilineages, their kinship relations and their marriage and family arrangements, in all these matters the two peoples were sufficiently close to permit these differences to be largely glossed over by both sides during the process of incorporation, involving as it did a good deal of linguistic and ritual interchange which occurred so gradually that it doubtless went unnoticed by most people. However, the superordinate position of the Alur and those most assimilated to them vis-à-vis all the rest received constant cultural expression. The Alur professed to regard the rest as bad-mannered and uncouth people who ate dirty and repulsive things like frogs, snakes and other reptiles, and even elephant meat. Although there were real differences in diet, many of the stated ones were fanciful and had meaning only as a dramatization of the cultural dimension of status differences. The Lendu in particular were derided for their practice of circumcision. "Your penis is red!" was said of them in scorn. Perhaps this was related to the greater disapproval of intermarriage between Alur girls and Lendu men than between Alur girls and Madi or Okebo, though it is surprising that there was no resistance to the uncircumcised Alur marrying Lendu girls. Some Lendu groups actually gave up circumcision under Alur influence.

While costume varied a good deal locally, and partly for obvious ecological reasons, there was a general distinction between the dress of the Alur and the rest. Alur men traditionally wore calf or antelope skins over their shoulders (1956: plate 27), sometimes with a small skin over their private parts, while men of the other peoples wore a fairly large skin between their legs which folded over a waist cord before and behind. Alur women wore a long fiber tail hanging between their buttocks and a very small, tight plug of leaves over their genitals in front. (1956: 92[plate 5], 270[plate 13]) The wives of some chiefs wore special aprons of dangling iron chains. Most of the Moru-Madi women wore much thicker bunches of leaves between their legs, covering their genitals in front and hanging from waist cords over their buttocks. Alur chiefs might confer the privilege of wearing calf or antelope shoulder skins on lineage heads of the subject peoples. Chiefs themselves had various other special garments exclusive to themselves: lion and leopard skins, barkcloth cloaks trimmed with colobus monkey fur, and crowns of cowrie shells. On the other hand, the *ambaya* (1956: 173 [plate 11]) cult of the Lendu, which is concerned with divination, fertility, dance, and other rituals, is espoused by noble Alur as well, and they wear its red feather emblem on festive occasions. There was no significant ecological counterpart of the different ethnic groups. The ecology itself was very varied, but its divisions did not correspond with distinct ethnic areas and was not strictly relevant to the question of incorporation. But there was a significant exchange of special products between different areas which to some extent knit together both Alur of different zones and the subject peoples with them, although all were practically self-sufficient locally for their basic subsistence. Fish were most plentiful in the Nile and Lake Albert and salt also came from the lowlands. On the other hand cattle only flourished in the high grasslands. Big game including elephant ivory was also more plentiful in the Nile Valley and in the west where the plateau sloped down towards the Congo forest. There were many other differences in emphasis on natural resources reflecting local variation of rainfall, temperature, soil fertility, entomology, and so forth. (1956: 10-14) The basic contrast of fish in the Nile valley and cattle in the highlands has persisted with, superimposed upon it during the last two or three decades, an increasing concentration on growing cotton as a cash crop in the midlands, and with less success in the lowlands. In the highlands cotton will not grow, and their dense populations developed a correspondingly heavy involvement in labor migration chiefly into rural Buganda to grow cotton on land rented or sharecropped from the Ganda. (1956b) Mainly during the last decade the economy of the highlands has been supplemented by successful planting of arabica coffee by the Alur. There were a number of European farms and plantations in Congo Alurland which provided local employment but did not seem to arouse the degree of hostility often associated with them in East Africa. Surface iron-ore deposits did not concentrate the Okebo, who seem to have been widely scattered through Alurland. There were few if any Okebo in the Nile valley, but all Alur seem to have had them within possible reach, though many small chiefdoms did not necessarily include them. There were thus general economic exchanges over quite long distances in the case of salt, fish, or hoes and more locally in various vegetable food stuffs. Then there were the special exchanges and circulations based upon the network of chiefs and their tribute. This concerned local foodstuffs, their attempted monopoly of elephant ivory, lion and leopard skins, colobus monkey skins, certain prized antelope skins such as kob, and the hindlegs of all edible game animals killed, particularly buffalo and antelope. Chiefs imported bark cloth from

Bunyoro in exchange for ivory, and later it became their means of obtaining firearms. Economic exchanges knit together the numerous zones, ethnic groups, and chiefdoms of which Alur society was composed and formed an important aspect of that wider and more complex organization which chiefs brought to their non-Alur peoples, but economic and ecological complementarities were not closely tied to ethnic differences except in the case of Okebo ironworking.

The Alur, secure in their conceit of inherent superiority, valued but despised the other peoples. Although they categorized them thus, and their superiority was expressed in ritual and in the political subordination of the other groups, it is doubtful whether this obtruded too much in the ordinary everyday dealings of man to man. Especially when a whole group of subject people was highly assimilated to Alur language and culture, structurally equivalent to Alur localized lineages around it, their intrinsic lower status and foreign ethnic origin (however remote) did not obtrude except when specific ritual precedence, intermarriage, or other crucial determinants were actually in question.

The Lendu had the lowest status. This factor and their general dependence upon the Alur they seem to have recognized with resignation. Their very name for the Alur of Jukoth was "rain" (*zhi*). The neighboring Hema of Blukwa, who like the founder of Jukoth came from Bunyoro but went straight among the Lendu as rulers, adopting their language and losing their own, simply refer to the Lendu as *matzabali* ("my people"). The Madi were much more respected than the Lendu, but the Alur still regarded their culture as inferior and despised their lack of political specialization. Although their association with Alur goes back to the beginnings of distinguishable tradition, they never seem to have been subordinated in such numbers as the Lendu. Some fairly small groups became highly assimilated and some others accepted Alur chiefs' sons among them. But the majority remained on the fringes of Alur society, going to Alur chiefs for rain but otherwise remaining largely autonomous. The Okebo were different because their ironworking specialization provided a strong basis of self-respect for them all. They could accept their political subordination and their dependence on Alur rain, while happily pointing out that the Alur could not survive without them. The Alur regarded Europeans during the colonial period as simply having taken over their own mantle as rulers, while the Okebo regarded them as having taken over their mantle as technological specialists! It is important to note that the early administrators of the Belgian Congo (who did not have the more spectacular political structures of the interlacustrine Bantu immediately before their eyes as in Uganda) also regarded the Alur as "civilizers of the hordes." (Quix 1939)

Although ritual occasions expressed the subordinate status of the subject peoples, they also expressed their membership as integral parts of Alur society. The ancestral shrine of a chief consisted of two miniature huts, one on the right for his chiefly ancestors and all the Lwoo, to be served by the living Lwoo; one on the left for the spirits of the non-Lwoo, the *lwak* (masses) or *jumiru* (serfs) and to be served by them. At Alur birth and marriage ceremonies and in the lengthy ritual preparations for Alur dances, or in the supernatural protection of villages, among recognizably Nilotic Lwoo elements there are important Moru-Madi (usually Lendu) components. On the other hand local groups of Lendu, Okebo, or Madi could easily carry on many distinctive ritual practices of their own, sometimes crudely approximating their terms and meanings to supposed Alur equivalents. Many topographical names all over Alurland are recognizably Lendu, though it is not always easy to distinguish Lendu from possibly cognate Madi or Okebo words, especially when they have already been considerably mangled by adoption into Alur speech.

Since the Republic of the Congo obtained its independence in 1960, the Congolese Alur must have depended vitally upon the maintenance of the power of chiefs as the principal local force for order and security, with even the resuscitation of some aspects of their political authority. No detailed information is available, although it is known that they have been subject to occasional attack by marauders of different political factions in which at least one major Alur chief has lost his life. The early Lumumbist influences were obviously hostile to chiefs and traditional authority, as their more extreme succeeding organizations have also been. But the struggle to restore law and order and the authority of the central government has obviously meant renewed reliance on chiefs with traditional legitimacy as the most stable local agents. There is no evidence or reason to suppose that this has significantly affected the relationship of Alur to Lendu and Okebo, though it would have been fascinating to study those relationships during this exceptional period. The new administrative chiefs whom the Belgians put over the Lendu and Okebo, who were disentangled from serfdom under the Alur, paid Alur chiefs the ultimate compliment of imitating their regalia and making them the model for their conception of chiefship.

In Uganda the central government has remained stable, but the climate has also been more favorable than in the rest of East Africa to maintaining some recognizable dignity and status for traditional chiefs, if not necessarily formal bureaucratic power. This has obviously been due to the pervasive influence of Buganda and its hereditary Kabaka in the Uganda state. Noting the successes achieved by the Ganda and their king in dealing with the British, all other peoples in Uganda were keen to emulate them if they had any basis for doing so, in the shape of hereditary rulers, however humble. The privileges of Buganda in the state structure have had a ripple effect through the western kingdoms of Ankole, Toro, and Bunyoro to remoter peoples such as the Alur. The relevance of this is that it bolsters the solidarity of the Alur as a self-cognizant people of distinct language and culture. It also had the effect of making all tribal peoples in Uganda see the occasion of independence as the moment in which they must make their final bid for such recognition as they might hope to receive. The Sebei won recognition as a new district, but here a halt was called and the guerrilla campaign by the Konjo in the Ruwenzori mountains has not won such a prize. There has been a determination by the central government to hold all boundaries (with the notable and unique exception of the Lost Counties of Bunyoro) for fear of the avalanche of demands which would follow any sign of flexibility.

Thus, the highly assimilated non-Lwoo groups among the Alur will certainly remain Alur. Lendu, Madi, or Okebo, who still speak their own languages and are conscious of a separate identity but reside in administrative counties which are recognized as Alur, have no hope of winning any separate recognition. Nor has Alur dominance any possibility of administrative extension. But in the Alur counties the Alur language will be used in primary schools, and it is likely that a somewhat diluted Alur culture will envelope non-Alur in those areas. Even the Alur themselves have no secure official recognition for their language in Uganda, which already suffers from a plethora of more than a half-dozen officially recognized local languages in radio, the press, schools, and government communications. The Alur situation is symbolized by the fact that they are not allowed a program of their own on Uganda radio, but have the right to an Alur announcer among those serving the general Lwoo program which is supposed to embrace Alur, Junam, Acoli, Lang'o, Palwo, and Padhola (Dama), but is in fact dominated by Acoli and Lang'o and is not always understood by the rest.

The Alur see themselves as maintaining and reinterpreting their traditional status when they hire Madi, or even Lugbara rather than Alur to work their cotton fields for wages, or when they regard themselves as meriting managerial rather than manual employment away from home. However, the day of the Alur as grand incorporators is obviously over. They could and did turn groups of other people into Alur quite successfully without excessive violence or injustice and at a level more profound than that of the merely political.

But their traditional ideology of subordination is out of tune with the egalitarian public ideology of contemporary Africa—less rigid, it is true, than that of the Rwanda Tutsi or the Rhodesian Europeans, and much more analogous to that of the Islamic northern Sudan in relation to the Christian and pagan south. The Alur will now exercise their talents and intelligence as minority members of the multitribal Uganda elite from which the transcendence of ethnicity will gradually spread through the society. But it will not effectively penetrate geographically remote communities, such as those of the rural Alur, until their subsistence economies are much more completely transformed and their basic level of schooling is raised to that critical point which everywhere in Africa leads to heightened mobility and increased urban involvement.

Hereditary kingship and chiefship have certainly fallen into disfavor more recently with the defeat and flight of the Kabaka of Buganda in 1966 and the stripping of their officially recognized status from other hereditary rulers by the Government of Uganda. However, the most important traditional chief of the Uganda Alur has not held any governmentally recognized office for some time and constitutes no threat to the political regime of independent Uganda, so that educated and urban Alur are still able to combine loyalty and service to the Uganda Government with a profound attachment to Alur chiefship as a fundamental part of their cultural heritage.

REFERENCES

Beattie, J. 1960. *Bunyoro: an African kingdom.* New York, Holt, Rinehart and Winston.

Crazzolara, J. P. 1950, 1951, 1954. *The Lwoo.* Volumes I, II, III. Vernoa, Editrice Nigrizia.

Evans-Pritchard, E. E. 1940. *The Nuer.* Oxford, Clarendon Press.

Girling, F. K. 1960. *The Acholi of Uganda.* London, Her Majesty's Stationery Office.

Quix, J. P. 1939. "Au pays de Mahagi." *Congo* 1(3): 276-294; 1(4): 387'-411.

Richards, A. I. (ed). 1960. *East African Chiefs* (Chap. 13, "The Alur"). London, Faber.

Southall, A. W. 1954a. "Alur tradition and its historical significance." *Uganda Journal* 18(2).

1954b. "Alur migrants." in A. I. Richards. *Economic development and tribal change.* pp. 140-160. Cambridge, Heffers & Sons.

1956. *Alur society: a study in processes and types of domination.* Cambridge, Heffers & Sons.

Forthcoming (a). "Twinship and symbolic structure." In J. La F. Sackur (ed.). *Festschift for Audrey Richards.* London, Tavistock.

Forthcoming (b). "Cross-cultural meanings and multilingualism." In *Social Implications of Multilingualism in Eastern Africa.* Ninth International African Seminar, Dar-es-Salaam, December, 1968.

5

THE POLITICAL INCORPORATION
OF NON-NYAMWEZI IMMIGRANTS
IN TANZANIA

R. G. Abrahams

INTRODUCTION

The area which I call Unyamwezi consists of the Tabora and Nzega Districts and the eastern half of the Kahama District of the former Western Province of Tanganyika.[1] It covers an area of about 34,000 square miles in which the Nyamwezi are, for the most part, both the politically dominant and the numerically preponderant tribe. The Nyamwezi are a Bantu-speaking people who numbered 363,258 in the official census of Tanganyika in 1957. As such they are the second largest tribe in the country, being smaller only than their closely related northern neighbors the Sukuma. Most, though by no means all, Nyamwezi live in Unyamwezi, and many other tribes are also represented in the area. The Sukuma, Sumbwa, and Tusi form the largest "foreign" contingents in a total population of around 450,000. More detailed figures are presented later in the paper.

Most of the inhabitants of Unyamwezi are farmers, though some Tusi do not practice agriculture. Various staple crops are grown including maize, sorghum, bulrush millet, and cassava. The year falls into two main seasons, a rainy season from around October until April and a dry season. The average rainfall is slightly under 35 inches per year, but rain is unpredictable from year to year and is often very poorly distributed. Land is for the most part plentiful but is in general of poor quality. Various cash crops have been tried with little success, and for more than a century the people have sought wealth as porters, traders, and laborers outside Unyamwezi. Cattle, though numerous, are mainly to be found in the Nzega district, where, as in northeast Kahama District, there has been much Sukuma immigration. Sukuma and Tusi tend to be the largest cattleowners in the region. Sheep and goats are

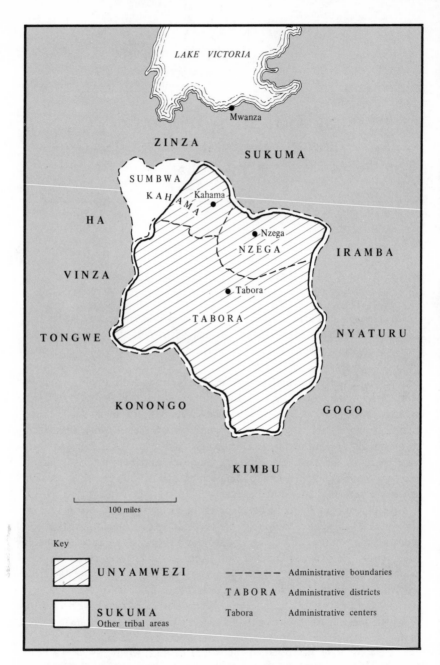

MAP 1. UNYAMWEZI AND SURROUNDING TRIBAL AREAS

much more evenly distributed, and chickens are found in most homesteads. The language normally used in the internal political organization of Unyamwezi, and indeed in most contexts of social life, is Nyamwezi itself, though some immigrants speak their own language among themselves. Most immigrants appear to have little difficulty acquiring sufficient Nyamwezi for their needs, and there are almost always fellow tribesmen with a knowledge of Nyamwezi who can initially serve as interpreters for them should this be necessary. In addition most men in the region speak good or fair Swahili, though this is true of relatively few women outside the towns and the rural area around Tabora. Swahili is the language used in communications between the people and the central government, and also in economic transactions with some Asian traders, but with the exception of the Tabora area, discussed later, it is rarely heard in discourse between rural Africans.

There are 31 chiefdoms in Unyamwezi, and every rural African is a citizen of a chiefdom. As such he is automatically involved in the set of relationships which link together a Nyamwezi chief, his subordinate officeholders, and their subjects. In addition, people are linked to each other by relationships of neighborhood, by common membership in secret societies, and by ties of kinship and marriage including membership in domestic groups. Interpersonal ties of friendship also exist. Almost all social life in Unyamwezi takes place within the framework of these different sets of relationships, and it is meaningful to talk of the social personality of an individual as the sum total of the different roles which he derives from his participation in them. Although there is some overlap between the different sets, both in their personnel and in the functions which they serve, it is necessary to realize that they are all distinct and that the differences between them receive explicit recognition in the social organization of the people. Thus, though some members of a village may have kinsfolk living there, the village as a whole is not a kinship unit, and neighborhood relationships are recognized as being distinct both from kinship ties and ties of common citizenship derived from the villagers' subordination to one chief and village headman.[2]

It may be noted here that Nyamwezi are not generally averse to foreigners as a class, and their long history of travel outside the region is almost certainly partly responsible for the absence of any rigid xenophobia among them. They have, moreover, never been politically united as a tribe, and fighting between Nyamwezi chiefdoms appears to have been as common in the past as that between them and their various non-Nyamwezi neighbors. Finally, as I shall try to show, their chiefdom system and other aspects of their social organization are on the whole well adapted to the incorporation of most types of immigrant.

THE TRIBES OF UNYAMWEZI

In Tanganyika, as in many other parts of Africa, there is no simple exact answer to the question of what constitutes a tribe. In the present paper, I shall use the term to refer primarily to the groups to which people assigned themselves in the official census of 1957 and in such public documents as court registers and files. Membership in such groups is typically passed on from father to son, and each such group considered here has its own home tribal territory or territories and, in most cases its own language and distinctive customs. I may add that I usually experienced no difficulty in eliciting a person's tribe in Unyamwezi, and people not infrequently volunteered the information in explanation of a particular piece of behavior. There is some evidence that people may change their tribal customs and, occasionally, their tribal affiliation in the course of time, and more will be said about some such changes later in the paper.

According to official census figures, the total African population of U-nyamwezi numbered 452,523 in 1957. The main features of the tribal composition of this population can be seen in Table 1. Tables 2a, 2b, and 2c give some picture of the local distribution of tribes in the region. It is in fact

TABLE 1. MAIN TRIBES OF UNYAMWEZI
(BASED ON 1957 CENSUS)*

Tribe	Numbers	Percent of Total
Nyamwezi	242,697	54
Sukuma	61,758	14
Sumbwa	34,309	8
Tusi	17,647	4
Iramba	17,311	4
Others	69,920	16
Total	443,642	100

*A small number of Sukuma, Tusi, and Iramba may have been excluded from these figures owing to inclusion under the category "unclassified" in some census areas.

TABLE 2a. POPULATION OF TABORA DISTRICT (BASED ON 1957 CENSUS)*

Tribe	Numbers	Percent of Total
Nyamwezi	70,421	43
Tusi	11,105	7
Sumbwa	9,739	6
Kimbu	9,697	6
Konongo	9,271	6
Ha	8,053	5
Sukuma	6,183	4
Manyema	5,192	3
Fipa	2,192	1
Others	30,145	19
Total	161,998	100

*The figures include the population of Tabora town which is made up as follows: Nyamwezi 3,660; Manyema 2,016; Sukuma 526; Zaramo 436; Bemba 328; Tusi 293; Nyasa 256; Ngoni 251; Fipa 245; Yao 242; Sumbwa 234; unclassified 3,518; total 12,005.

impossible to find a chiefdom in which fewer than four tribes are represented. Everywhere the Nyamwezi tend to be the largest tribe, though there are a few local exceptions to this general rule. Some tribes, such as the Iramba and the Kimbu, are found mainly in those chiefdoms which border their own country. Sukuma and Sumbwa are more widely distributed, and some Tusi are found in most areas where the herding of cattle is possible. Figures for the relatively small chiefdom of Busangi in northern Kahama District and for the large chiefdom of Busongo in northeastern Nzega District will serve as examples of the distribution of tribes in a chiefdom. In Busangi, out of a total 1957 population of 4,711, Nyamwezi numbered 2,359; Sukuma 1,080; Sumbwa 973; Rongo 119; Tusi 106; all others 74. In Busongo, out of a total 1957 population of 71,551, Nyamwezi numbered 34,764; Sukuma 28,160; Iramba 5,123; Sumbwa 1,439; Tusi 449; Taturu 348; Turu 235; all others 1,032. Comparable situations are found in most villages within a chiefdom. More-

TABLE 2b. POPULATION OF NZEGA DISTRICT
(BASED ON 1957 CENSUS)*

Tribe	Numbers	Percent of Total
Nyamwezi	119,760	59
Sukuma	42,531	21
Iramba	17,311	8
Sumbwa	9,714	5
Tusi	4,413	2
Kimbu	2,406	1
Others	7,620	4
Total	203,755	100

*The figures include the population of Nzega town for which separate 1957 figures are not available. In 1952 the African population of the town was 351, and it was still small at the time of fieldwork.

TABLE 2c. POPULATION OF THE EASTERN PART
OF KAHAMA DISTRICT* (BASED ON 1957 CENSUS)

Tribe	Numbers	Percent of Total
Nyamwezi	52,506	61
Sumbwa	14,856	17
Sukuma	13,044	15
Tusi	2,129	2
Rongo	1,049	1
Others	3,196	4
Total	86,780	100

*Owing to the abstraction of these figures from the figures for the local census areas in eastern Kahama District, the category "others" probably includes a few Sukuma, Tusi, and Rongo. The figures include the population of Kahama Town which was given in the census as Nyamwezi 690; Sumbwa 238; Others 550; total 1,478.

over, with the partial exception of the Tusi who occasionally live together on the outskirts of a village, the homesteads of the representatives of different tribes within a village are typically intermixed rather than forming discrete subdivisions of the settlement.

As may be seen from the map, many of the outside tribes represented in the area have territories which border upon Unyamwezi. The Manyema and some of the Tusi are the chief exceptions. The Manyema, who originally came from beyond Lake Tanganyika in the Congo, are mainly descendants of carriers and slaves brought into the region during the last century. Most of them are settled in Tabora District. Many of the Tusi come from Ha country in the west, but some of them have come into the region from more distant interlacustrine areas to the northwest.

DIFFERENCES AND SIMILARITIES BETWEEN THE TRIBES

It is impossible within the limits of a single paper, and indeed within the limits of my fieldwork data, to present an adequate, detailed account of differences and similarities between the Nyamwezi and each of the many outside tribes whose members may be found in Unyamwezi. Instead, in the present section I shall mainly discuss the position with regard to the Sukuma, Sûmbwa, and Tusi who, as I have mentioned, form the largest and most widely distributed foreign contingents in the population of the area. From the point of view of culture and social organization, these three tribes in fact constitute a reasonably good sample of the groups incorporated in Unyamwezi. The Sukuma are quite the most similar to the Nyamwezi of all the tribes represented in the region, while the Tusi are one of the most distinctive groups there. The Sumbwa fall between these two extremes, and much that I shall say about them here appears to be applicable in general terms to a majority of other tribal groups found in the region.

There is no doubt that the Nyamwezi and Sukuma are in many ways a single people. They speak the same language with some differences of dialect, and the dialect of a northern Nyamwezi is closer to that of a southern Sukuma than to that of a southern Nyamwezi. The two tribes are, moreover, very similar to one another both in their general culture and in their social and political organization. The boundary between Unyamwezi and Sukumaland is that between the Western and Lake Provinces of Tanganyika, and, as one might expect, this boundary is a relatively arbitrary one. The Shinyanga District of Sukumaland was for many years a part of Western Province, and the ruling families of some northern Nyamwezi chiefdoms share common descent with some southern Sukuma ruling families.

Despite the great overall similarity between the two peoples, however, there are also some differences between them. More favorable ecological conditions in Sukumaland have enabled the Sukuma to develop a more powerful economy based on cotton growing and on cattle owning, and there are also a few regional differences in kinship and political organization which more or less correspond with the boundary between the two tribal areas. Thus, the kinship terminology, although similar for both peoples, is not applied in exactly the same way in both areas, and the strong Sukuma commoner associations, the *basumba batale*, are lacking in Unyamwezi.[3] Finally, the boundary between the Lake and Western Provinces is of considerable importance in itself in certain contexts, even though it is a relatively arbitrary one. Mwanza and Tabora, the administrative centers of the two provinces, are situated about 100 miles to the north and south of the boundary respectively, and much of the governmental and economic business of the Provinces is directed from these centers, so that in many aspects of their lives the backs of the two peoples are metaphorically turned upon each other.

Under normal circumstances, the similarities between the Nyamwezi and Sukuma clearly facilitate the assimilation of members of the two tribes into each other's territories. The similarities have not, however, prevented the development of some peculiarly difficult problems in the incorporation of Sukuma into Unyamwezi within recent years. I shall say something about these special problems in a later section. Here it is sufficient to note that they have been intimately connected with an unusually high rate of immigration of Sukuma cattleowners into certain parts of the country.

Usumbwa, the country of the Sumbwa, borders upon northwest Unyamwezi. In the somewhat scanty literature about the area, the Sumbwa are usually described as a branch of the Nyamwezi, and some Sumbwa claim that they are in fact the original Nyamwezi. Similar claims are also sometimes made by the Konongo who lie to the southwest of Unyamwezi. However this may be, the Sumbwa today appear to differ considerably from the Nyamwezi both in their language and in certain other aspects of their culture and social organization. Linguistically, the people seem to be closer than the Nyamwezi to some of the southern tribes of the interlacustrine region such as the Ha, the Haya, and the Zinza. Traditions of subordination to the Haya kingdom of Karagwe in the earlier part of the nineteenth century provide a possible reason for this. The Sumbwa in Usumbwa grow at least one crop, eleusine, which is not normally found in Unyamwezi, and, largely owing to the prevalence of tsetse in the area, they possess very few cattle. In their kinship system, they are said to allow marriages between certain categories of kinsfolk, whereas marriages between kinsfolk are not normally permitted among the Nyamwezi. Their political system also differs in some details from that of the Nyamwezi, with the result that I have found it necessary to exclude the Sumbwa chiefdoms of Kahama District from my earlier study of Nyamwezi political organization.[4]

It would, however, be unwise to place too much emphasis upon these differences between the Nyamwezi and the Sumbwa in the present context. Like most immigrants, Sumbwa experience comparatively little difficulty in learning to speak Nyamwezi, and the two languages apparently tend to merge on the borders of the two countries. Both peoples are basically agricultural in their economy, and their residence patterns and village organization are more or less similar. Intermarriage between members of both groups is found and is not, to my knowledge, subject to any generalized disapproval. Again, both peoples have broadly similar political systems in which law and order is maintained to a considerable extent through the chiefdom organization, and neither Sumbwa nor Nyamwezi society is rigidly class-stratified. Lastly, both peoples share a number of secret societies, so that a Sumbwa coming into Unyamwezi does not usually find it difficult to continue his cult life as a member of such a society.

The situation with respect to the Tusi is rather different. Before outlining it, however, it may be noted that the name "Tusi" is used somewhat loosely in Unyamwezi to refer both to Tusi from Ha country and to the related Hima, Huma, and Tutsi from such countries as Ankole, Buzinza, and Ruanda. Such peoples also tend to describe themselves as Tusi when in Unyamwezi. In addition, it appears that the name "Tusi" is occasionally used by and to refer to people who, although they come from "Tusi" areas, might nonetheless not normally be classed as Tusi, Hima, and the like in their home territory.

The people called and calling themselves Tusi tend to differ from the Nyamwezi in a number of important respects. Firstly, they are primarily pastoralists. A considerable number of them do not engage in any agriculture whatsoever, and some of them live in small Tusi communities on the outskirts of Unyamwezi villages, rather than within the settled area of the village. Linguistically, they speak closely interrelated languages of the interlacustrine group. They also differ from the Nyamwezi in their kinship system which is patrilineal, as opposed to the more bilateral organization of the Nyamwezi, and permits certain marriages between kin. Finally, they come from highly stratified societies in which they typically form the aristocracy, though it should be stressed that they are in no sense politically or socially dominant in Unyamwezi.

Perhaps even more important than such substantive differences between the Tusi and the Nyamwezi are the Tusi values which accompany such differences. The Tusi are in general anxious to maintain their identity as a distinct group in Unyamwezi. They do not appear to favor intermarriage with non-Tusi, though some of their women occasionally marry men of other groups. Tusi men, in my experience, almost without exception marry Tusi women, and they sometimes travel long distances to their home country in order to find a wife if one is not readily available in Unyamwezi.[5] They join some of the local secret societies, but they have their separate Swezi spirit cult, despite the existence of a Nyamwezi-Sumbwa Swezi society in the region.[6]

Under these circumstances, it is not surprising that the Tusi are one of the least well-integrated elements in the population of Unyamwezi. More will be said in later sections about special problems which their presence in the region raises.

To close this section, I shall say a little about one of the other tribes of Unyamwezi, the Rongo, who specialize in blacksmithing and bow-making. Some of them are also active hunters, making their own ammunition and repairing their own muzzle-loading guns. The Rongo, who are mainly found in northern Unyamwezi, are the only tribal group who specialize in an important craft within the region. They appear to come originally from Sumbwa and Zinza country, and their culture appears to be similar to that of the Sumbwa. They are often classed generically with the Sumbwa and the Zinza as *banyamweli*, or westerners. Some of them engage in relatively little agriculture, relying upon their ability to purchase food from the profits of their iron work and hunting. In the past, before the introduction of large quantities of European hoes and axes, they were an extremely important group in the economy of the region. Nowadays, however, their position has been undermined by such imported goods, and they themselves prefer to buy these goods rather than produce them by hand. They are, however, able to gain some income from making bows and arrows, repairing guns, hunting, and making certain nonimported iron tools and artifacts such as small cattle bells and the long-bladed axes used for making local stools. Like the Sumbwa, they present no special problems of integration into the wider community in which they live.

NYAMWEZI POLITICAL ORGANIZATION

In the previous section, the main similarities and differences between the Nyamwezi and the three largest and most widely distributed "outside" tribes in Unyamwezi were discussed. Something was also said about the position of a specialist tribal group, the Rongo. I turn now to consider certain features of the Nyamwezi political system which are relevant to the incorporation of outsiders in the area. Two main sets of features need to be distinguished in this context. Firstly, there are various rights and obligations of chiefdom citizenship which apply to all members of a chiefdom irrespective of their tribe. Following Parsons, these may be described as "universalistic" features of the system. Secondly, there are a number of "particularistic" features of the system which allow for special treatment of subgroups within a chiefdom.[7] I shall start by outlining the universalistic elements of chiefdom organization.

As was mentioned earlier, every rural African who lives in Unyamwezi is a citizen of a chiefdom, and as such he automatically has certain rights and obligations vis-à-vis the chief and other officeholders in the chiefdom and his fellow subjects. Among the most important of his obligations are the need to pay taxes, the need to respect and obey the chief and his subordinate rulers, and the need to keep the peace. Among his most important rights are those to secure tenure of land, to have his disputes settled by the courts, and more generally to be protected by his rulers against any usurpation of his privileges as a citizen. Of great importance in the past, but rather less so in recent years, was the right of citizens to the ritual services of the chief and other rulers who, by sacrifice and other ritual means, were believed able to procure good rainfall and prosperity for their subjects. Most of these rights and obligations are, broadly speaking, similar to those which would be held by any non-Nyamwezi citizen of Unyamwezi in his home country, and the system thus provides a readily understood framework in which the inhabitants of the region can carry on their life in an orderly and secure fashion irrespective of tribal differences between them.

The universalistic nature of some of these features of Nyamwezi chiefdom organization receives overt expression at the installation ceremonies of chiefs. In the public part of these ceremonies, which any member of the chiefdom may attend, the new chief is formally addressed by one of the ritual officers of the chiefdom. In the course of this address, the chief is told that he no longer has a father or a mother, and that all the people, including these, are now his children. He is admonished not to hesitate to share his food with any of his subjects, and he is told that he must be just in his court, neither favoring the rich nor maltreating the poor. He is warned that the prosperity of the country is in his hands and that he should follow the customs of his predecessors. Similar speeches are made to the chief by visiting rulers who attend the ceremonies. The subjects gathered there are also told that they must help and honor their new ruler.

I turn now to look at some of the particularistic features of the chiefdom system. One of the most important of these in the present context is the tolerant acceptance of some differences in customary law between the members of the different tribal groups within the region. This is particularly the case in relation to what one might call the domestic or private as opposed to the public and more overtly political domain of social life in Unyamwezi. It is clearly recognized by all concerned that different tribes have different customs and that, providing there are no unwelcome public consequences, members of these tribes need not all follow the same rules in every sphere of their behavior. If a Tusi, for example, says that he does not eat chicken, people do not say that he should do so because he is a citizen of a Nyamwezi chiefdom in which the majority of the inhabitants eat chicken. Again, it is apparently the case that Tusi who are friends will sometimes allow each other access to their wives.[8] As far as Nyamwezi are concerned, this is a custom which they themselves do not practice, but they do not seem to feel that Tusi in the region ought to cease to practice it. Similarly, non-Nyamwezi are not enjoined to follow Nyamwezi customs of inheritance, nor are they legally bound to pay bridewealth according to the Nyamwezi pattern for such payments, since the form and amount of bridewealth paid in Unyamwezi is basically a matter of mutual agreement between the parties to a marriage themselves. Thus the Tusi, whose bridewealth customs differ considerably from those of the Nyamwezi, are not expected to marry according to Nyamwezi custom, and they may even bring their marriage disputes to the chiefdom court and have them settled in accordance with their own practices which are explained to the court by a neutral Tusi assessor. Sometimes such a person is called upon *ad hoc,* but in several chiefdoms one of the elders is, in fact, a Tusi.

This reference to Tusi court elders in some chiefdoms brings me to the second main particularistic feature of the system, namely the existence of special representatives for one or more tribal groups within some Nyamwezi chiefdoms. The only reasonably regular occurrence of such representation is, in fact, with respect to the Tusi who are, as I have said, the most distinctive of the larger "outside" groups in the area. My information on this topic is not very full, but as far as I can tell, the situation is as follows. It appears that, until relatively recently, all chiefdoms in which sizable Tusi minorities were living had a recognized Tusi leader, known as *ntwale wa Batusi*, who served as a general intermediary between the Tusi population of the chiefdom and the chief. His position was, at least in some Tabora District chiefdoms, a paid office recognized by the central government. Nowadays, governmental recognition of the *ntwale's* position is rare, and a number of chiefs have bypassed this problem by appointing such men, or occasionally another Tusi, as a paid court elder in their court.

The only comparable case which I have found with respect to other tribal groups within the region concerns the Sukuma. In one Kahama District chiefdom in which there had been a high rate of Sukuma immigration, the chief adopted the unusual procedure of allowing the predominantly Sukuma population of one of his recently settled northern villages to choose their own headman. He did this as a gesture of good will towards them, though in fact they chose the person who would most likely have been made headman in any case, namely the man who had first cleared bush in the new settlement. This is, however, the only case which I have met of special treatment for Sukuma immigrants, and the group concerned forms only a section of the Sukuma population of the chiefdom.

It may be added here that there is no institutionalized bar upon the holding of headmanships by non-Nyamwezi in the region. That comparatively few of them do so is largely because many of these offices are held by members of the Nyamwezi ruling family of a chiefdom who, it should be noted, form only a small proportion of the Nyamwezi population of the areas they rule. Some headmanships are, however, held by personal followers of a chief and first clearers of the bush, or the descendants of such men, and a reasonable proportion of these office holders seem to be non-Nyamwezi.

It appears from the above material that the Nyamwezi chiefdom system provides a relatively flexible and undemanding framework for the incorporation of non-Nyamwezi elements into the population of the region. That it should do so is in keeping with another feature of the system, namely the strong interdependence which exists between the rulers of the area and their subjects. I have described elsewhere the form which this interdependence takes (Abrahams 1967a: Chapter VII). Here it is sufficient to point out that Nyamwezi chiefs, for their part, obtain considerable benefits from the possession of a large subject body, and that they are therefore generally anxious to maintain and if possible increase the size of the population of their chiefdoms. The population of the area, both Nyamwezi and non-Nyamwezi, is a fairly mobile one, and the system appears to be well designed to allow any Nyamwezi chiefdom to serve as a possible catchment area for a diverse body of new subjects.

To close this section, a little may be said about the place of non-Nyamwezi residents in Nyamwezi villages with particular respect to the system of neighborhood relationships which I mentioned earlier. In a previous publication (Abrahams 1965) I pointed out that such relationships in northern Unyamwezi provide a secondary framework for political organization, the main feature of this being the existence of a well-developed system of informal neighborhood courts. In other parts of the country relationships between neighbors are recognized as a distinct category but their political role appears to be relatively attenuated. The main point in the present context is that neighborhood obligations in all parts of the country apply to members of the local community concerned irrespective of their tribe. Thus neighbors as such, rather than neighbors of particular tribes, are expected in northern Unyamwezi, for example, to help each other thresh bulrush millet, build houses, attend funerals, and participate in the system of neighborhood courts. The only people who, in my experience, are not involved in such neighborhood cooperation are those Tusi who do not reside within the settled area of Nyamwezi villages. As will be seen in the next section, however, the extra-village residence of such Tusi is a source of conflict in the area.

Neighborhood relationships thus provide a further universalistic framework for the incorporation of foreign elements into Nyamwezi social and, in northern Unyamwezi, political life. As far as I can ascertain, members of the tribes concerned have little difficulty adapting to this system. Although adequate data is lacking for most areas, except Sukumaland where a similar system to that found in northern Unyamwezi prevails, it appears that at least some of the other tribes in question have comparable forms of neighborhood organization in their home territories.[9]

FURTHER ASPECTS OF SUKUMA AND TUSI IMMIGRATION

In the previous section I described how Nyamwezi political institutions are in general well adapted to the incorporation of foreign elements in the population, and I discussed the special treatment of the Tusi and some Sukuma in the region. In the present section, I shall look more closely at some aspects of Sukuma immigration into northern Unyamwezi, and I shall also say a little more about the position of the Tusi in the area.

As I have already mentioned, there has been a high rate of Sukuma immigration into northern Unyamwezi within recent years. Thus the Sukuma population of Kahama District, which has always tended to live in the eastern, Nyamwezi, part of the District, was recorded as 4,902 in the official census of 1948, whereas the figure had increased by almost 200 percent to 13,380 by 1957. In Nzega district, the figures for this period are less startling, with a rise of nearly 25 percent from 34,803 to 42,531. The rise since 1931, however, when the Sukuma population was recorded as 3,537, has been extremely high, even granting some inaccuracy of the census. Although exact figures are lacking, it is clear from a variety of evidence that a large proportion of these Sukuma immigrants into northern Unyamwezi are cattle owners and that many of them possess comparatively large herds of cattle. The main attraction of the region for them has been the availability of good grazing land, and in Kahama District this has been coupled with the absence of a formal system of cattle culling.

At least in northern Kahama District, where the rate of immigration has been highest in most recent years, the influx of Sukuma cattle owners has created certain difficulties. The immigrants appear to have entered too quickly and in too large numbers to permit their gradual absorption into the existing population, and some chiefs find it hard to exercise adequate control over them. This task is rendered the more difficult by the fact that the Sukuma like to settle in the better grazing areas which are often situated at a considerable distance from chiefdom headquarters.

The main difficulty which chiefs have experienced in this respect has been in tax collection, but there has also been a more general tendency for some of the immigrants to live their own lives without reference to the chiefdom system, including the chiefdom courts. Some chiefs have been more successful than others in handling this situation, though none of them appears to have found the problem easy. The more successful ones have made a strong effort to get to know the immigrants, and they have paid fairly frequent visits to the areas of Sukuma settlement in order to do this. It was one of these chiefs also who, as I described, allowed some of his Sukuma subjects to choose their own headman. Less successful chiefs have tended to pay less attention to the problem, and in one case this contributed seriously to the downfall of the chief in question. In such cases, it is not uncommon to find Sukuma immigrants who have never seen their chief, and some of them are not even sure of his name. In general, it appears that while the problems posed by this large-scale Sukuma immigration are not insuperable, they have nonetheless stretched the resources of the chiefdom system and the chiefs themselves to an unusually severe degree.

In my earlier discussions of the Tusi, I have mentioned that they are one of the least well-integrated elements in Unyamwezi's population. I have also noted that they receive special treatment as a minority in some Nyamwezi chiefdoms, and I have described how Nyamwezi tolerate a number of differences between their own customs and those of the Tusi. It must, however, be admitted that despite this tolerance the Nyamwezi exhibit some dislike of the Tusi, and particularly the most separatist elements amongst them, and this dislike provides one of the very few cases I have encountered of a definite Nyamwezi prejudice against the members of another tribe. Although my information for the eastern part of Unyamwezi is relatively weak, it appears that a comparable attitude is also adopted there towards some of the local Nilohamitic-speaking Daturu pastoralists.

Although it is not always obvious at first sight, a main source of this antagonism of the Nyamwezi to the Tusi appears to be the fact, already noted, that some of the Tusi do not live together with the other inhabitants of the region but pursue a dominantly pastoral existence in encampments on the outskirts of the ordinary villages. Typical expressions of the prejudice against them take the form of statements made by Nyamwezi chiefs and commoners alike that Tusi are in general bad citizens and in particular extremely active cattle thieves. When one points out that members of other tribes in the area, including Nyamwezi and Sukuma, also steal cattle, one is told that the Tusi are especially bad in this respect. I must confess that I do not possess the necessary figures for testing whether the Tusi actually steal cattle more often than do members of the other tribes within the region, and it is possible, considering their pastoral interests, that they in fact do so. It appears unlikely, however, that such figures in themselves would be sufficient to account for Nyamwezi attitudes towards the Tusi. First, if one questions Nyamwezi about Tusi cattle stealing, they often tend to phrase their answers with respect to Tusi residence patterns rather than in terms of statistics. "Why," they ask, "do Tusi like to live among themselves away from other people, if not better to pursue their cattle-thieving activities?" Secondly, although the Nyamwezi are, as I have said, quite tolerant of many Tusi customs there are some additional Tusi practices which seem to them repugnant. The Tusi are apparently much freer sexually with the wives of their close kinsmen, and particularly those of their sons, than are the Nyamwezi, and the people like to quote this fact against them as an example of their bad behavior.[10]

The Tusi, then appear to tax the hospitality of the Nyamwezi in a rather different manner from that described for the Sukuma immigrants. In the latter case the rate of immigration seems to have been a most important variable, which has counterbalanced the strong cultural similarities between the Nyamwezi and Sukuma, although the Sukuma tendency to live well away from chiefdom headquarters has also been significant. In the Tusi case, it appears that the cultural distinctiveness of the Tusi, and its residential correlates have been the major factors involved.

PROCESSES OF CHANGE

So far in this paper I have concentrated on giving a more or less static account of the position of avowedly non-Nyamwezi citizens in Nyamwezi chiefdoms. I turn now to a brief discussion of some past and present changes in the composition and behavior of the various tribes within the region, beginning with the Nyamwezi themselves.

According to the traditions of the people, about three hundred years ago Unyamwezi was an uninhabited country abounding in all sorts of game, and the ancestors of the present ruling families began to move into the area about this time. It appears, as I have mentioned, that the country has never been politically united. Rather, it seems to have always been divided among several separate ruling dynasties, most of which possess a number of chiefdoms at the present time. Each dynasty claims distinct origins and entry into the country. Thus one claims to have come from Kenya, another from Uganda, another from the eastern part of Tanganyika, and yet another from the region of Lake Tanganyika in the west. Always they came as hunters. In some cases, the dynasties claim to be descended from members of still extant tribes such as the Kamba of Kenya and the Kimbu. In other cases, the tribes concerned no longer exist, at least under their old names. Most Nyamwezi claim some connection, however tenuous, with a ruling dynasty of the region, though they often live in chiefdoms which do not belong to it. This last is, of course, consistent with the fairly high mobility of the population of the area. Such mobility also seems to go some way towards explaining the considerable, though by no means complete, cultural homogeneity which the Nyamwezi display despite the mutual independence of their chiefdoms and the claimed distinctive origins of the ruling dynasties. A full solution of the ethnological problems posed by this situation is not available at present and seems, in fact, unlikely to be found. The main point in the present context is that the dominant tribe of Unyamwezi, the Nyamwezi themselves, appears to be the product of a long process of amalgamation of rather diverse elements.

It is difficult to assess the extent to which this amalgamative process is still taking place. I personally came across only one case where a person of non-Nyamwezi parentage claimed to be Nyamwezi, and it is probably significant that the parents of the man concerned were both Sukuma. He explained his description of himself as Nyamwezi in terms of his long residence in the country. There is, however, one case where large numbers of people appear to have changed their tribal affiliation temporarily for purposes of the official census. This involves the Kimbu living in southern Tabora District. In the census of 1931, 23,323 Kimbu were recorded and many were said to be living in the area in question. In 1948 their numbers had apparently fallen to 14,873 and they were not listed as a separate Tabora District tribe. In the census of 1957, however, their numbers increased to 31,149 and nearly 10,000 of these were reported to be living in Tabora District. To a small extent, these discrepancies may be accounted for by the admitted inaccuracy of the 1931 Tabora District census, but it is almost certain that many Kimbu in Tabora District in 1948 described themselves simply as Nyamwezi and reverted to their Kimbu nomenclature in 1957. Whether a reverse trend will again take place is hard to say without more detailed study of that part of Unyamwezi.

With the partial exception of the basic rules of chiefdom and village organization, where these are not already customary to immigrants, the adoption of Nyamwezi custom by non-Nyamwezi in the region seems to be neither very common nowadays nor, in the light of the degree of tolerance prevailing there, especially necessary. Probably the most important case is that of some of the Tusi who have abandoned their traditional exclusive pastoralism and have taken up residence in Nyamwezi villages. Some of them have also begun to adopt patterns of marriage payments which are rather closer to those of the Nyamwezi than are their traditional ones. Unfortunately, I do not possess useful quantitative material upon this question, but it seems likely that half or more of the Tusi in the area have been involved in such changes. It is, moreover, difficult to ascertain to what extent the changes in question are a direct result of residence in Unyamwezi, since Scherer has reported some comparable phenomena for the Ha area from which many Tusi have migrated into Nyamwezi country. (Scherer 1965: 14)

Lastly, mention should be made of the rather special conditions which obtain in the rural area immediately surrounding the town of Tabora. Since the beginning of the present century a large number of people in this area have taken to Islam, and the population, both male and female, is for the most part bilingual in Nyamwezi and Swahili, using both languages in everyday conversation. Although Islamic custom has been modified in various ways to fit more closely with the cultural patterns of the region, these factors of religious and linguistic change have clearly served to even out many of the distinctive features which normally mark off the different tribal groupings of the region from one another.

CONCLUSION

In this paper I have discussed some of the main features of the position of non-Nyamwezi immigrants in Unyamwezi. I have shown that the population of the area is composed of members of a number of different tribes, and I have described the differences and similarities between the more important of these and the Nyamwezi. I have argued that Nyamwezi chiefdom and village organization is on the whole well-adapted to the incorporation of such peoples, and I have suggested that a major feature of this situation is the high degree of tolerance which Nyamwezi extend to non-Nyamwezi immigrants. I have, however, pointed out that some Tusi and, in certain areas, Sukuma immigrants pose special problems. In the course of my discussion I have found it useful to distinguish between universalistic and particularistic aspects of the political system, and between a domestic or private domain of custom, on the one hand, and a political or public domain on the other. I have also briefly discussed some past and present processes of change within the region.

Two final points may be made here. First, it appears from my discussion of the special problems posed by the Sukuma and the Tusi that cultural homogeneity is not enough in itself to guarantee successful incorporation, and that cultural diversity does not alone necessarily make such incorporation difficult. Other factors such as rate of immigration and residence patterns may be of at least as great if not greater importance.

Second, it is clear from the material presented that the inhabitants of Unyamwezi are only "tribesmen" in particular contexts, and that membership in a particular tribe is more or less irrelevant in many areas of social and political life within the region. This is a point which has been made strongly in analyses of urban social systems (Epstein 1958, Gluckman 1961), but its applicability to many rural areas is less often stressed. Nor is it simply a matter of the units involved in the rural social system being subdivisions of a tribe, as might be the case among such peoples as the Tiv of northern Nigeria. In Unyamwezi, as in many other parts of Africa, the social and political units in question tend to obliterate tribal boundaries rather than to form subcategories within them.

NOTES

---

1. The writer carried out anthropological fieldwork among the Nyamwezi between 1957 and 1960 as a Junior Research Fellow of the East African Institute of Social Research. The present tense in the text refers to the period of fieldwork.

2. For further details of Nyamwezi neighborhood organization see Abrahams 1965.

3. For an account of these Sukuma organizations see Cory 1954: 77-78 and *passim* and Revington 1938.

4. See Abrahams 1967a which is a revised version of the study referred to. For an overall survey of Nyamwezi, Sumbwa, and Sukuma see also Abrahams 1967b.

5. Scherer (1965: 47) records a similar pattern for the Tusi in Buha.

6. For a discussion of the Swezi cult in the Nyamwezi area see Bosch 1930: 202-217 and Cory 1955. Beattie 1957 gives an account of the cult in Bunyoro.

7. This distinction is roughly similar to but not exactly coincident with that drawn by Fortes (1958: 6).

8. See also d'Hertefelt 1962: 60 and Oberg 1943: 585.

9. On the Sukuma see Cory 1954: 67 and *passim*. Scherer (1962: 195) mentions the importance of neighborhood relationships among the Ha, and I myself was told in the field that the Sumbwa have a comparable system to that of the Nyamwezi.

10. See also Scherer 1965: 51, 177 and Maquet 1961: 42-43 for corroborative material from Buha and Ruanda.

REFERENCES

Abrahams, R. G. 1965. "Neighborhood organization: a major sub-system among the northern Nyamwezi." *Africa* 35 (2): 168-186.

1967a. *The political organization of Unyamwezi.* Cambridge, Cambridge University Press.

1967b. *The peoples of greater Unyamwezi.* London, International African Institute.

Beattie, J. 1957. "Initiation into the Cwezi possession cult in Bunyoro." *African Studies* 16: 150-161.

Bösch, P. 1930. *Les Banyamwezi.* Münster, Anthropos Bibliothek.

Cory, H. 1954. *The indigenous political system of the Sukuma and proposals for political reform.* Kampala, East African Institute for Social Research.

1955. "The Buswezi." *American Anthropologist* 57(5): 923-952.

d'Hertefelt, M. 1962. "Le Rwanda." in A. A. Trouwborst, M. d'Hertefelt, J. H. Scherer. *Les anciens royaumes de la zone interlacustre méridionale.* pp. 15-112. London, Oxford University Press. (Another edition of this book is published by the Musée royal d'Afrique centrale Terruren.)

Epstein, A. L. 1958. *Politics in an urban African community.* Manchester, Manchester University Press.

Fortes, M. 1958. Introduction to J. Goody (ed.), *The developmental cycle in domestic groups.* Cambridge, Cambridge University Press.

Gluckman, M. 1961. "Anthropological problems arising from the African industrial revolution." in A. Southall (ed.), *Social change in modern Africa.* pp. 67-82. London, Oxford University Press.

Maquet, J. 1961. *The premise of inequality in Rwanda.* London, Oxford University Press.

Oberg, K. 1943. "Three systems of primitive economic organization." *American Anthropologist* 45: 572-587.

Revington, T. M. 1938. "Concerning the Banangoma and Basumba Batale societies of the Bukwimba Basukuma." *Tanganyika Notes and Records* 5: 60-62.

Scherer, J. H. 1962. "Le Buha," in: A. A. Trouwborst, M. d'Hertefelt, J. H. Scherer, *Les anciens royaumes de la zone interlacustre méridionale.* London, Oxford University Press. (Also published at Tervuren.)

1965. *Marriage and bridewealth in the highlands of Buha (Tanganyika).* Groningen.

6

MARRIAGE POLICY AND INCORPORATION IN NORTHERN GHANA

Jack Goody

INTRODUCTION

The problem of political incorporation arises when a central government is established over peoples of diverse culture, as in many colonial, precolonial, and postcolonial states in Africa. Or when large-scale migration, forced or free, brings on the scene an alien population, as in the Americas. Or thirdly, by the process of internal differentiation that is continually taking place within all social groups.[1]

The cultural differences to which these three processes give rise have a number of implications for the political system. Minority cultures, for example, are often foci of discontents against the regime and the pattern of ethnic differences is frequently reflected in political parties and in political decisions.

Since it is in most cases impossible to dissociate political and cultural factors, I shall examine the processes of assimilation as a whole, paying particular attention to marriage policy, which has a profound effect upon the integration of persons into a social system. Since processes of incorporation only operate over the long run and since they are so varied in kind, it will first be necessary to outline a general framework within which the more detailed study of some groups in northern Ghana can be considered.

Human communication itself involves some degree of incorporation, since attitudes often become modified in the very process of interaction. In this way the barriers and differences between persons and groups are continually being ironed out by social intercourse. Indeed, it has been claimed that one function of the taboo on sexual relations between brother and sister is to create alliances between the members of different kin groups and thus reduce their isolation. Where such kin groups form dwelling units, marriage usually

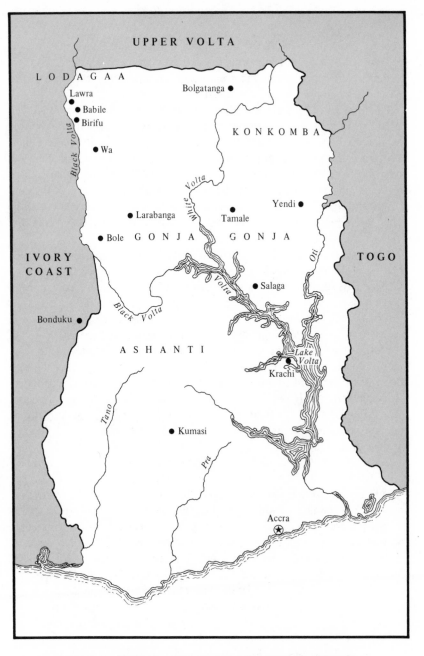

MAP 2. TRIBAL AREAS OF NORTHERN GHANA

involves a residential shift for one of the partners and hence the physical incorporation of an outsider into the domestic group of kinsfolk. And it is particularly the children of these unions that provide cross-cutting links between the groups to which the husband and wife belong.

This process of cultural assimilation is paralleled by one of internal differentiation. In complex societies some such differences inevitably result from the process of production and the division of labor which it entails. Others arise from the development of more elaborate forms of organization and some too from the varied access to cultural capital that literacy affords. Even in the simpler societies, diacritical features develop around the constituent groups and roles (for example totemic emblems and sumptuary laws), while other variations in behavior arise from the same process of cultural drift that produces the dialects of a language.

The process of internal differentiation may of course lead to the splitting of groups; differences within a single polity then become differences between polities. This distinction is to some extent a relative one. Of course, even within a single system, economic and social differences may be so radical as to threaten the existing order; of such a kind are Marx's contradictions in a capitalist society. In distinguishing between internally and externally generated differences, I do not wish to mask these points. Nevertheless it does seem useful to set aside those kinds of cultural difference that arise directly out of the contact of peoples, either through temporary visits or more permanent migrations. If only because of the manner in which they originate, these differences tend to be more extensive in kind and to lack (initially at any rate) the element of consensus that marks the growth of difference within a single polity.

Migration has been defined as "the physical transition of an individual or a group from one society to another." (Eisenstadt 1954: 1) This definition tends to assume what is now largely true, the division of the entire world into boundary-maintaining nation states, inclusive segments of the world's land and people. But to encompass earlier migrations, particularly those in stateless societies, we need to take account of the movement of peoples into empty and unclaimed lands, into the interstices between existing social groups. The resulting juxtaposition of ethnic groups requires the establishment of some kind of social relationships, of friendship, antagonism, or more usually a mixture of both. On the other hand, it does not raise the problem, in any radical way, of the incorporation, absorption or assimilation of the migrants in a single political system.

Following Eisenstadt (1954: 1) we may distinguish three main aspects of the migratory movement:

(i) initiating factors, including the motivation of the individuals concerned,

(ii) the nature of the migratory process itself,

(iii) the absorption of the immigrants.

It is the last of these upon which I wish to dwell, although it must be borne in mind that the way in which incorporation proceeds may be greatly influenced by other aspects of the migratory process: for example, whether the dominant motive is to escape oppression or to find new farms, whether the move takes place individually or in groups, whether the sex ratio is in balance or imbalance. A factor of fundamental importance is clearly the respective social structures of the migrant and receiving groups.

Amongst acephalous peoples, immigration means rapid assimilation—there is no room for major cultural differences. In Northern Ghana, a great deal of movement has taken place among stateless peoples (and still does), partly because of ecological factors such as the impoverishment of the soil, the incidence of disease,[2] or the pressure of an increasing population; partly because of internal conflicts over inheritance, succession, or status;[3] and partly too because of pressure from centralized states and their slave-raiding offshoots.[4] Among the Isala the result is seen in the varied origin of the clans, Fulani, Mossi, Gonja, Mamprusi. But there, as in the case of the Tallensi or the LoDagaa, diverse elements are fused into a relatively homogeneous culture. (Rattray 1932) Even Muslim traders got drawn into the acephalous melting pot and emerged, like the Mafobe Dagarti of Jirapa (Goody 1954: 32) or the Hen'vera clan of Isala (Rattray 1932: ii, 472), as pagan farmers arranged in polysegmentary lineages.

Nowadays in these areas one finds stranger settlements, known by the Hausa term *zongo*, scattered along the main traffic routes. But in earlier times, before the establishment of European overrule, it is doubtful how far small communities could have sustained an independent identity in acephalous societies; if they did, it was by creating a completely separate existence where relationships with the local population were confined to market activities. Indeed the new *zongos* that have formed near such communities are still characterized by juxtaposition rather than incorporation, except in the limited context of trading activities. Nowadays they also tend increasingly to attract government services and consequently act as a magnet for the educated elements in the local population.

It is not only Muslim groups that undergo downward assimilation into acephalous societies; at times a similar process takes place with segments of the dynasties of centralized states who start by dominating but are later absorbed into the local system, the social structure of both groups becoming modified in the process. In northern Ghana incorporation of this kind often occurs on the periphery of the savannah states whose fluid boundaries are sometimes the result of the ebb and flow of raiding, conquest and retreat, and sometimes of the resurgence of local forces, the strength of "commoner opposition" to chiefly privilege. The process forms a recurrent feature of the politico-military history of northern Ghana, and is reported for the Tallensi, Nankanne Builsa, Kusase, and for some Wala groups.

Another form of incorporation was a common feature of Gonja as of other West African states, namely, the incorporation of slaves. Not only did the children of slave concubines have the full status of their fathers, but the descendants of the union of two slaves eventually became freemen and the memory of their origin gradually disappeared over time. But this complex problem is peripheral to this essay on the incorporation of groups, and demands to be treated more fully at another time.

The units of an acephalous society tend to be homologous and politically equal (Fortes and Evans-Pritchard 1940: 13); in the long run there is but one slot into which migrants can fit. Centralized societies on the other hand are invariably stratified, and in most preindustrial societies stratification is political in kind, that is, access to the kingship (and usually the major offices of state) is confined to a minority group. Only the postmonarchical party systems of modern times provide formally open means of obtaining political office, though under capitalism the economy (or at any rate its commanding heights) is still marked by a degree of ascriptive ownership of the means of production. In modern states new migrants have usually the same rights of political control (for example, the vote) as other citizens, though it may be more difficult for them to obtain political office. But in societies where officeholding is legally restricted the new migrants must either displace the existing rulers or accept a politically inferior status.

If they displace the governing elite (or create a new one), they do so by force or the threat of force. They create (or take over) a conquest state, of which the colonial system is one major variant. Though colonization may occasionally grow out of contractual agreement, war is its usual midwife. And the result, in every case except that of free occupation, is a politically stratified society, with the newcomers holding the reins of authority. Colonization, insists Maunier, is emigration plus government, whether this be in colonies of settlement ("habitable colonies") or colonies of rule ("colonies for exploitation," "skelton colonies"). But it is also government that is subordinated to that of the mother country, which remains (initially for colonies of settlement and perpetually for colonies of rule) the homeland to which many of the migrants see themselves as eventually going back.[5]

In monarchical systems, such as prevailed in African states, the expansion that follows military conquest takes place not by means of the extension of bureaucratic rule (though the rudiments of such may perhaps be discovered in nineteenth-century Nupe and Ashanti)[6] but rather by dynastic expansion into adjacent areas.[7] A notable example is to be found in the spread and eventual fission of the Mossi (Mole-Dagbane) states from their Mamprusi homeland. Ritual ties persisted, even when government had effectively passed to the former segments of the ruling dynasty.

When home territory and dynastic offshoot are spatially separated, political ties tend to be more quickly broken off. For, under the prevailing conditions, the new state, whether formed by the losing faction in a succession dispute, by a group of mercenaries or freebooters, or by a dissatisfied outpost of empire, is independent of the mother country for the recruitment of personnel, the provision of capital, technological services, as well as for the materials of conquest, that is, the means of destruction. And the actors themselves are soon likely to want to discard rather than retain political and sentimental ties with their earlier homeland.

Gonja was just such a conquest state. A group of "Mande" horsemen first settled to the north of the Bono kingdom in the sixteenth century and later established their own state above the Black Volta. Separated by great distances from their homeland and coming as a warrior band rather than as family migrants, they doubtless took their women from the new locality in which they found themselves and the children of these unions adopted their mothers' tongue. Mande was abandoned and Guang substituted; the assimilation of the migrants, at least linguistically, originated in the absence of women of their own kind. The conquerors had therefore to marry the conquered and linguistic change was in a downward direction.

When the Gonja state expanded northward across the Black Volta, it wrested from the Mossi-speaking states (Dagomba, Nanumba, Wa, Mamprusi, and Buna)[8] a territory as wide as present-day Ghana itself. While driving out the earlier rulers, the conquerors (the NGbanya) took over their subjects, who consisted of a number of small groups, distinct both in language and in culture. In their midst, the new ruling estate established a number of divisional centers, from which chiefs were dispatched to govern their alien villages.

Traditions of subject peoples such as the Vagala make it clear that political incorporation was initially effected by force of arms; indeed, such is almost invariably the case, since any state system has to establish an effective monopoly of force, not simply for military reasons but in order to back up the decision-making process. It is because they fail to achieve such a monopoly that many union governments are so ephemeral.

But in time military government gave way to a rule which was, at least partially, based upon consensus. While all important chiefships remained firmly in dynastic hands, an element of popular choice (not simply dynastic election) crept into the system of succession; or, at any rate, the approval and blessing of representative commoners constituted an intrinsic part of the installation of a new chief.[9]

The political incorporation, by conquest leading to partial consent, was followed by cultural assimilation. In general, the commoners retained their own language. Although in central Gonja some of these groups adopted the language of the ruling estate,[10] most were compact and solidary enough to retain their own speech forms. Gonja (*Gbanyito*) was used as the language of administration, and such records as were kept were written in Arabic and Hausa; but social intercourse was very often conducted in the language of the commoners. In those Gonja divisions where a plurality of languages exist, multilingualism is frequent and even members of the ruling estate can be heard conversing among themselves in a commoner tongue.

Language, the prerequisite of all complex cultural achievement, has a certain inflexibility when compared to other forms of cultural expression. For, except within prescribed limits, you cannot mingle codes. If two groups come together they either keep the languages separate and so limit effective intercourse (unless they practice multilingualism) or else they adopt one and reject the other. You may get major changes in vocabulary over time, as in post-Norman England; but you cannot compromise with basic systems as you can (and indeed have to) mix systems of marriage, law, and the like.

There is no known law which will predict the direction of linguistic change in a conquest situation; one can point to the variables, dominance, numbers, sex ratios, imtermarriage, usage and self-image, but not to the relationship between them. Political dominance is certainly not enough to ensure the acceptance of one's language as the means of communication. If one looks at northern Ghana, the incoming groups (whether they have been settlers or conquerors) have generally accepted the language of the indigenes. But while they have accepted, they have also imposed; the area round Tamale seems formerly to have spoken Kpariba, a Tem language resembling Konkomba, while in eastern Gonja the language adopted by the Mande invaders is now being accepted by many of the other groups in the area.

Part of the explanation has to do with the relative numerical strength of the groups concerned. A small group, even if in a dominant position, will tend to lose out; language exists primarily as a tool of communication and only secondarily as an emblem of group existence. For similar reasons, a mass migration allows the participants the opportunity to cling to their language.

Another factor is the sex ratio. If the incoming group is more than just a handful, and at the same time heterosexual in composition, then it can operate as a breeding unit; such an endogamous group can retain its language and other aspects of culture even under adverse conditions. But if the group consists only of males, which would tend to be the case in situations of conquest, trade, or hunting, then there is always the problem of the "mother tongue," or, more significantly, the language of peers; women are generally less the explorers of new social territory than the consolidators of the old.

I argue later that marriage policy is the most important single factor in the change of language (and other cultural features) since it usually provides the social context within which this basic skill is acquired.

Meanwhile two other factors require consideration. The first is usage: if a language has special significance in religious behavior, either for ritual or for writing, then it gains an added resistance to change. The second has to do with what I speak of unsatisfactorily as the self-image of the group. In some cases language assumes a heightened value as a symbol of group activity, and intense efforts are made to retain or revive the native tongue, despite the heavy pressures making for its extinction; the rescue operation carried out upon the Celtic languages is an example of what I have in mind.

Such a factor, vague as it is, seems to be needed to explain the strength of commoner tongues in western Gonja (Bole) and their disappearance in the central (Buipe) area. The main commoner group in the west of the country is the Grusi-speaking Vagala, whose traditions claim an Isala origin.[11] While contact with the NGbanya has undoubtedly modified many other features of Vagala culture, the language itself flourishes. Indeed it is spoken in many compounds of members of the ruling estate, whose mothers often belong to that group. Many Vagala men display great pride in their language, and their traditions recount how their ancestor Bangmaara strongly resisted the coming of the NGbanya, who succeeded in conquering them only by a trick.[12] Even today, the Vagala play little part in the main Gonja festivals, except as spectators, and they retain some of the spirit of opposition to authority that marks the members of many stateless communities.

This "commoner opposition" is notably stronger here than in those parts of Gonja where there is no linguistic differentiation between rulers and ruled. This opposition is not openly "purged" in any public ritual of rebellion but forms a recurrent theme of conversation and is often expressed in linguistic terms. Vagala elders sometimes refused to answer my Gonja greetings and often insisted on addressing me in their own tongue, knowing I could not understand.

I have described the Vagala situation at some length not because it is typical (in many respects it is not) but because I want to refer to this example in discussing other aspects of the problem of cultural accommodation in Gonja.

With regard to language, the situation is one of separateness. Whereas Gonja (Gbanyito) has but few remnants of Mande vocabulary, possibly no more than Twi,[13] Vagala is closely related to its parent tongue, Isala;[14] neither Vagala nor Gonja is much influenced by the other, even though the languages are spoken in the same town (Bole) and by the same people.

But in other areas of cultural expression, the situation is often very different. Occupationally, the NGbanya have remained rulers and the Vagala peasants; militarily, they have kept largely to their earlier weapons, and the same is true of other aspects of their technology. But in these respects their equipment and behavior was representative of a geographical region rather than of any particular group. On the other hand, the Vagala have adopted much of the material culture associated with the centralized states and with Islam; guns have tended to displace bows, and cloths to outmode skins and fibers. Economically, both groups have adapted to local conditions and cultivate local staples, especially yams. The Gonja have ceased to depend upon rice and the Vagala upon guinea-corn, although both crops retain a certain religious significance in offerings to the gods.

Religious assimilation requires special treatment. When the NGbanya, who were probably pagan Bambara, established their conquest state, they were accompanied and helped by Muslims of Dyula origin. A mid-eighteenth century history, the *Gonja Chronicle*, contains an account of the conversion of the ruling estate, and European sources of the early nineteenth century refer to the Muslim kings of divisions such as Buipe and Daboya.[15]

Whatever the situation in the eighteenth century, most Gonja rulers of recent memory were eclectic in their religious practices and beliefs. Like their Christian and Hindu counterparts, even formally Islamic societies have their syncretistic elements.[16] But for the Gonja, New Yam festivals and the yearly celebrations of local shrines are as important, though not always as public, as the regular Muslim festivals. Muslims, whether by descent or by conversion, occupy different social roles from the princes and have different tasks in national ceremonies. While many princes pray in private, to sit with the Muslims on public occasions or to attend the Friday mosque is to forfeit any rights to chiefly office. In 1937, Jawulla, Chief of Kpembe, was removed from office when he asked leave to make the journey to Mecca. No chief can become a *karamo*, it is often said, though this is not universally true, especially nowadays. On the other hand, no chief entirely rejects Islam as do some commoner groups, like the Vagala; he has to maintain a judicious balance between the various divisions of his realm, religious as well as kinship, and for reasons of belief as well as of political expediency. But the most outstanding sphere of cultural assimilation is in domestic life. The kinship system of the NGbanya bears little relationship either to the Bambara with their dominantly patrilineal kin groups (Pacques 1954) or to the Akan with their strong matrilineal clans (Fortes 1950); although succession to office and estate membership are transmitted agnatically, unilineal descent groups are of peripheral importance and indeed it is difficult to speak of "corporate" kin groups at all.

The Vagala provide an even more striking instance of cultural change through assimilation.[17] In the main features of the kinship system, their parental group, the Isala, resemble the Tallensi and the Dagaba (Rattray 1932): strong patriclans, high bridewealth, widow inheritance, and the prohibition of cross-cousin marriage. However, the Vagala have no important descent groups, low marriage payments, prohibited widow inheritance, and preferred cross-cousin marriage. The reversal is striking and complete. And in all these features, the Vagala resemble their overlords the NGbanya as well as their fellow commoners from other ethnic groups within the state.[18]

This contrast points to one possible conclusion: that the social organization of both conquerors and conquered, of both dominant and subordinate groups, has undergone major changes in a single direction at the domestic level; differences have been ironed out and the disparate systems mutually adjusted one to another.

The result, in terms of kinship, inheritance, and marriage, is broadly consistent with Islamic practice, and it should be remembered that the third "estate," that of the Muslims, have basically the same practices. The Islamic custom of paternal parallel cousin marriage and bisexual inheritance tends to break down the boundaries of clanship (though neither custom is at all common in Gonja). Islamic practice favors the transfer of marriage gifts (*sadaq*) to the wife rather than bridewealth to her kin; and while widow inheritance is permissible, the levirate is discouraged.[19]

But there are many variations in marriage and inheritance among Islamic peoples, and many more committed Muslim societies retain features such as matrilyny (for example, the Wolof and northern Tuareg) and exogamy (for example, the *dyamu* of the Mande) which are incompatible with Muslim law and custom. Nor has the Muslim religion as such had any direct effect upon the commoner communities of Gonja, despite the congruence of their kinship institutions.

RESTRICTED AND UNRESTRICTED CONUBIUM

The most significant factor in this process of change is not Islam itself but the incorporation of diverse groups in a single polity, marked by unrestricted connubium. Systems of stratification in Africa stand in marked contrast to those of Eurasia, and particularly to the caste societies of the Indian subcontinent. For endogamy is rare anywhere in Negro Africa. It is found only where northern whites are dominant over southern blacks. The example of the Union of South Africa has parallels among the Saharan Tuareg and the Bahima of Ankole, as well as in Ethiopia (Shack 1966: 8); and it is a pattern that was copied by Freetown Creoles. (Banton 1965: 136).[20]

Among the Tuareg of Timbuctu, as in other caste societies, it is the "purity of women" that is at stake (Yalman 1963); women cannot marry down. (Miner 1953: 23) The Negro Bela are agricultural slaves of the Caucasian Tuareg pastoralists; a Bela can never marry a Tuareg girl. The Negro Gabibi, who are said to have a slave origin, are agricultural serfs of the Caucasian Arab merchants; again a Gabibi cannot marry an Arab girl. (Miner 1953: 20,24) But unions of male Tuareg with female Bela are not uncommon and give rise to an interstitial estate known as the Daga.

A similar situation obtained among the Ankole of Uganda. As among the Tuareg and Arabs of Timbuctu, there was a sharp economic, cultural, and ethnic division between pastoral rulers and subject farmers. No Bairu peasant could marry a Bahima girl; the union was repugnant and the bridewealth unobtainable, since the Bairu were not permitted to own productive cows. (Oberg 1940: 130) "Marriage" was equally impossible between a Bahima man and a Bairu girl, since it was illegal to alienate cattle to the lower orders. But such women did become concubines of a sort, again giving rise to a group of "half-caste," known as Abambiri.

Otherwise endogamy exists only in some skilled occupational groups in Senegal, Mali, and Niger (though groups of in-marrying smiths are found over a much wider area of Africa). In the eastern part of the Western Sudan, that is, in Northern Nigeria, the system of stratification is more flexible and does not inhibit marriage between social estates. Marriages within certain degrees of kin are prohibited and the unions of cross-cousins are often favored, but, from the standpoint of stratification, conubium is unrestricted, not simply in law but in practice too. Men are eclectic in their choice of wives and do not confine their marriages either to their own, or to any other, social estate or ethnic group.

I do not wish to imply that Gonja marriages never have any immediate political or religious significance. The reigning chiefs do marry the daughters of neighboring rulers, but they can more often be heard to express a distinct preference for commoner wives who are reckoned to be less transitory partners than women of the ruling estate. (E. Goody 1962) In former times, slave concubinage was common for much the same reason, and a prominent chief once remarked to me, "You know, all our mothers were slaves." An exaggeration, it is true, but one that brings out the same kind of preference for "low" marriage that exists in the extensive kingdom of Bariba in northern Dahomey (Cornevin 1962: 163)[21] and in many other states of West Africa (although it was probably uncommon for a free woman to marry a slave).

In Gonja, the long-established Muslim groups (for example, the "Gonja" Muslims) are almost as eclectic in their marriages as their chiefly counterparts. While there is a tendency for a woman's first marriage to be made with a man of the Muslim estate, their brothers are not so inhibited. As the senior Imam in Gonja recently remarked in explanation of his own maternal origin, "Here, we Muslims (*Karamo*) marry commoners (*Njumo*), the commoners marry chiefs (*NGbanya*) and the chiefs, Muslims." In any case, the marriage ceremony includes a rite which converts the girl to Islam.

Open conubium increases the intercourse between the various groups in the society and hence modifies the social institutions of all. For example, if frequent intermarriage occurs between two groups, one practicing agnatic, one uterine inheritance, then property inevitably tends to accumulate in the hands of the former, and a whole series of further changes is likely to occur in order to meet this situation.[22] Such a process of change seems to have been at work in various parts of Gonja. But the changes are clearest in the case of marriage payments.

In the acephalous societies of northern Ghana, the marriage payments are high.[23] Whereas among the commoner groups, many of whom appear to have had a common origin with their acephalous neighbors, the prestations are greatly reduced. For reasons of reciprocity, they have been brought down to the Gonja and Muslim level; instead of the transfer of bridewealth to a woman's kin, we find marital gifts made to the woman and her parents, which are not returnable if the union is dissolved.

Free intermarriage in a stratified system also tends to emphasize a woman's attachment to her own natal group; in old age she is likely to be drawn back to an environment in which she can revert to the customs, beliefs, and privileges of her youth, rather than continue to live in a conjugal setting when her days of childbearing are over. And for similar reasons, less emphasis is likely to be placed upon the unilateral allocation of children to one parent rather than another; in Gonja, kinship fostering plays a dominant part in maintaining the links between siblings separated by spatial and social distance, and indeed by the very fact of marriage.[24]

In other words, the incorporation of structurally diverse groups with frequent intermarriage leads to a mutual adjustment of domestic institutions (which is the sphere most directly influenced) and results in a kinship organization based upon the lowest common demoninators. The result is the kind of "bilateral" system found, and for much the same reasons, in other centralized states in Africa, the Hausa (Smith 1959: 243) and Nupe of northern Nigeria, the Dagomba of northern Ghana and the Lozi of Zambia, all of which have incorporated groups of widely different social structures.[25]

I would stress that the important factor is frequent intermarriage rather than open conubium alone. In most states no legal restrictions are placed upon intermarriage, but in contemporary societies, all of which, whatever their ideology, have some system of social stratification, the strata normally prefer to marry among themselves; as in the earlier Eurafrican slave societies of the Americas, sexual intercourse rather than marriage is the characteristic relationship with women of the lower orders.

RURAL MIGRATION

I have so far been dealing with the processes of mutual adjustment arising out of the establishment of the Gonja state, an exercise which is inevitably somewhat speculative since there are too few records to enable us to make a satisfactory reconstruction of Gonja society in the seventeenth and eighteenth centuries.

However, immigration into the area continues at the present time, and the Gonja, like any other ethnic group, have to decide upon their relationships with these newcomers—just as the strangers themselves have to decide what to do about the Gonja.

The character of contemporary migration into Gonja depends largely upon whether it is rural or urban,[26] or more precisely, according to the intended occupation of the immigrant, whether farming, trading, government service, or some specialist activity such as herding, smithying, drumming, dyeing, or distilling.

The rural migration is of farming groups of shifting cultivators[27] and is concentrated in the western and eastern extremes of the country.[28] In the west the migration of Lobi (LoBirifor) from the Ivory Coast began around

1917 and reached its peak in the 1940s, when they became the most numerous element in the Bole Local Council area.[29] The Konkomba migration from the Oti plains in eastern Dagomba began somewhat later and shows little sign of slackening.[30] The reasons for these migrations were many. The Lobi were prompted by a desire to escape the poll tax imposed in French colonies. Moreover, the area of western Gonja into which they moved had been devastated two decades earlier by the activities of Samory, the Mandingo warrior; it was fertile, as local soils go, and few inhabitants survived. The migration built up rapidly and the LoBirifor were joined by the LoDagaa (or Lobi-Dagarti) from the more heavily populated Lawra district east of the river, who had come across these empty lands on their way to work down the mines, on the railways, or in the cocoa farms of southern Ghana.

In the east, the Konkomba seem to have been motivated mainly by the desire to obtain better yields, and the actual move often followed a period of wage labor on farms in the Salaga-Krachi area. Better yields meant more cash, which could then be used to purchase manufactured goods or to circumvent the traditional system of infant betrothal which forced the junior generation into heavy dependence upon the old and meant the postponement of marriage until the age of 35 or 40.[31] So the search was not simply for new lands and for better yields, but also for a larger cash income. The move coincided with the introduction of motor transport to northern Ghana in the early 1920s. The bulky food crops of the north could now be transported at economic rates to the markets of southern Ghana, where the increasing prosperity of cocoa farmers and the larger percentage of the labor force engaged in nonagricultural pursuits led to a great demand for farm produce, especially yams. It was not accidental that the Lobi and Konkomba, whose staple foods are cereals, were moving into areas better suited to the cultivation of yams, to become the most prosperous farmers in the north.

Both groups were ambivalently welcomed by the Gonja, whose chiefs were keen to increase the numbers under their command, for political as well as for financial reasons. But the newcomers maintained a virtually separate existence, their joint activities being largely confined to the market and the court. For both groups came from strongly "acephalous" peoples who resent the authority vested in chiefs, and indeed in governments generally. Having been for centuries the prey of slave raiders, they adopted a particularly hostile attitude towards the representatives of those states which had mounted attacks against them; indeed, given the technological imbalance in weapon systems, their only safeguard had lain in continual vigilance and a constant readiness to take up arms in self-defense—and in an emergency to flee across a

convenient river. Their hostility to and suspicion of outsiders, their attachment to the bow and arrow which they always carried, their homes built like
fortresses, all this had a firm basis in reality.

The settled Gonja are uneasy about these more mobile farmers and, like
settled Europeans and the nomadic gypsies, fear them both on account of
their supernatural powers and their easy recourse to violence. Even Gonja
commoners, who have taken on the clothing associated with Islam and the
centralized states, look down upon them as naked bushfolk, more used to
skins than to cloth, to bows than to guns.[32] As a result, Gonja of all estates
strongly discourage marriage with these new migrants and the number of such
unions is very small.

It seems doubtful whether a migration on this scale could have taken place
before the advent of British overrule at the beginning of the century placed
severe restraints upon the political activities of the Gonja. Before the Lobi
and Konkomba were more valuable as potential slaves than as subjects. Colonial rule gave them some new freedoms. In this as in other respects, new states
are heirs to their colonial predecessors and independence has not greatly
altered the position of these peoples. But proud and industrious, oblivious to
considerations of status, the Lobi and Konkomba are making a useful contribution to the economy of Ghana as well as to their own pockets; their voice
will soon be heard and the Gonja hierarchy, which has neatly adapted to the
new dispensation, will receive a rougher jolt from these new migrants whom it
has rejected than from the old ones whom it has assimilated long since.

URBAN MIGRATION: THE BOLE ZONGO

If we turn from rural to urban migration, we need to take account of two
further variables: firstly, the length of residence in the new environment,
intended and actual, and secondly, the nature of the urban center.

The more recent inhabitants of Bole consist of traders, migrant laborers,
and administrative personnel. The laborers are few in number. The administrative personnel, who are educated, regard themselves as temporarily stationed there and have elaborated their own "civil service" life, socially separate from the local inhabitants. Most of the strangers have come by way of
trade, though in many cases this has now ceased to be their major occupation.

All trade involves migration and, lying in the savannah country to the
north of the Akan-dominated forest, Gonja was a natural area for the exchange of forest produce with the livestock and manufactured goods of the
north. Bonnat, one of the first European visitors, was told that the great
trading town of Salaga formerly had a population of some 40,000, plus a

daily average of 10,000 strangers entering and leaving the town during the dry season.[33] The figure is doubtless greatly inflated, but temporary migrants were nevertheless of great importance to the social organization of Gonja, whose total population in 1960 was but 118,000. An influx of long-distance traders of this kind required a considerable degree of organization of the caravans themselves, of the main centers of trade,[34] and of their provisioning. In the larger towns along the routes, men from the trading nations settled down to provide food, lodgings, and assistance for their countrymen, to act as landlords, middlemen and agents in the complex network of trade in which so many were fully engaged. These settlers were often men grown tired of the constant traveling, who had no explicit intention of making their permanent home in a new land. They had come, and they stayed on, principally for economic reasons, becoming landlords and brokers.[35]

Nevertheless, such men formed the nuclei of the "tribal" quarters of the *zongo* or strangers' settlement. *Zongo* is Hausa for a "ward" and it describes the strangers' sections that are found in so many towns throughout West Africa, especially those situated along the main roads. Many of these *zongos* are of recent origin; the conditions that followed the establishment of colonial rule enabled traders to expand into areas previously denied them, and increased incomes from cash crops and wage labor made such expansion more profitable than hitherto. Babile *zongo*, next to the LoWiili settlement of Birifu, is just such a new development, separated from the autochthonous community because, in such a region of dispersed compounds, strangers have to create their own nucleated townships. But some 50 and 120 miles to the south, the towns of Wa and Bole have long-established traders' quarters. And in other places, such as Salaga, Bonduku, Nalerigu, and the ancient towns of Begho and Ghana,[36] there was a physical division between the King's town and the Traders' town, the former consisting of "locals," the latter of "strangers," and often enough the two towns also represented a religious dichotomy between pagan kings and Muslim merchants.

I raise the question of the social morphology of the settlement into which the migrant fits because of its effect on the process of incorporation. In a town of the size and separateness of present-day Salaga, with its population of 4,000 and situated some two miles from the King's town of Kpembe, it is possible for the inhabitants to lead a relatively self-contained existence. Marriages can be made within the town and there are few pressures to conform to local custom or participate in Gonja ceremonies. For trading purposes Hausa was more useful than Gonja and persists even as a first language among part of the community.

Even so, some adaptation to local conditions has taken place; the older residents in Salaga, the Bornu of Nfabaso, the Hausa of Sonipe, and the inhabitants of Lompor, speak Gonja as their mother tongue; indeed, when he stayed there in 1888, Binger referred to all these groups as Gonja. (1892: ii, 95) And it is precisely these groups that have the highest rate of intermarriage with the local population.

The same distinction between "assimilated" and "nonassimilated" immigrants is found in the western Gonja capital of Bole and is again linked, as one would expect, to length of residence.

The earlier migrants live in Nyimunga, a section of the old town, where their buttressed, Sudanese-type dwellings are similar in construction to the flat-roofed compounds of the chiefs and commoners.[37] The quarter is made up of peoples of various ethnic origin, the memory of which is retained in their patronymics, in their tribal names and in their oral traditions. But linguistically, and in most other ways, they are Gonja, even though, in certain contexts of social action, they are referred to as Ligby, Dyula, Wala, or Hausa.

People answering to just these same tribal names are found in the *zongo* itself, the new part of Bole which includes the market area and where the houses are of the separate Ashanti type, built in cement or mud-brick, with sloping roofs of thatch or metal sheets. But the Hausa or Ligby who live there interact more with other residents of the *zongo* than they do with the old Hausa or the old Ligby of Nyimunga.

Nevertheless, incorporation is a continuous process which is beginning to take effect even among the newer migrants. In order to obtain a measure of assimilation, I examined the marriages of all residents in the Zongo ward of Bole (Ward 5) recorded in the tax registers of the Local Council and the results are listed in Tables 1 and 2.

I have no precise figures that enable me to relate length of residence with degree of intermarriage, but in any case the differences which these tables bring out cannot be explained on the grounds of time alone. The significant variable seems to be the marriage policy of the groups themselves.

At one end of the scale, we have the Yoruba (locally known as Lagosians) who are here a completely in-marrying group. Their daughters' marriages are arranged with other Yoruba living at great distances. At Christmas, 1965, two of Moses's daughters were to be married to Yoruba husbands at Bolgatanga, some 190 miles away. The same man, who has lived in Bole for 17 years, refuses even to respond to greetings in Gonja. On his walls hang Nigerian calendars displaying the photographs of prominent Yoruba politicians, while his transistor radio keeps him in constant touch with his distant homeland.

TABLE 1. IN-MARRIAGES AND OUT-MARRIAGES IN BOLE ZONGO

Ethnic group of husband	In-marriage	Out-marriage	Total
Ashanti	3	5	8
Dagarti	4	0	4
Dagomba	3	4	7
Ewe, and the like	2	1	3
Frafra	1	0	1
Gonja	23	3	26
Hausa	4	2	6
Isala	0	6	6
Lobi	1	1	2
Mossi	7	6	13
Songhai	2	8	10
Wala	6	2	8
"Wangara" (Smith)	0	1	1
Yoruba	19	0	19
Total	75	39	114

TABLE 2. SUMMARY OF IN-MARRIAGES AND OUT-MARRIAGES IN BOLE ZONGO

Husband's group	In	Out
Gonja	23	3
Non-Gonja	52	36
Total	75	39

Moses has no intention of becoming a permanent inhabitant of Gonja or of contracting any persisting ties with its inhabitants. Indeed his occupation of shopkeeper would be hampered if he did so. One of the main reasons why the Gonja, like other inhabitants of northern Ghana, have difficulty in establishing stores in their own localities (and I have known some spectacular failures) is because of their wide network of kinship ties and obligations; a large number of people are linked to them in ways that are incompatible with the cool calculation of the profit and the loss, and with the preference for cash transactions or monthly settlement that are required in this highly competitive business of petty trading.

As in-marrying, as culturally distinct, and as homeward-looking as the Yoruba are two other "expatriate" groups in Bole, one "higher," one "lower" in the dominant scale of values, namely the Europeans and the Fulani. Neither of these groups appears in the list of *zongo* marriages, since the former (2 marriages) live in the "residential quarter" and the latter (4 marriages) live next to their cattle kraals on the outskirts of the town. In both groups, the marriage range is as wide as that of the Yoruba, and their kin relations are therefore equally dispersed.

In all three of these instances, the absence of out-marriage is a function not only of the homeward orientation of the groups, the theoretically temporary character of their migration and their desire to retain cultural distinctions, but also of the specialist roles demanded of their wives.

Yoruba women undertake a great deal of petty trading. In Bole, they looked after the bulk of the market stalls, while their husbands minded the stores and traveled to Kumasi to purchase supplies; in Salaga, they did the early morning rounds of the nearby King's town of Kpembe, which had neither market nor shops. These trading activities require knowledge, skill and determination; at marriage, wives are set up as traders by their husbands, who then provide them with a loan so that they can select, at cost price, those goods from his store which they think likely to sell.

Fulani women have equally specialized roles, since it is they who are responsible for milking the cattle, making the butter, and selling the products in the local market. For though they have no cattle of their own, their husbands are all pastoralists who, like the Yoruba, have come to acquire some capital and then return home.

European women also have special tasks and expectations which make it difficult for women of other groups to fill their roles or for them to fill the roles of other women in the locality.[38]

At the other end of the scale of intermarriage lie the Isala, Mossi, Songhai

(Zaberima), and the Ashanti. But even though most interaction is greater between the residents of the *zongo* than with other inhabitants of the town, out-marriage is overwhelmingly with the Gonja rather than with women of other ethnic groups (Table 3).

TABLE 3. OUT-MARRIAGE OF NON-GONJA MALES IN BOLE ZONGO

With Gonja	30
Songhai — Hausa	4
Isala — Degha (Mo)	1
Ashanti — Hausa	1
Total	36

Songhai men are the only ones to contract any number of out-marriages to non-Gonja women; and these are with their closest cultural neighbors, the Hausa, and can therefore be considered the best alternative to actual in-marriage. The Isala and Degha are also the closest pair from a linguistic and cultural standpoint.

Apart from the few Ashanti, the out-marrying groups are also the assimilating groups. Their migration histories show that they usually come singly, often selling their labor rather than marketing goods. Two of the groups, the Mossi and the Songhai, live outside the boundaries of Ghana, and the representatives in Bole doubtless come from the commoner elements in those stratified societies. In the past, the Isala (or "Grunshi") were often raided for slaves and so form a significant, though mainly concealed, portion of the population of Gonja, as of Ashanti. These groups have therefore a strong incentive to assimilate and the Gonja do not reject their advances.

Any policy of intermarriage requires both demand and supply; that is to say, in the absence of force, a willingness on the part of both conubial groups. While Gonja marry Isala and Mossi, they express aversion to the idea of marrying Fulani and Lobi.[39] Since the figures give no idea whether one party or both, one sex or both, were responsible for the absence of intermarriage, I tried out a preliminary survey of marriage preferences, based on a nonrandom sample.[40] The responses are summarized in Table 4.

TABLE 4. MARRIAGE REJECTIONS OF BOLE MEN
(BOLE, AUGUST 1965)

Respondents		Tribe Rejected								
Tribe	Number	"Dagarti"	Fulani	Gonja	Hausa	"Lobi"	Mossi	Yoruba	No Rejects	Total Responses
"Dagarti"	10	–	6	4	–	7	2	4	3	26
Degha (Mo)	1	–	1	–	1	1	–	–	–	3
Fulani	1	–	–	–	–	–	–	1	–	1
Gonja	9	4	8	–	5	8	4	7	–	36
Hausa	1	1	1	1	–	1	1	1	–	6
Isala	1	1	1	1	–	1	1	1	–	6
"Lobi"	1	–	1	1	1	–	1	1	–	5
Mossi	1	–	–	–	–	–	–	–	1	1
Songhai	1	–	–	–	–	–	–	–	1	1
Vagala	2	–	1	–	2	2	2	2	–	9
"Wangara"	1	1	1	–	–	1	1	1	–	5
Yoruba	1	1	1	1	1	1	1	–	–	6
Total	30	8	21	8	10	22	13	18	5	105

The most rejected groups are the Lobi and Fulani. None of the Fulani evidenced any desire to marry outsiders; in any case they were decisively rejected by other groups. I had at first thought that their rejection in the centralized states (for the same is reported for the Mossi) was associated with the fear that pastoral penetration might be the forerunner of military conquest; news of events in northern Nigeria certainly spread rapidly throughout the western Sudan, and other states may have wished to prevent the kind of takeover that occurred in the *jihad* of 'Uthman dan Fodio at the beginning of the nineteenth century. But the "Dagarti" and other acephalous peoples also reject such marriages, though often admiring the beauty of Fulani girls. As I have earlier remarked, their anxiety appears to be related to the fears that settled peoples so often have of their nomadic neighbors, whose greater freedom of movement and different culture make them seem dangerous, unreliable, and "shifty" in every sense. But particularly, perhaps, they fear that the mobility of these strangers will deprive them of their wives or sisters, their children or their nephews.

The other main ethnic group of rejected partners (rejected for marriage, though not necessarily for sex) are the "Lobi" (LoBirifor). For aesthetic reasons, Lobi women wear lip-plugs of up to an inch in diameter in both their upper and lower lips, but this practice does not endear them to the more sophisticated inhabitants of Bole and Wa. Nor does their comparative nakedness and the use of shea-butter to anoint their bodies. All of these features, combined with their farming life, lead others to dismiss them as "dirty."

The distinction between "Lobi" and "Dagarti" (Lo and Dagaa) is largely a matter of the position of the speaker relative to a whole series of cultural differences, and no hard-and-fast boundary can be drawn between them.[41] So that the lack of any marriages between Dagarti and Gonja (Table 1) may be due to the fact that, although these men refer to themselves as Dagarti, others think of them as Lobi. However, it is the case that the Gonja do not show the same antipathy for the new migrants from the Lawra district (the LoDagaa) that they do for those from the Ivory Coast (the LoBirifor), and there is no doubt that the former will be more rapidly incorporated, both into the marriage system and into the contemporary scene, especially since many of them were strongly influenced by schools and missions before they migrated southwards.

The next most frequently rejected group is the Yoruba, mainly I think in response to Yoruba separateness and the knowledge that, for a man, such a marriage would be even more fragile than most unions in Gonja, with the additional possibility of losing all one's children, or alternatively one's sister's children.

I have as yet few responses from women, and the only additional comment I can offer here is that a woman's marriage policy becomes more liberal the older she gets. However, there is no evidence to show that Gonja women who make *zongo* marriages are any lower in status than those who marry their own kind. In the first place, there are many important men in the *zongo* who hold positions of economic, religious and, nowadays, political power. In any case, as in Ashanti and Techiman, Gonja women of the ruling estate were eclectic in their choice of mates, also having perhaps some sexual preference for the men from the north.

The situation of open conubium and free intermarriage that obtains in Gonja, Hausaland, and most of Africa, contrasts strongly with the city of Timbuctu and the Ankole of Uganda, closed where conubium is practiced by the ruling groups. Although high-status men have liaisons with lower-status girls, the sexual and marital relationships of their women are severely restricted; as Yalman has remarked of India, there is a "structural necessity to safeguard the women in a caste system." (1963: 48)[42]

The apparent correlations of such a system are significant, for in both Timbuctu and Ankole you find considerable ethnic heterogeneity. In Timbuctu, intergroup marriages are few and "sexual relations are primarily organized through prostitution." (Miner 1953: 277, 280) So that distinct groups, each with their own languages and traditions, operate in virtual separation one from another except in the field of market activities. The situation is basically the same as Furnival's well-known description of a plural society:

In Burma, as in Java, probably the first thing that strikes the visitor is the medley of peoples—European, Chinese, Indian and native. It is in the strictest sense a medley, for they mix but do not combine. Each group holds by its own religion, its own culture and language, its own ideas and ways. As individuals they meet, but only in the market-place, in buying and selling. There is a plural society with different sections of the community living side by side, but separately, within the same political unit. Even in the economic sphere there is a division of labour along racial lines . . . There is, as it were, a caste system, but without the religious basis that incorporates caste in social life in India . . . The obvious and outstanding result of contact between East and West has been the evolution of a plural society (1948: 304-5).

That the continuing ethnic diversity of Timbuctu depends largely upon marriage policy can be seen from the history of one of its main elements, the Arma. These are the descendants of the Moroccan army, consisting partly of renegade Christian gunmen, that crossed the Sahara and conquered the upper Niger in 1591. As an entirely male garrison of professional soldiers, some thousand miles distant from their base, they were forced to take their women from the vanquished Songhai, whose language they had also to adopt.

A similar contrast with contemporary Timbuctu is seen in Hausaland, where the Fulani conquerors, freely intermarrying, acquired the Hausa language, and ethnic distinctions all but disappeared. Among the Interlacustrine Bantu of Uganda, the same contrast exists between the Ankole and the Buganda, even though the ruling dynasties claim a common origin. In Ankole closed connubium is associated with the retention of ethnic differences, and in Baganda, open conubium with their disappearance.

This process of cultural incorporation through marriage usually works both in a downward and in an upward direction, leading to a reconciliation of diverse cultural practices. Where the groups involved are solidary, and by this I mean to exclude the case of slaves whose incorporation makes but little contribution to cultural change, each gives something to the resulting culture. As a result the process of Islamization that in the West African savannahs often accompanies inclusion in a centralized polity, is perhaps less unidirectional than the corresponding process of Sanscritization that occurs in India, where social and sexual intercourse with the religiously impure is severely restricted.

CONCLUSIONS

In the acephalous societies of Northern Ghana, political incorporation means cultural assimilation. In the state systems this may entail no more than coresidence, though the degree of cultural assimilation clearly affects a man's political role.

In these differentiated societies, there is a sense in which incorporation is never complete, except for the dominant minority; the significance of membership of the body politic varies with status, and alienation is in part a function of the divison of labor, including differential access to armed force. Nevertheless, if we stick to immigrant groups, it is clearly possible to make a rough assessment of the degree and rate of incorporation among them.

While there are a number of factors involved in these differences in incorporation, marriage policy is overwhelmingly the most important; for most purposes the situation in Northern Ghana can be summarized in the proposition that the rate of incorporation (I) varies directly with the rate of out-marriage (OM); that is, I = OM. For out-marriage is more than an index of assimilation; it is the main mechanism whereby integration is achieved. This it does in two interrelated ways, by affinity and by kinship.

In terms of affinity, marriage and the domestic environment create the kind of cathexis (though the hostilities are numerous) that generally leads to the mutual adjustment of attitudes,[43] and such accommodation may flow over to more distant affines. In terms of kinship, marriage usually establishes the domestic group that forms the template of culture, the unit of socialization, that is, of cultural incorporation.

In nation states socialization is partially shifted on to the school, which becomes an indispensable medium of cultural indoctrination; quite apart from the teaching of national history and literature, there is the saluting of the flag, the saying of prayers, the lining of streets and the celebrating of state occasions. It is the school on which new nations, like the old, rely for the inculcation of national unity as against tribal or religious solidarity. Here we are dealing not with the assimilation of immigrants (whose presence is often discouraged) but with the incorporation of the diverse elements brought together by European conquest. For "Balkanization" is a function not so much of colonial rule as of precolonial divisions.[44] The new nation states are the heirs to colonial governments in their boundaries as in other respects, but the problem of incorporation becomes more acute when power no longer rests in the hands of outsiders, who, as far as the internal balance of peoples is concerned, are mainly, though not entirely, ethnically neutral.

In pursuit of national unity, which is often fragile enough, the new states of Africa try to eliminate sectional politics, whether based on religion, tribe, or region, and have usually opted for a one-party state. Meanwhile, a corollary of the stress of national unity is the emphasis placed upon the sanctity of existing boundaries, anomalous as these may be.

But the problems of incorporation are a challenge to old nations as well as to new. Some are frankly incorporative (though always selectively so), seeking new members from outside rather than waiting for natural increase alone. Others are exclusive, attempting to maintain the "purity of the nation," unwilling to mix with peoples of other physical features or cultural habits, for social and doctrinal as well as for racial reasons.

The social problems, at least, are not altogether imaginary. If we look at the process of decolonization, the greatest difficulties in the final stages of the progress towards independence have often been in those countries with major internal problems of assimilation, for example, in Guyana, Fiji, Mauritius, and Zimbabwe. Though countries like Brazil have gone some way towards solving problems of this kind, largely by marriage policy, it is not surprising that many others attempt to avoid difficulties by expelling, excluding, or limiting other breeds, or by promoting slogans such as "one country, one faith, one people." Indeed the insistence on national, or even continental unity (the European idea or the O.A.U.) may have the side effect of racializing politics and thus militating against the fuller incorporation of nation states or regional groupings into even wider political units.

If incorporation increases with the rate of intermarriage, then the sociopolitical implications are clear. The unity of a state can be nurtured by encouraging marriage between the most socially distant members of the nation, tribal groups in West Africa, immigrants in Europe. Alternatively it can be fostered by discouraging the immigration of physically, culturally or doctrinally distinct peoples. But on a wider canvas, in terms of a world strategy, the distinctions continue to exist, whether or not immigration occurs, and a major mechanism for dissolving them, if this goal is a desirable one, is by increasing marital and sexual relationships. International cooperation can be promoted through international copulation. To achieve such ends, nationally or internationally, barriers to intermarriage should be broken down, and the union of cousins, cross and parallel, should be proscribed, like other in-marriages. The legal enforcement of exogamy presents obvious objections and difficulties; but positive sanctions, such as tax relief, could be equally effective in the long run as a way of increasing the import and export of women.

As Tylor long ago pointed out, endogamy is a policy of isolation and the progress of mankind has depended to a significant measure upon the substitution of marrying-out for killing-out. Tylor realized that every marriage was by implication a political act.[45] Nor was this true only in the childhood of mankind. "Even far on in culture," he wrote, "the political value of intermarriage remains. 'Matrimonial alliances increase friendship more than aught else,' is a maxim of Muhammed. 'Then we will give our daughters unto you, and we will take your daughters to us, and we will dwell with you, and we will become one people,' is a well-known passage of Israelite history." (1889: 267) This statement expresses in concrete terms what is meant by marriage policy, the consequences of which I have tried to examine for the Gonja and some other African peoples.

APPENDIX

In March, 1966, I had an opportunity to follow up the preliminary survey of marriage preferences in a rather more systematic way, helped by some University students from Gonja; the earlier questionnaire was administered by two Europeans, with Dagarti and Vagala assistants. I mention the identity of the interviewers (who were all well known in the community), since this is bound to affect the responses on so sensitive an issue.

The survey was carried out both in Western Gonja (Bole) and in Eastern Gonja (Kpembe-Salaga). The results are summarized in Tables 5, 6, and 7.

The data are largely consistent with the preliminary study. In Bole, the most rejected groups were: Fulani, Lobi, Dagarti, Hausa, and Yoruba. The Dagarti are less desirable as marriage partners than in the earlier survey, partly because of changes in the interviewing staff (who were now non-Dagarti); in any case, this figure is likely to fluctuate because of the difficulties in discriminating them from the Lobi (the problem of the "LoDagaa continuum"). The Hausa also appear as more rejected, the Yoruba as less.

TABLE 5. PATERNAL PREFERENCES FOR DAUGHTERS'
MARRIAGES (BOLE, MARCH 1966)

Respondents		Tribe Preferred										
Tribe	Number	Ashanti	Dagarti	Dagomba	Fulani	Gonja	"Grunshi"	Hausa	Lobi	Yoruba	For Love	Total Responses
Ashanti	2	2	–	–	–	1	–	–	–	–	–	3
Gonja	7	5	1	5	–	7	3	5	–	3	–	29
Isala	3	1	–	–	–	3	–	–	–	–	–	4
Vagala	10	8	3	9	–	10	4	3	2	–	–	39
Yoruba	3	–	–	–	–	–	–	–	–	1	2	3
Total	25	16	4	14	–	21	7	8	2	4	2	78

TABLE 6. PATERNAL REJECTIONS FOR DAUGHTERS' MARRIAGES
(BOLE, MARCH 1966)

Respondents		Tribe Rejected										
Tribe	Number	Ashanti	Dagarti	Dagomba	Fulani	Gonja	"Grunshi"	Hausa	Lobi	Yoruba	For Love	Total Responses
Ashanti	2	–	1	1	1	–	1	1	1	1	1	8
Gonja	5	2	5	1	5	–	4	1	5	1	–	24
Isala	3	–	2	1	3	–	2	3	2	3	–	16
Vagala	8	1	4	1	7	–	3	2	5	1	1	25
Yoruba	3	–	–	–	–	–	–	–	–	–	3	3
Total	21	3	12	4	16	0	10	7	13	6	5	76

N.B. The preliminary survey asked about the respondent's own marriage,
the later survey for his daughter's; there seemed to be some advantages in a
less direct approach.

TABLE 7. PATERNAL REJECTIONS FOR DAUGHTER'S MARRIAGES (KEMBE-SALAGA, MARCH 1966)

Respondents		Tribe Rejected											Total Responses
Tribe	Number	Ashanti	Dagomba	Fulani	Gonja	"Grunshi"	Hausa	Nchumuru	Yoruba	Konkomba	No Rejects	Reject All	
Ashanti	4	—	1	3	1	2	2	—	3	3	1	—	16
Busanga	2	—	—	—	—	—	—	—	—	—	2	—	2
Dagomba	2	2	—	2	—	2	—	2	2	1	—	—	11
Ewe	1	—	—	—	—	—	—	—	—	—	1	—	1
Fulani	3	3	3	—	3	3	1	3	—	3	—	—	19
Gonja	27	7	1	13	—	10	6	9	14	13	3	—	76
"Grunshi"	4	1	—	3	—	—	1	2	3	2	1	—	13
Hausa	1	—	—	—	—	—	—	—	—	—	—	1	8*
Konkomba	5	4	4	5	—	4	4	4	5	—	—	—	30
Mossi	1	—	—	1	—	—	1	1	1	1	—	—	5
Nawuri	1	—	—	—	—	—	—	—	—	—	1	—	1
Nchumuru	1	1	1	1	—	1	—	—	1	1	—	—	6
Yoruba	4	1	1	—	1	1	1	1	—	1	—	3	31*
Total	56	19	11	28	5	23	16	22	29	25	9	4 (32*)	219

*Total possible rejections = 8 for each respondent. Thus each unit in the column "rejects all" stands for 8 "responses" and is included as such in the totals.

In Eastern Gonja, the results conform more closely to the original survey. It is the Yoruba who are most rejected, followed closely by the Fulani. Then come the Konkomba, who occupy the same structural position as the Lobi-Dagarti; they are the new, immigrant farmers from acephalous communities. After them come the "Grunshi" (exslaves) and the Ashanti (exconquerors).

In the Kpembe-Salaga material, the preferences were the mirror opposite of the rejections. Throughout the district, the politically dominant minority was held to be the most sought-after marriage partners, other than one's own group, except by the in-marrying Fulani and Yoruba; the Gonja are rejected only by the Yoruba, the Fulani, and by one Hausa and one Ashanti.

There is one figure out of keeping with the general picture, namely the Yoruba in Tables 5 and 6 who stress "marriage for love," an attitude that stands in contrast to the actuality of most Yoruba unions. The discrepancy can perhaps be explained by the fact that the respondents were relatively young and were not anxious to appear different (even though they behaved so), especially as foreigners at a time of political crisis: the Nkrumah government had just been overthrown.

The Yoruba are probably the most deliberately organized of the alien Africans living in Ghana; most parts of the country, including Bole and Sala-ga, have been visited by Nigerian High Commission staff who have encouraged their nationals to take out passports.

NOTES

---

1. This article has also appeared in *Comparative Studies in Kinship*, published by Routledge and Kegan Paul, 1969. I wish to thank the Trustees of the Leverhulme Foundation for a grant which enabled me to continue my fieldwork in Ghana in 1965 and 1966. For a general account of the LoDagaa, see J. Goody 1956, and of the Gonja, J. Goody 1967.

2. The LoDagaa migration, formerly into the northern Ivory Coast and Upper Volta, now into Western Gonja, is mainly caused by pressure on the land.

3. The migration stories of the Degha and other Grusi-speaking peoples often relate how the migrants left their homeland following a quarrel over the ownership of the head of a dog they had jointly sacrificed.

4. The southward movement of peoples (the Degha, Vagala, Tampolense) to form the Grusi wedge was probably the result of pressure from the Mossi (Mole-Dagbane-speaking) group of states, especially Mamprusi, Dagomba, and the Mossi themselves. An indication of the devastation caused by the activities of these states can be found in a contemporary Hausa account of the wars which were conducted by the Songhai freebooter, Gazari, his successor Baba-tu, and their "overlords," the Dagomba, in Isala country during the latter part of the nineteenth century. (G. A. Krause, 1928: 53-60)

5. In every colony we therefore find the colonizers as the conquerors, the governors, "the exploiters, the progeny of old countries, coming from afar, and claiming to bestow on the new countries the benefits of the development of their riches. And we find the earlier occupiers, the dominated, the governed or the colonized, who, by the very fact of their country's being occupied, are reduced to a position of legal or actual tutelage. From this point of view, colonization seems to us both a primitive and a general phenomenon." (Maunier 1949: 6)

6. Nadel 1942; Wilks 1967.

7. The recognition of common interest also led to a system of international alliances, and military force to a network of tributary relationships, but neither relationship meant emigration, and "government" was only peripherally involved in the collection of tribute.

8. Being an offshoot of Wa, the dynasty of Buna originally spoke Dagari, but like the NGbanya, they adopted the language of the indigenes, in this case Kulango. (Goody 1954: 13)

9. The public expression of such approval is an important part of the installation ceremonies of the Mossi states. For example, in the Wa division of Wechiau, the chief is actually enrobed by the representatives of the Muslim and commoner estates, the Imam, and the Earth Priest.

10. The Mpre and Mpur adopted the language of the ruling estate; in Eastern Gonja, the Nanumba Earth Priest of Salaga, and possibly some early Konkomba inhabitants, made the same change.

11. The other main commoner language in the Bole area is Safalba, a language of the Mossi group. Many of the inhabitants can understand all three; in addition, others speak Ligby, Hausa, and English. In some types of song such as *Aguro*, a singer's prestige is enhanced by the number of languages he can use. For a stranger, the linguistic situation is bewilderingly complex.

12. The only published account of the traditions of the Vagala of Bole is given in Rattray. (1932: ii, 516)

13. For Gonja, see Duncan-Johnstone 1930: 30, quoted in Goody 1954: 12; for Twi, see Wilks 1962.

14. See word lists in Rattray 1932, where it is stated "there is no doubt that the Isala, Vagala and Tampolense were originally one stock." (i, 122)

15. Goody 1954: 36ff; Dupuis 1824: 248.

16. For West Africa, see Trimingham 1959: 40 ff.

17. Throughout this essay I have distinguished between a change in culture and a change of culture. A group of people moving from one locality to

another may adopt the practices of their hosts *in toto*, and so effect a change of culture; but in the process they are also likely to modify the receiving society in some way (and so produce a change in culture). It is the second that is usually referred to as social (or cultural) change; the former is a type of social (or cultural) mobility. Mobility is often connected with change but has no necessary relationship to it.

18. The implications of this contrast are discussed in two papers written in collaboration with Esther Goody, "Cross-Cousin Marriage in Northern Ghana" and "The Circulation of Women and Children in Northern Ghana."

19. Greenberg 1946; Trimingham 1959: 127ff, 165ff.

20. In 1894 Bishop Ingham wrote of the Creoles and immigrants: "The latter form a class for the most part below them. They are their servants. Illicit connection there may be, but not intermarriage." (Banton 1965: 136)

21. Lombard, quoted by Cornevin (1962: 163-4), states that "the king took his wives from families of low status."

22. According to my inquiries, the patrilineal Guang speakers of Larteh in southern Ghana attempt to forbid the marriage of their daughters with the matrilineal Akan since their offspring would be without inheritance. Huber also records that among the neighboring Krobo, no father would formerly give his daughter in marriage to an uncircumcized man "which, *in concreto*, means to a member of the *Akan* tribe" (1963: 96); Huber attributes this to long-standing enmity, but property considerations would certainly explain the same phenomenon.

23. See Tallensi (Fortes 1949), LoDagaa (Goody 1956, 1962), and Isala (Rattray 1932).

24. Goody, E. 1960: chapter 6; 1966.

25. Neither the definition of bilateral nor the comparative analysis can be expanded here.

26. The 1960 Census Report on *Statistics of Towns* (1964) includes as urban those communities with a population of 5,000; only one Sonja town, Damongo, reached this figure. But before 1874, the population of Salaga was perhaps 8 times this size and in 1888, the first European visitor to Bole described it as bigger than the well-known market town of Bonduku.

Numbers, however, are not all. The Gonja themselves make no terminological distinction between towns and villages; both are *nde* (sing. *kade*). But in most divisional capitals of Gonja, however small, an ethnically mixed population gives a certain cosmopolitan air; and the structure and ambience of a town like Bole are certainly different from those of the farming villages that surround it.

27. The term "shifting cultivator" requires some comment. Many LoBirifor and Konkomba live in relatively permanent villages, farming the surrounding land by rotation and by fallow. But if yields drop and circumstances allow, most of them are quite prepared to abandon their elaborate compounds and move to foreign parts.

28. See Tait 1961. The Konkomba inhabited what was formerly Togoland under U.K. Mandate, which was later included in Ghana after a U.N. plebiscite.

29. The figures in the 1960 census for the whole of Western Gonja are: "Gonja," 30,670 (49.1 percent), Lobi 10,390 (16.6 percent). In 1948, there were 7,333 Lobi in Gonja. The 1931 census does not record ethnic distribution.

30. The figures in the 1960 census for Eastern Gonja Local Council are: "Gonja," 18,800 (33.7 percent); Konkomba, 16,050 (28.8 percent). In 1948, there were 7,832 Konkomba in Gonja, including the part under U.N. trusteeship.

31. Tait 1961; J. and E. Goody, "The Circulation of Women and Children in Northern Ghana."

32. Weaving, which is common in the Vagala villages of Western Gonja, is completely unknown to the LoDagaa, to the LoBirifor and to the Konkomba, among whom all cloth is foreign.

33. M. J. Bonnat, *Liverpool Mercury*, June 12, 1876. In 1940, the population of Timbuctu was only 6,000 and Miner claims that it was never more than double this figure (1953: 14).

34. On the organization of the caravans, see the Hausa documents collected by G. A. Krause 1928, especially No. 41. (Mustapha and Goody, 1967).

35. On the roles in trading communities, see Cohen (1965) and Hill (1966). The large number of persons engaged was partly due to the bulky nature of the commodities and partly to the absense of wheeled transport. South of Salaga, donkeys were of little use, owing to the presence of tsetse, and goods had to be manhandled, usually by slaves or pawns.

36. Bono-Mansu, capital of the forerunner of Techiman, was also perhaps a twin town.

37. The Eastern Gonja have round thatched huts, set in an open circle, rather like the neighboring Dagomba. A striking example of the mutual adjustment of which I have spoken is the fact that in Eastern Gonja, chiefs, Muslims, and commoners all have round huts, while in Western Gonja they all have flat-roofed compounds.

38. Except for a priest, whose role prescribed celibacy, the Europeans were transients rather than migrants and their roles too diverse to consider here.

39. The Lobi-Gonja marriage recorded in Table 1 was exceptional in character and lasted only a short while. I am indebted to Yakubu Saka for his help with this survey.

40. I am grateful to Keith Hart and Birgitte Rode-Møller for their assistance in administering the questionnaire, and also to Esther Goody for her help and advice. The smallness of my numbers is due to the lack of time at my disposal; but the investigation needs to be pursued in greater depth, with more subtlety and with better statistical techniques. See Appendix for later information.

41. For a discussion of the complexities involved see Goody, J. 1956: chapter I. Like the LoDagaba, the LoBirifor inherit movable property matrilineally, so that intermarriage raises some of the same problems it does for the Krobo, the Guang, and the Akan.

42. I use the word caste without religious implications (such a system has no warrant in Islam) to indicate one of a hierarchical series of endogamous status groups.

43. There appears to be no adequate study of the attitudes of spouses before and after marriage, but there is plenty of evidence of the high correlation of social and political attitudes between husband and wife (91 percent agreement in Newcomb's restudy of Bennington students) and of the adjustment of attitudes of strangers one to another (Newcomb 1962; see also Homans 1950).

In its most general form, that of balance theory, the process has been summed up as:

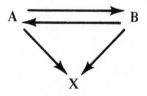

A and B are social persons, X a social object. Where A's attitude to X and B's attitude to A are positive, then B's attitude to A will, given continuing interaction, tend to change in the same direction. (Newcomb 1953)

44. In the establishment of their rule, colonial governments united rather than divided, although in the exercise of power, they often exploited cleavages in order to gain their ends.

45. The political implications of contemporary marriage are explicit in the policy of the major world powers. The Soviet Union clearly disfavors the out-marriage of its women, while at the height of the Cold War, affinal connections with former citizens of Russia were enough to place an Englishman's visa in jeopardy, should he wish to visit the United States.

REFERENCES

Banton, M. 1965. "Social alignment and identity in a West African city," in H. Kuper (ed.). *Urbanization and Migration in West Africa.* Berkeley and Los Angeles.

Binger, L. G. 1892. *Du Niger au golfe de Guinée.* Paris, Librairie Hachette.

Cohen, A. 1965. "The social organization of credit in a West African cattle market." *Africa* 35: 8-20.

Cornevin, R. 1962. *Histoire du Dahomey.* Paris.

Dupuis, J. 1824. *Journal of a residence in Ashantee.* London.

Eisenstadt, S. N. 1954. *The absorption of immigrants.* London.

Fortes, M. 1949. *The web of kinship among the Tallensi.* London.

1950. "Kinship and marriage among the Ashanti," in A. R. Radcliffe-Brown, and D. Forde (eds.). *African systems of kinship and marriage.* London.

———, and E. E. Evans-Pritchard (eds.). 1940. *African political systems.* London.

Furnivall, J. S. 1948. *Colonial policy and practice.* Cambridge.

Goody, E. 1960. Kinship, marriage and the developmental cycle among the Gonja of Northern Ghana. Ph.D. thesis. University of Cambridge.

1962. "Conjugal separation and divorce among the Gonja of Northern Ghana," in M. Fortes (ed.). *Marriage in Tribal Societies.* Cambridge.

1966. "Fostering in Ghana: a preliminary survey." *Ghana Journal of Sociology* 3.

Goody, J. 1954. *The ethnography of the Northern Territories of the Gold Coast, west of the White Volta.* London.

1956. *The social organization of the LoWiili.* London.

1962. *Death, property and the ancestors,* Stanford.

1967. "The overkingdom of Gonja," in *West African Kingdoms*. D. Forde, and P. Kaberry (eds.), London.

———, and E. Goody. 1966. "Cross-cousin marriage in Northern Ghana." *Man* 1: 343-355.

Greenberg, J. H. 1946. *The influence of Islam upon a Sudanese religion*. New York.

Hill, P. 1966. "Landlords and brokers: a West African trading system." *Cahiers d'Etudes Africaines* 6: 349-366.

Homans, G. C. 1950. *The Human Group*. New York.

Huber, H. 1963. *The Krobo* (Studia Instituti Anthropos, 16). St. Augustin, near Bonn.

Krause, G. A. 1928. "Haussa-Handschriften in der Preussischen Staatsbibliotek." *Mitt. Seminars für Orientalische Sprachen* 31.

Maunier, R. 1949. *The sociology of colonies: an introduction to the study of race contact*. First French ed. 1932-1942. London.

Miner, H. 1953. *The primitive city of Timbuctu*. Princeton.

Mustapha, T. M., and J. Goody. 1967. "The trade route from Kano to Salaga." *Journal Hist. Soc. Nig.* 4: 611-616.

Nadel, S. F. 1942. *A black Byzantium*. London.

Newcomb, T. M. 1953. "An approach to the study of communicative acts." *Psychological Review* 60.

1962. *The acquaintance process*. New York.

Oberg, K. 1940. "The kingdom of Ankole in Uganda," in M. Fortes, and E. E. Evans-Pritchard (eds.). *African Political Systems*. London.

Pacques, V. 1954. *Les Bambara*. Paris.

Rattray, R. S. 1932. *The tribes of the Ashanti hinterland*. Oxford.

Shack, W. A. 1966. *The Gurage*. London.

Smith, M. G. 1959. "The Hausa system of social status." *Africa* 29: 239-252.

Tait, D. 1961. *The Konkomba of Northern Ghana*. London.

Trimingham, J. S. 1959. *Islam in West Africa*. Oxford.

Tylor, E. B. 1889. "On a method of investigating the development of institutions; applied to laws of marriage and descent." *J. Anthrop. Inst.* 18: 245-269.

Wilks, I. 1962. "The Mande Loan element, in Twi." *Ghana Notes and Queries* 4: 26-28.

1967. "Ashanti government in the 19th century," in D. Forde and P. Kaberry (eds.). *West African Kingdoms*. London.

Yalman, N. 1963. "On the purity of women in the castes of Ceylon and Malabar." *J. R. Anthrop. Inst.* 93: 25-58.

7

INCORPORATION IN BORNU

Ronald Cohen

INTRODUCTION

Incorporation in Bornu is evident in two different theaters of action. First, and most apparent, there is the set of processes by which the ancient kingdom has become a local political unit within the larger one of Northern Nigeria and the Nigerian nation as a whole. Secondly, there are the ways and means by which the Kanuri of Bornu have incorporated surrounding groups and members of these groups into the orbit of their own society and its culture. The first aspect is recent and dramatic, and I have documented the most salient aspects of it in previous publications. (Cohen 1962a; 1967; in press [i]) The second aspect is much less dramatic and certainly less well known, although it has been going on for centuries in Bornu as the Kanuri have become the dominant political force in the Chad basin.

In what is to follow, I will lay stress, then, on the ways in which the Kanuri have incorporated others and then summarize some of the major aspects of Kanuri incorporation into modern Nigeria. Finally, I shall attempt to ask some questions about what it is that is not incorporated, or only minimally so in the contemporary era, and attempt to explain the reasons for this.

THE HISTORICAL BACKGROUND[1]

The Bornu kingdom developed in the fifteenth century as a successor state to that of Kanem. In the early kingdom the leading clan and its royal lineage along with their followers were forced to flee when a rebellious Kanem group, the Bulala, captured the dominant position in the Kanem kingdom. After settling in Bornu, the royal clan of the Magumi Sefuwa and their followers set up a capital, Birni Gazargamu, in the northern part of the country and from this base began conquering the local pagan tribes whom they dubbed collectively as the "So." (Cohen 1962b) From this time onwards, outsiders in Europe and the rest of West Africa were aware of a powerful, centrally organized kingdom in the Bornu area and of its people, the Kanuri, who professed Islam and considered themselves part of an expansionist kingdom in the Chad basin.

The kingdom maintained a dominant position in the area throughout the fifteenth and sixteenth centuries while the seventeenth and eighteenth centuries are often spoken of as a time of relative decline. Whether this is true or not, the fact remains that for the first time in its long history, the Bornu state was seriously threatened at the beginning of the nineteenth century by the rise of the Fulani empire of Sokoto. This emergent kingdom stimulated local Fulani in Bornu to rebel against Kanuri hegemony in the western part of the kingdom. After several serious defeats, including the loss of their capital city (1808), the Kanuri were able to put down this revolt. They were aided in this by a Kanembu sheikh, Al-Kanemi, or Shehu Laminu as he is known locally. This man utilized his position to found the second Bornu dynasty, although he never proclaimed himself royal during his lifetime. This was done by his son, Umar, in 1846, when the last of the royal heirs to the old dynasty was finally killed.

The second dynasty ruled until 1893, when it was overturned by an invader from the east named Rabeh. This man had been a lieutenant of Suleman, the son of Zubeir Pasha, a notorious slave raider in the Sudan. When Suleman was vanquished by Gordon's forces in the 1880s, Rabeh led a group of soldiers across Africa and finally arrived in Bornu in 1893. He defeated the Kanuri and set himself up as the founder of a third dynasty. Unfortunately for him, the scramble for Africa was being initiated in Europe and he was eventually killed by the French in 1900. When the British set up modern Bornu, they put the Kanembu Shehus back in power, thus restoring the second dynasty which is the one that rules the emirate today.

POLITICAL INCORPORATION WITHIN THE KINGDOM

Throughout the history of Bornu, although its sphere of influence has expanded and contracted through time, there has grown up the concept of a territory which we may call Bornu proper, or the sovereign state. Outside of this area were the tributaries whose allegiances waxed and waned through time. The northern and eastern borders of the sovereign state were clear-cut and easily defended because they were rivers—the Yo on the north and the Logon-Shari complex to the east. Given modes of warfare, transportation, and defense, it was natural that such barriers should become the borders of this powerful realm. On the west and the south, no easily demarcated boundaries existed and the history of incorporation in these areas is less clear-cut or easily defined.

However, modes of incorporating isolated settlements, ethnic groups, or nomadic pastoralists developed within the borders of the kingdom that served to link such peoples to the state hierarchy. This particular mode of incorporation was the fief system. (see Cohen in press [i]) Under this system, local settlements with their own leaders were linked to a Kanuri noble through the noble's local representative (*chima gana*). The local representative had a voice in the selection of local leaders and could in extreme cases depose rebellious or recalcitrant ones. If the local settlement expanded and was successful, the local leader could be taken to the capital by the *chima gana* to see the senior fief-holder (the *chima kura*) and be taken by this latter noble into the court of the of population actually living on the land provide the highest migration rates, the highest being one of the central areas, with a density of population of well over 200 to the square mile and 27 percent of adult men absent at any one time. These areas, therefore, have the Kanuri as well as non-Kanuri villages. Ethnicity was not a specific membership criterion population. The latter includes everyone of a particular area, whether present or time, such units absorbed the developing national culture of the Kanuri and in this sense became part of an expanding Kanuri ethnic unit. Differences of dialect, hair style, local architecture, perhaps even a specialized set of occupations, might persist or even develop, but for purposes of membership in a polity these territorially defined fiefs were subparts of the kingdom.

Ethnic groups who were nomadic or seminomadic transhumance pastoralists and were less identified by their settlement than by their named segmentary grouping were absorbed in other ways. Within the kingdom such groups were assigned to nobles in the capital who then made agreements with the headmen of these nomadic groups. The headman, then, served as the client of the noble, linking his own ethnic group through the noble to the Bornu throne. The noble collected tributes and informed the headman about administrative matters, such as military levies and the most appropriate areas for pasturage, and the like. In return, the group was given the protection of the Bornu state, could use its judicial hierarchy as an appeal court system, and was allowed a great deal of cultural autonomy in matters of language, dress, and even female circumcision (clitoridectomy) which was and is practiced by the Shuwa nomads of Bornu even though the Kanuri abhor the custom.

These two systems of fiefship defined two separate modes of absorption into the Kanuri state and its emerging national culture. First there were those whose ecological adaptation was primarily that of village agriculturalists, such as the Ngau, Budduwai, Monga, and other local groups. These groups came in time to regard themselves as Kanuri. Secondly, the more predominantly pastoral peoples, especially the Fulani and Shuwa nomads, remained ethnically separate and indeed are so today.

However, this is an oversimplified picture of what actually occurred, because in effect the two fief systems were interchangeable. Thus a settled group might disperse. This could result from depredations made into a local area by disease, warfare, or even from slave raiders. The original population could disperse or migrate as a whole and its past unity be maintained for some time through a local chief who had the right to collect minor tributes even though some of his former townsmen had joined onto other chiefs' settlements. In this sense the dispersed group was treated as if it were an ethnic group whose headman linked it to the Bornu state. Such flexibility allowed for the maintenance of sovereignty, even though serious changes had occurred in the territorial basis of political organization.

On the other hand, nomadic groups such as the Fulani of western Bornu (see Stenning 1959) might settle into villages and become seminomadic transhumance pastoralists who also raised crops near a home village. In such cases their village would be regarded as a settled fief for distribution among the title nobility of the Bornu court. Thus the two different types of fief, *chidibe* (territorial) and *jilibe* (ethnic-based), were interchangeable with one another.

Two other factors were also important in determining the degree of incorporation. These were the position of pastoralism in the traditional culture and whether or not the incorporated group was Islamic. Traditionally, many of the peoples of the Bornu area kept cattle and still do so today, especially in the Mongonu area near Lake Chad. However, only the Shuwa Arabs and the Fulani derived from cultures that were, at least when they entered Bornu, dominantly pastoralist and nomadic or transhumant in their ecological adaptation. Furthermore, these two peoples were both Muslim by religion and thus thought themselves to be the cultural equals of the Kanuri. The result of this has been that even when such peoples have settled into permanent villages, they have kept their language, many of their unique customs and even used their own sociopolitical terms to describe local leaders. Thus the headman of a Fulani settlement was and is today called *Lamido*, not *Bullama*, *Lawan*, or *Mbarma*, which are the equivalent words for the position among the Kanuri.

On the other hand, groups to the south and southeast of Bornu whose original culture base was that of segmentary patrilineal lineages and clans and whose languages are related to the Bantu family of African languages were absorbed over the centuries into the Kanuri nation. They dropped their language, adopted Islam, and lived in villages and fiefs of the Bornu state. This latter process is still going on and can be observed in southern Bornu towns such as Damboa where the Marghi look just like the local Kanuri. They dress the same, speak the language easily with only a trace of accent, and live in households and wards that are structured socially and politically in exactly the same way as the Kanuri around and to the north of them. On the other hand, although they have embraced Islam, they brew millet beer, as do non-Muslims in other Kanuri towns, and some of their kinship norms include a number of non-Kanuri features. Thus almost all Kanuri report that they should and do joke with their wife's younger sister; almost all of the "Kanuri-ized" Marghi of Damboa report that they do not. I would conclude from this evidence that the incorporation of this group has brought them into Kanuri sociopolitical structure at the level of ecology and village organization but that within the family there are still non-Kanuri practices extant. The brewing of beer indicates that they are still regarded, to some extent, by their Kanuri neighbors as pagans and members of an inferior minority group even though they profess Islam. Certainly it is easy to elicit such statements about Marghi inferiority from the local Kanuri.[2]

INCORPORATION OUTSIDE THE KINGDOM

In the precolonial era, Bornu was not only a sovereign state, but an imperial expansionist one as well. This meant that she had developed modes and techniques for incorporating other states and peoples into her empire. Thus, beyond or often at her borders and differing more or less with her in their local culture, was a series of societies which came within the sphere of influence wielded by Bornu in the Central Sudan. Techniques of incorporation varied according to the sociopolitical complexity of the dependency, its historical relations to Bornu, and its position with respect to Bornu's complicated set of international relations with other powerful states and empires of the Sudan.

Directly to the north lay the Saharan trade routes beset by desert raiders who threatened the peaceful passage of commerce. One third of the way across the central route from Lake Chad to Tripoli is the town of Bilma, for centuries and even today an important center for the Saharan salt trade. From the sixteenth century onward, Bornu colonized this town with its own people in order to control the trade. Tubu nomads, who settled in Bilma, have become Kanuri-ized and even today the town is thought of as being dominantly Kanuri in culture.[3] However, to the northeast of the lake and from there west are a series of major towns ending at the far western extremity with the large entrepot of Zinder. All of these, but especially Muniyo and Zinder, became tributaries of Bornu and were pledged to maintain the trade routes and abstain from raiding caravans and towns under Bornu hegemony.

Although these northern towns gave their names to the tributary relationship, it is important to note that each of them was in fact the center or capital of a state, having its own subordinate towns, villages, and nomadic populations. Thus Zinder is supposed to have included over 2,000 town areas and each of the town areas had satellite hamlets within its own jurisdiction. (Richardson, Vol. II: 226) In other words, these were in effect states who sent tributes annually and at other times, especially after slave raids, to the capital of Bornu. In return, Bornu generally came to their aid if they were attacked from elsewhere. Their autonomy was reflected in the fact that the ruler of these states could try nonappealable capital cases without reference to Bornu, whereas fully incorporated groups within the Bornu state involved all citizens in an appeal-court system through the political hierarchy and capital cases were supposed to be taken to the royal court of Bornu.[4] Furthermore, although Bornu could advise these states concerning their relations to others, it could not insist—unless a subordinate state acted against another tributary also under Bornu's protection. Thus, the Bornu rulers were hopeful and indeed formally requested that Zinder carry out hostilities against Maradi to the west. However, the ruler of Zinder refused because he was, and had been for a long time, on friendly terms with Maradi. (Richardson, Vol. II: 228; for Maradi, see M. G. Smith in Daryll Forde and Kaberry 1967). On the other hand, when Zinder attacked Daura, the Hausa state to the south, it was understood that approximately 400 of the western towns of this particular state were under Sokoto protection and that Bornu would therefore not punish Zinder for such raids, especially if part of the booty were sent back to the Bornu capital. There were times when Zinder tried to attack Daura more indiscriminately, using the excuse that the eastern parts of Daura had risen up against Bornu authority and were pagans to boot. (Richardson, Vol. II: 222) Depending upon its own fiscal and international situation, Bornu might look the other way or insist that slaves taken from its protectorate area be allowed to return to their own homes. On one such occasion, at least, Zinder complied and the slaves were returned. (Richardson, Vol. II: 238)

Perhaps the most important factor affecting the relations between Bornu and such tributary states was the internal struggle and competition for power among the royal contenders within the subordinate state itself. Let me give several examples, mostly from the Kanuri-speaking tributaries of Zinder and Muniyo.

In the 1840s the ruler of Zinder, who had a history of recalcitrance towards Bornu, led a series of successful uprisings.[5] Eventually, the Shehu of Bornu was able to quell this revolt as he had others in the past. In so doing, he deposed the monarch (Ibrahim) and put this latter person's younger brother on the throne.

However, no sooner was the new ruler installed, than he rebelled as well and the Bornu Shehu had to gather a large army, put down the younger brother, depose him, and restore the older one, Ibrahim, to the Zinder throne, while taking the younger one as hostage to Kuka, the nineteenth-century capital of Bornu.

This second deposition had occurred the year before Richardson's arrival and involved a three-month siege of the city with a force reported to be in the neighborhood of 60,000 Bornu soldiers. The Zinder people had built an entire mud wall around their capital within three days, and when under siege, the younger brother of Ibrahim had said he would willingly pay tributes in money, cattle, and slaves, but he would not go to Kuka. However, the older brother, Ibrahim, had gone previously to the Bornu capital and had thrown dust over his head in the presence of Shehu Umar of Bornu. He (Ibrahim) thus became again the ruler of Zinder. Even so, because of all this instability, a Bornu consul was appointed to remain in Zinder and overview the state. In 1851, when Richardson visited the town, the man appointed was a North African native of Fez, who had lived in Algiers and fought against the French. Informants reported to Richardson that this consul had taken a great deal of authority away from their traditional ruler, and Richardson suggests that the people and their rulers would probably not tolerate this situation much longer.

We are also told that the rulers of Zinder are the descendants of slaves of the ancient royal house of Bornu—the Magumi Sefuwa Mais. (Richardson, Vol. III: 193) I would suggest that although there was a constant tendency for tributaries to rebel, the excessive rebelliousness of Zinder in the 1830s and 1840s was due to their ancient allegiance to the former dynasty that was still in existence at least until 1846. Thus they were, in fact, refusing to be a tributary to the new royal house of Bornu. However, when no other alternative was available (for instance, after the old dynasty died out), the older brother, Ibrahim, swore obedience to the new Bornu rulers.

In the case of Muniyo, to the east of Zinder, another Ibrahim, the father of the ruler visited by Richardson in 1851 (Vol. II: 317), had killed seven of his own brothers who were appointed by Bornu to the throne of Muniyo.

Each time a ruler was killed, Bornu would send an army and appoint a new ruler, and the killer would disappear into the hill country. After each murder, Ibrahim would write to the Shehu of Bornu, saying "I am under God and you," which enraged the Shehu who then sent another army. "[At] last the Shehu, seeing the impossibility of continuing the war with such a vassal allowed him to have a quiet possession of Muniyo." (Richardson, Vol. II: 317) After this Ibrahim and his son served as loyal tributaries to the rulers of Bornu.

This internal intrigue was heightened when the tributary stood very close to both sides of a struggle. Thus, Barth (Vol. II: 482), in discussing a small principality in Kanem, says that this area was so completely dependent upon the relative supremacy of either Bornu to the west or Wadai to the east that there were always in reality two rulers—one actually in power, having been appointed by the latest conqueror and another member of the royal family waiting in the shadows with his followers. This second one was generally intriguing with the other great power in the area and waiting only until its armed forces should turn up so that he could publicly be acclaimed for his loyalty to the new overlords and be put on the throne. To a lesser extent this same situation seems to have applied to Baghirmi (Barth, Vol. III: 438), although they were a more powerful group and could always retreat to the east or west of the Shari River, depending upon which direction they were attacked from. Furthermore, Baghirmi rulers often paid tributes to both Bornu and Wadai, the largest portion going to the one who had made the most recent successful attack against their kingdom.

One interesting attempt to create an alliance was carried out between Bornu and the Walid Sliman (Suleman), a group of North Africans who emigrated to the Kanem area during the nineteenth century. Haj Bashir, chief advisor (Waziri) to Shehu Umar, agreed to supply this group with horses and arms if they would quell Tuareg raiders on the caravan routes, "but the great difficulty which the Vizier appears not to have overcome, was to subject the predatory excursions of such a set of people to some sort of political rule." (Barth, Vol. II: 65) Bashir kept the wives and mothers of the principal leaders of the Walid Sliman in Kuka, the nineteenth-century capital of Bornu, as hostages. This was not successful, however, and the group constantly preyed on innocent peasants and traders as well as fighting amongst themselves.

On Bornu's western borders, the well-known position of the Galidima can now be seen in context. Elsewhere (Cohen 1967; in press [i]; Cohen and Brenner in press), I have commented on the unique position of this noble-man, who, unlike other Bornu aristocrats, did not reside in the capital city, but was allowed to live in a consolidated fief at the western end of the kingdom, whereas other fief-holders held numbers of fragmented fiefs spread throughout the state. The task of the Galidima was to secure the western borders and the trade routes to Kano. In order to do so, he was allowed to maintain his own semi-independent area of Bornu more on the model of a tributary state than a completely incorporated segment of the Bornu territory.

To the west of the Galidima was the tributary principality of Matsina or Mashina. Here, again, on the border area, as in the case of Baghirmi, smaller states found themselves between two great powers, that of Bornu to the east and Sokoto to the west. And their internal politics were partly determined by this international position. Thus Barth (Vol. II: 165) reports on a civil war in the Gummel area after the death of the local ruler. When this man died (he had been during his lifetime under Bornu suzerainty), his two sons competed for the throne and the younger one asked for help from Sokoto. This help was forthcoming and the younger brother was able to depose the older one, who then exiled himself into Bornu territory under the protection of Matsina and, presumably, the positive sanction of both the Galidima and the Shehu of Bornu. The ruler of Matsina then gave the older brother a fief town of his own within the western Bornu area which was to be his official residence. From here he raised an army and eventually attacked and killed his younger brother, restoring himself to power in Gummel and bringing it and its surrounding towns back under Bornu's sphere of influence. (Barth, Vol. II: 175-176) He even defeated a Sokoto force sent against him and was able to raid and pillage "to the very gates of Kano." (Barth, Vol. II: 177)

A further point in these accounts, but not spelled out in any detail, is the nature of a linkage relationship of these tributary leaders and their estates to the Bornu court of central administration. Although all activity was carried out in the name of the ruler of Bornu, a number of writers comment specifically that the administrative link was not between heads of states but between the tributary state and a chief noble of the Bornu realm, even though allegiance was paid in principle to the Bornu throne. Thus, Zinder is described by Richardson to be the direct responsibility of Haj Bashir, chief minister, or Waziri, to Shehu Umar. (Richardson, Vol. II: 184) Furthermore, the guide sent to Zinder to direct Richardson to Bornu was a slave in the Bashir household. (Richardson, Vol. II: 196) Bashir also negotiated the alliance with Walid Sliman nomads noted above. Barth notes that the tributary of Mandara was the direct responsibility of Abdu Rahman, younger brother of the Bornu monarch. (Barth, Vol. III: 118) Indeed, so fiercely did Rahman feel this responsibility, that when Bashir, the chief minister, mounted an attack on

Mandara for its having behaved "in a refractory manner" (Barth, Vol. III: 118), which Rahman could not stop, it seems as if Rahman might have sent word secretly to his fief tributary warning him of the impending military expedition. When the expeditionary force reached Mandara, the monarch of that principality sent out word immediately that he would submit completely to Bornu and its wishes, thus avoiding a clash that would pit Rahman against a tributary ruler whom he considered to be under his own personal protection.

The folk view or cultural meaning of tributary states, reflected to some extent in the incident recounted above, can be seen more clearly in Bornu relations to small non-Muslim groups at the southern boundaries of this state. When Bornu forces raided for slaves and booty to the south there were a number of alternative results. First of all, the local people could run away, abandoning their village, flocks, and fields in order to save themselves, and then return later—impoverished but with their group intact. Secondly, they might try to resist by ambushing the attackers or fighting off a siege of their village. In this case, no quarter was given on either side, and if the Kanuri were victorious, they killed large numbers of the men and took the women and children as slaves. Thirdly, the Kanuri raiders might make an alliance with the local village or clan head. This headman would be brought in, throw dust over his head and pledge allegiance to the ruler of Bornu.[6] In some of these cases local headmen would then sanction raids on villages within their own areas and those of their neighbors, and then receive a few slaves as their part of the bargain. (see Barth, Vol. III: 254)

One of the most interesting features of such raids occurred when the Bornu troops would rush upon a group of fleeing pagans and then suddenly an order would be given to stop the raid. Kanuri leaders would shout "Amana, Amana!" and their followers would know immediately that this particular group had to be let alone. (Barth, Vol. II: 400-401) The word *amana* means "trust" or "in the trust of," and refers to two extremely important Kanuri institutions. The word can be used to describe the content of working superior-subordinate relations which involve disciplined respect. (Cohen 1965; 1967) To the Kanuri *aman* or *amana* is what makes such relationships work for the benefit of all concerned. Thus, ego can give respect to his social superiors by visiting them in their homes. This is called "giving respect" or *nona*. But only between father and son, client and patron, or trusted friends is there also *aman* or *amana*. Secondly, the word *amana* is also used to describe a foster child, especially a female under marriageable age, who is placed in ego's household. It means that those who did this trust ego to take care of their girl, to make sure her virginity is unimpaired and, as marriage negotiations develop, to make the best match, informing those who have decision-making authority for this marriage so that everything is done according to the jural rules governing marriage inception. It should also be noted that distributing young girls in this manner is often done by subordinates who place their own daughters in the house of their patrons or people with whom they would like to have a patron-client relationship. In other words, the concept of tributary is put into the same semantic category as that of general trust between superiors and subordinates as well as the relationship between a household head and a child he is raising "in trust" for someone else.

Up to this point, we have been describing the incorporation of groups into Kanuri society via the major political institutions of fiefship through subjection or by tributary status. However, there were and are other modes of incorporation by which individuals and small groups were able to move in and out of the Kanuri nation. In an outward direction, people were constantly moving from Bornu towards its outer boundaries and in so doing they spread Kanuri culture centrifugally in all directions. In some cases this seems to have been quite active colonization with an economic and political motivation, as in the case of Bilma to the north of Bornu. The motivation here was obviously a Kanuri desire to control the salt trade that was so importantly centered around and in the town of Bilma. In other instances, local colonies of Kanuri seemed to have arrived on the scene as a result of personal self-interest or even to have been brought there by force. Thus, Clapperton notes (*Bornu Mission*, Part 3: 622) that in Bedde country to the west of Bornu, he came across Kanuri who had been brought there by force of Fulani arms when their capital, Birni Gazargamu, fell in 1808. He notes that one of these captives claims to be a sister of the Mai or first dynastic rulers, and they are now (1820s) reconciled to their new home and have decided to remain there of their own free will.

Barth saw a number of Kanuri colonies. He describes one (Vol. III: 329) on the east (non-Bornu) side of the Shari River near present-day Fort Lamy. These people also seem to have run away from Bornu near the beginning of the nineteenth century to avoid the warfare ravaging their country at that time. To the south of Bornu the same author notes a number of Kanuri colonies set up, usually at sites where trade routes that crosscut one another met; as such, these were natural locations for the development of larger market towns. (Barth, Vol. II: 438; 443) At one point in this same area Barth even met with a group of colonists who were en route southwards toward the Benue River in order to set up a new town (Vol. II: 522). Whether or not such movements outwards produced a flow of Kanuri culture in the same direction was probably dependent on the size of the colony in relation to its surrounding non-Kanuri groups and to the socioeconomic and political importance of the area. Thus, Bilma, which is of intense importance, was retained within the Kanuri cultural orbit and constantly protected and expanded with the result that today it is a garrison of Kanuri culture in the southern Sahara and spreads this culture to surrounding peoples, especially those who settle in or near the town. On the other hand, settlements within the border area between Hausaland and Bornu have in the past hundred years lost their distinctive Kanuri cultural origins and become Hausa-ized. Even here, however, some influences are perceptible. Thus, Barth speaks of Gummel as a dominantly Hausa town inside the area of Bornu hegemony. The gate to the north of the town is called *chinna-n-yala*; these are two words—*chinna* (gate) and *yala* (north)—arranged into Hausa syntax by the use of the Hausa preposition *n* (of). (In Kanuri syntax, it would be *chinna yalabe*; the preposition in Kanuri is *be*, which comes at the end of a phrase: Barth, Vol. II: 168.)

Another place where such colonizing has had extremely significant effects, but about which we still know very little, is in the Biu area south of Bornu. Here, according to oral traditions, a group of Kanuri overlords were supposed to have settled several hundred years ago. These newcomers enforced conversion of the northern Bura-speaking groups to Islam and formed a centralized emirate society tributary to Bornu which came to be called Babur or the Emirate of Biu. The original Kanuri melted into the local population, presumably, maintaining some hold on an emergent noble class, and the southern Bura-speaking groups maintained an agnatic, acephalous system of localized clans and semiautonomous villages within each clan. Here, then, if this very sparse information is correct, Kanuri attempts at incorporation produced the seeds of a more complex Kanuri-like political organization, but the original Kanuri colonial overlords in the area were absorbed into the local (and developing) Babur cultural context.[7]

The Kanuri also incorporated groups and individuals who moved into their kingdom in a number of ways. We have already seen how this was done within the framework of the fief system, but other modes were available and performed a similar function. These can be summarized under the categories of clientship, slavery, marriage, and trade.

As I have pointed out elsewhere (Cohen 1965; 1967), perhaps the most important social relationships in Kanuri society were those modeled on the father-son dyad, but widened culturally to include clientship or any category of superior-subordinate relations. Chains of such relations formed the basis for political hierarchy in the state, and among the most trusted of subordinates were nonkin clients. Quite often non-Kanuri could enter into the society as trusted clients of nobles or the royal person himself, and thus establish a "client-house" whose agnatic descendants became Kanuri-ized and attached to noble families through the original client relationship of their founder. The Bornu consul, appointed in the mid-nineteenth century to supervise the affairs of Zinder, was such a man. As already noted, he was a North African, not a Kanuri. His superior was the Waziri, or chief minister, of Bornu, and he felt that he represented his superior's interests, which were also those of the Bornu state, while serving his residence in Zinder. His descendants are today Kanuri-ized residents of the Bornu capital (L. Brenner: personal communication). In Bornu today there are Kanuri-ized Shuwa, Fulani, Mandara, and others, whose ancestors entered Bornu society through such clientage relationships.

In traditional Bornu, large numbers of foreign slaves, usually from southern and southeastern pagan groups, were used as laborers in households and in the fields for agricultural labor. Although there were mechanisms for freeing such slaves, usually at the death of the master, they were mostly inherited and remained within Bornu. The general rule for slave status was clear-cut: sons of free men (even by slave women or concubines, *chir*) were free, while sons of male slaves retained their servile status. In other words, sons of non-Kanuri slave women were considered fully incorporated members of Bornu society, although in practice they had lower status than their half-brothers whose mothers were free.

Slaves could also be used by both the monarch and his nobles as important administrative aides and there was a large number of titled slave offices in the royal court of Bornu. A few of the most important ones were held by eunuchs, thus creating no slave lineages and increasing the power of appointment of their masters. In general, however, slave nobles were able to perpetuate their households and if their sons were competent they could, or at least one of them could, succeed to his father's office. Thus, today, a number of noble Kanuri are the descendants of royal slaves. Their ancestors accepted Islam long ago and they consider themselves today to be fully Kanuri in cultural heritage. Other nonslave nobles sometimes pass slurring remarks about the slave origins of such people, but in general they have a high status in the society as a whole.

At the lower levels of society, nobles and/or Bornu rulers could establish slave settlements in rural areas, either in their own fiefs or in someone else's (with the fiefholder's permission). These slave towns often still bear the name "slave town," and are made up today of a core group of Kanuri-ized descendants of the original slaves who were captured from pagan groups elsewhere and settled in this particular place.

The institution of marriage also allowed for the importation of non-Kanuri women into the society. Kanuri marriage is virilocal and to a variable extent patrilocal as well. Marriage between Kanuri men and women from other Muslim ethnic groups, although not widely practiced, has always occurred. Such women learn the ways of Kanuri household life, husband-wife relations and, even if they divorce, may elect to stay in Bornu and remarry into another Kanuri household. The large numbers of Kanuri men who incorporate non-Kanuri ethnic terms into their names is an indication of the foreign provenience of their mothers and provides some measure of the ubiquity of these non-Kanuri marriages. Thus, two of the royal princes of Bornu are both called Abba Kiari after a paternal (royal) grandfather. The elder is called Abba Kiari Kura or Abba Kiari-the-elder; while the younger brother is called Abba Kiari Shuwa or Abba Kiari-the-one-with-the-Shuwa-mother. Such women generally maintain contacts with their own affines, maintain use of their native language, and visit their own kin as often as they can. However, over a period of time in Kanuri society, they drop many of their non-Kanuri ethnic traits. Interestingly, the last thing to change seems to be the hair style, which is an ethnically distinct trait in this area.

In major Kanuri towns, but especially in the capital, it has always been customary, as indeed it is all over the Sudan, to have special quarters laid aside for foreign traders. This is still true today. In precolonial Bornu a large contingent of such traders were the North African Arabs and the Hausa. Although their strangers' quarters were isolated pockets of foreign culture, and remained so, they were also sources from which new members, wives, and slaves might be received into Kanuri society and possibly incorporated fully over time.

One final mode of incorporation practiced traditionally and still carried on is that of voluntary conversion to Islam by members of pagan tribes who are living in Bornu. This type of incorporation is solemnized at a circumcision ceremony at which a group of Kanuri boys, aged seven to twelve, are cut. At such times, pagans of any age can ask to join the ceremony as newcomers and be received into adult male Kanuri society as converts to Islam. Although people viewing such conversions laugh and joke about it and the non-Kanuri ethnic origins of the convert are still remembered—he has taken an important step. If he then marries a Kanuri woman and tries to become a Kanuri-speaking Muslim, his children and, even more so, his grandchildren will become fully absorbed into the society.

In summary, then, incorporation into Kanuri society of other peoples within Bornu proper took place within the political structure of their fief system, through clientship relations to foreigners, slavery, and marriage. Traders from abroad were maintained as foreigners, but there was a constant leakage from this group into Kanuri society. Outside Bornu, tributary states were kept within Kanuri hegemony through the use of military power, while "trust" and protective relations were set up with pagan groups to the south. In some cases, such as that of Biu, tributaries run by Kanuri colonizers or consuls broke away from Kanuri rule and set up semi-autonomous kingdoms modeled on that of Bornu but modified by the nature of local sociopolitical structures. In a number of cases, Kanuri migrants turned up beyond the borders of Bornu proper. These may be called "colonies" set up for purposes of controlling a specific trade, as in the case of Bilma, or more privately organized migrations for reasons of personal safety or aggrandizement. In this latter case, Kanuri culture is lost over time by the migrant, except in the special case of Bilma, but he has imported some Kanuriness to the local scene, spreading Bornu cultural influence outwards from its center.

BORNU'S INCORPORATION INTO MODERN NIGERIA: A SUMMARY[8]

The coming of British colonial rule to Bornu created a territorially based political hierarchy within the kingdom, weakened the power of the monarch, ended the imperial ties to tributary states, as well as the slave trade, and faced Bornu's foreign trade southwards to the Atlantic coast. Out of these changes, plus the politics of independence, has come modern Bornu's incorporative position in Nigeria.

The British officials, not only in Bornu but throughout the emirates of Northern Nigeria, changed the fief system under the leadership of Lugard, so that a small group of nobles was assigned to districts throughout each kingdom. (see M. G. Smith 1960; Cohen in press [i]) These districts were made up of numbers of village area units that corresponded roughly to precolonial fiefs. In Bornu local leaders were appointed to these village headships while nobles from the capital took over as district heads under the Shehu. At first, the Shehu himself was allowed to collect the cattle tax, principal source of the emirate revenues, through his own slave followers at the capital. However, by 1914 these taxes too were incorporated into the duties of district heads, who then taxed both nomadic and settled populations within their own districts. This completed then, by 1914, the creation of a territorially based hierarchy from Shehu to district head to village area head to ward and hamlet heads and, hence, to household heads into which all aspects of the native administration could be lodged or attached.

From these changes two problems emerged that are not yet solved a half-century later. The first revolves around the relations between the village area head and his superior, the district head. District heads came originally from the royal court—they were former nobles and fief-holders. But except for the Galidima, who held Nguru, a consolidated fief that was made into a district, all other district heads went to constructed territorial units or districts that had been made up from a series of fiefs whose nineteenth-century affiliations to fief-holders were not similar to those of the present and were certainly not necessarily that of traditional subordination to the new appointee to the district headship. Thus, a district head might go out to his district, which contained 20 to 25 towns, each of whose town head owed subordination to twenty different nineteenth-century nobles. Now suddenly this new person was to be the political superior of these twenty village area headmen, and he had the task of creating a working administrative unit from a region that had had no previous political unity. Often district heads sent out their own followers to the various towns for which they had responsibility. These men, called *chima* (the nineteenth-century word for fief-holder), often became the "real" town heads, who used the British appointee as a puppet. In other cases, village heads could be persuaded to attach themselves as loyal followers to the new district head, while in still other cases, a district head and Lawan would intrigue to get rid of one another. In this latter case, the district head would complain to his superiors and to the British touring officers about a particular village head, while the village head would do the same on his part. Both tried to use whatever support they could muster in the royal court and in the end one of them might be transferred, retired, or dismissed; although a stalemate could also result if the village head had powerful friends in the kingdom who could protect him at the royal court. Because district heads constantly shift from one district to another, this problem of creating a viable administration is still present in Bornu at the district level. One district head admitted that six of his village area heads were appointees of the previous incumbent and that he had great difficulty in bringing them into his own organization of the district, since they were active followers of the previous district head, who had been promoted to a larger district in the emirate. (see Cohen 1962)

The second problem stemmed out of the presence of the British in Bornu and persists today (until 1967) in the provincial-government structure and its relations to the emirate or Native-Authority government, which is a subpart of the provincial administration. (Presumably the creation of a northeastern state in this area with its own state officials will not change this problem to any significant degree.) Starting with the British, and carried on into a Nigerian-staffed provincial government after independence, the basic standards for good or adequate political performance by officials of the emirate are Western in origin. Thus, district chiefs are viewed, officially at least, as people who receive salaries and must abjure exacting tributes or delivering tributes throughout the kingdom. They should deliver all tax revenues to the treasury as agents of government and certainly not take any portion of the tax revenues for redistribution to loyal followers or gifts to superiors. However, as I have pointed out elsewhere, district heads must take part of the tax money, or they will not be in a position to maintain the organization necessary to collect taxes. (Cohen 1962) Furthermore, if their tax receipts fall, Western standards are used to judge the district head as inefficient and he may be punished by pressures on the Native Authority from the provincial administration. Furthermore, the British provided an alternative hierarchy to whom appeals by the ordinary people could be made if the Kanuri authority system was deemed unsatisfactory. Provincial officials also had to translate regional or national policy directives into action at the local level and, therefore, pressure the emirate officials to carry out such directives. The result of a number of these conflicting standards on performance of the emirate officials was and is that members of the political hierarchy of the emirate are sensitive to the wishes of superiors rather than to the rules by which the political game must be played. This creates tensions when people do in fact refer to rules, and provides potentiality for change because of the ease with which modernizing directives may be incorporated into the system if they emanate from top people in the emirate government. (see Cohen 1962)

From at least 1914 onwards, when the present emirate government was set up, the Shehu's council under the chairmanship of the Waziri has performed the function of an expanding local cabinet. (Cohen 1967; in press [ii]) After World War II, when tax revenues increased rapidly because of the rise in the world price of groundnuts, cabinet activities have become increasingly complex and the Native-Authority departments under each counselor have become large bureaucratic organizations, with representatives in each district capital working under the guidance of provincial departments who have relations with regional and federal authorities. The local civil-service departments are organized into central offices in Maiduguri, the emirate capital, with representatives throughout the district capitals. This means that the clear-cut lines of authority from Emir, or Shehu, through the district head to village head is made more complex. Not only is the Bornu emirate set into a provincial (and now a northeast) state government, but the local-authority structures of capital to district to village must interact with representatives of the judiciary, the schools, the public works department, the veterinary and forestry departments, and so on. These representatives require the cooperation of the emirate authority structure but they are to some extent independent and responsible to their own hierarchies within each department for the success of their programs. Ultimately it is their activities that effect social and economic change and their programs that unite Bornu into a modernizing nation whose goals are conceived at the federal as well as the local level.

When this bureaucratic expansion is put together with the fact that the present Shehu came to his office in 1937 and is over ninety years of age, the conclusion is inescapable that much of the day-to-day decision-making is now being carried out in the Council, often with the help of technical experts from the provincial, regional, federal, or even foreign governmental sources. In other words, Bornu has gone a long way towards the development of a constitutional monarchy. However, the question remains as to whether the next incumbent of the royal role will try to regain power for the throne, or whether the Council will be able to maintain and expand its powers. Another possibility is that the local Native Authority government, or at least the Council, will eventually become a representative body, using the electoral process for recruitment instead of appointment by the provincial or state authorities in consultation with the Council and the Shehu as is now the case. (see Cohen in press [ii])[9]

The colonial era saw the rapid end of Bornu's imperial power and a collapse of the trans-Saharan trade. Because tributary states, such as Zinder or Kanem, came under the colonial rule of France, the tributary relations between Bornu and these states ended in 1900. However, certain formalities continue. Thus, in the 1950s, when the French appointed a new district chief in Niger, it was a necessary part of the formal investiture ceremony that a robe of office be given to the chief by the Shehu of Bornu. Thus, even though the two areas were under the rule of two colonial powers, precolonial relations were still in existence, at least at a symbolic level. Bornu relations with people on their southern, eastern, and western boundaries were also taken over by colonial officials and these areas were divided into subsectors of Nigerian provinces or, in the case of the eastern areas, into the protectorate of the Cameroons.

For all intents and purposes, relations with previous tributaries ceased and became unimportant when these areas came under the authority of different sets of colonial officials. However, in the case of Dikwa to the southeast, another Kanuri emirate was set up and a member of the Bornu royal family was placed on the throne. In a number of cases in the last fifty years, the

Bornu monarch has been recruited from this "junior" emirate, to the south-east of the present one. Since the population of Dikwa emirate is dominantly non-Kanuri, Dikwa itself can be seen as a semi-independent Kanuri colony in which the Kanuri are still attempting to incorporate non-Kanuri into their expansionist ethnic group. (see S. White 1963) Another important exception is that of the emirate of Biu, to the south of Bornu emirate, but within the same provincial administration. In the modern period, especially the last two or three decades, there has developed a competitive situation between these two political units for the fruits of modernization in the province as a whole. This can be seen in the large numbers of students from Biu that are in schools in the provincial capital and the widespread quota system that is employed so that they will not take up all available positions, some of which must be left for Kanuri. Whereas in the precolonial period, these two units could not have been competitors because of the superior power of Bornu, now within a provincial administration and a national and a regional unit that is senior to both of them, they can become specific interest groups competing for a share of the modernizing resources of the nation.

In the economic sector, the British very quickly discouraged and eventual-ly stopped the trade in slaves and other goods across the desert. For a while this trade was carried on in a clandestine fashion around the east end of Lake Chad because German and French authorities were evidently less forceful in their antipathy to it. One informant spoke of making his last raid for slaves in the winter season of 1920-21, but claims to have given it up after that because of the vigilance of colonial officials. In other areas, European trading companies were established who introduced Western currency and whose efforts, backed by government, very soon joined Bornu to the import-export trade of Nigeria. As cash cropping in groundnuts expanded and the local market for import goods, especially textiles, also expanded, Bornu joined a world trade community through its membership in an emerging Nigerian national economic structure. (Cohen 1967) At first this trade was handled by a few European companies and a cadre of Levantine middlemen who became the major distributors and buyers through their small businesses to and from African producers and consumers. Another group who came in to fill this small retail trading role was the Ibo from eastern Nigeria. They also carried on a fish trade from Lake Chad to other parts of Nigeria and played a significant role in the transport industry through their ownership of trucks that brought goods in and out of the Bornu area. As elsewhere, in Nigeria they also manned federal services such as posts and telegraphs, hospitals, and clerical staff in the trading companies in the provincial departments. Although expatriot staff formed the management level of the European trading companies up to 1960, these positions rapidly went to the Nigerians and very often Ibos in the post-independence period. Up until the late 1940s and 50s, local Kanuri did very little to change these arrangements. Kanuri trade within the emirate was handled within traditional and semitraditional ways. (Cohen 1967) However, with the growth of Nigerian political parties and local politicians whose horizons were expanded to the national level, pressures began to be exerted on the non-European, non-Northern Nigerian middlemen. By 1956, the local N.P.C. party organization was pressuring to restrict the activities of Levantine and other non-northern traders, such that northerners would have first buying access to the groundnut crop. By the 1960s this was accomplished and today the cash-crop buyers in Bornu are for the most part Kanuri, who deal directly with the European trading firms, and these latter enterprises handle the export crop as agents of the Nigerian marketing board.

The Bornu emirate government encourages such activity by providing licenses to Kanuri traders. It has also encouraged a local building industry by spreading out small contracts to a large number of licensed Kanuri contractors. This emphasis, then, on local development by the emirate government is designed to provide opportunities for the Kanuri to take up positions in a developing economy that were filled at first by outsiders. In the wider political realm, the emirate government simply adapted at first to the colonial regime. But as time went on, and especially as independence became a decided possibility, Kanuri leaders felt compelled to demand their share of offices and jobs at the national and regional Nigerian levels. And they have been successful.

There are now and have been Kanuri in almost every federal cabinet. There are Kanuri diplomats abroad and in senior posts in the army. The first Nigerian governor of Northern Nigeria was a Kanuri. To the Kanuri leaders, and even ordinary people, these are matters of great pride. Today the idea that some of the most successful Kanuri will find expression for their capabilities outside Bornu is taken for granted. On the other hand, at least one leader in the last ten years has resigned from a federal cabinet post to become the Waziri, or chairman of the emirate government council of Bornu. In other words, he felt that the chief political job at the emirate level was more important than a federal cabinet post. This local loyalty is reflected in attitudes to working outside Bornu. In 1966 we asked a sample (N = 886) of school and nonschool young people of both sexes, rural and urban, whether they would leave Bornu against the wishes of their family to obtain a good job; 75 percent said they would not, while 14 percent claimed they would. These figures are no different for school and nonschool populations, although more of the school group felt ambiguous about the choice and could not make up their minds. In other words, the vast majority of young people in Bornu prefer to remain in their own ethnic area, if their families wish them to, which is most often the case, even if opportunities are better elsewhere in the country.

For those who do want to leave Bornu and take advantage of a national or regional labor market, Western education is by far the most important means for accomplishing such ends. The difficulty in using education as a simple measure or pathway into wider Nigerian or Northern Nigerian society lies in the recruitment procedures utilized throughout the area. Although it has been suggested (A. M. H. Kirk-Greene, "Qualifications and the Accessibility to Office," African Studies Center, UCLA) that Northern Nigeria in general has had a movement from ascribed to achieved recruitment criteria, especially in government service, the situation is and always has been much more complex. Traditionally, even among those in the upper classes, competence had to be demonstrated, or a person was either passed over in favor of his more adequate kin or the power and prestige of the offices he held waned in the kingdom itself. The ranks of the bureaucracy inside Bornu were always open to successful newcomers through clientage and/or slavery. Thus, Haj Bashir, the very powerful mid-nineteenth century Waziri, is said to have had very mediocre beginnings but was able to build himself up to become one of the most powerful men of his day. (Cohen and Brenner, in press) On the other hand, as Bornu has moved into its modern position in contemporary Nigeria, the standards of competence have not so much changed from ascribed to achieved as they have expanded. Today in the local emirate government a man must be competent at his task in a modern technical sense, and demonstrate as well a clear-cut understanding of what it means in traditional terms to be a member of the Kanuri state elite. Without both of these qualifications, he is judged incompetent by his superiors. These criteria weaken somewhat as one moves outside the emirate. Thus, in longer interviews with secondary-school boys, who claimed that they would rather find work after graduation outside Bornu, the most common explanation given for their preference was that they felt that traditional recruitment procedures within Bornu would militate against their success in the local area. Conversely, they felt that outside Bornu in the northern region of Nigeria or even the federal capital of Lagos, it might be possible for them to rely more on Western standards of job recruitment that they had been taught to value in their secondary school backgrounds. However, even this insight is often incorrect, since they may find, as some of them have already reported, that when looking for positions outside Bornu, they are in fact being manipulated by powerful Kanuri leaders, who have decided to put so many Bornu boys here or there in the regional or federal bureaucracy.

Despite these difficulties, Western education does provide a means by which young Kanuri can and are moving out of their society into a larger Nigerian context, albeit this entire movement is not simply a matter of individuals doing what they prefer.

This brings us to a final point concerning modern incorporation in Bornu, that of ethnicity or cultural identity. The Kanuri are a deeply proud people. They widely believe their own culture and its special vehicle, the Kanuri language, to be superior to most of the other ethnic groups around them. This pride is also expressed in a sense of their own historical greatness and its longevity and in their religion. In the cities of Bornu today, many (indeed a majority) of the young people speak Hausa, and in relation to the rest of Nigeria, they feel a oneness with their fellow Muslims to the north. This, of course, goes along with a feeling of enormous social distance with non-Muslim southerners, especially Ibos. Whether Kanuri separateness as a distinct cultural unit will continue, given the rapid spread of Hausa, the rise of urbanization and the growth of Western education, is difficult to say, and hard data on these trends are still relatively rare. However, for the majority of the population of Bornu, ethnic identity is very strong today and shows no sign of weakening. As long as it is expressed in the political organization of an emirate, whether the emirate be within a province or a northeast state as it now is, there seems no doubt that Kanuri as a semiseparate group within Nigeria will continue to have an identity and a semiseparate cultural character.

CONCLUSIONS

The Kanuri of Bornu began their history as a conquest state and over the centuries developed a series of well-defined means to incorporate other peoples into their political system, which led often to cultural incorporation as well. Their fief system within the borders of the state was based on the territorial and nomadic status of those being ruled. The borders of this state were defined geographically to the north and east by rivers and politically by the fact that the ruler of Bornu had power of life and death over his subjects. Outside these borders were subject peoples who came within Bornu's sphere of influence. For the most part, these groups were territorially based, but in a few cases they were nomads. Thus, the two types of internal fiefs were reflected in two types of external relations to tributary groups maintained by the Kanuri. Their tributary status was demarcated by the fact that their leaders could try capital cases without reference to the Bornu court. As a group, these tributary peoples formed another border outside Bornu, not in geographical but in sociopolitical terms. The politics of such relations involved Bornu in the internal factional disputes of these areas, especially when the royal succession was at stake. Territorial fiefs within Bornu were incorporated culturally, while nomadic groups, who were Muslim, kept their own cultural distinctiveness. Tributaries, being more distant were able to maintain cultural distinctiveness, although those to the north seem to have accepted many Kanuri cultural influences. Incorporation also took place through conversion to Islam, marriage, slavery, trade, and the founding of Bornu colonies outside its own borders. Today, many of these modes of recruitment into Kanuri society still operate. Thus, conversion and marriage are still means by which newcomers enter Kanuri society.

In the twentieth century Bornu lost her tributaries. Consolidation of fiefs into districts has brought problems of relating the emirate government to those in authority beyond its boundaries as well as between members of the emirate hierarchy within Bornu's own political structure. It has also produced the conditions for a constitutional monarchy. Finally, it has afforded an opportunity for advancement to those who wish to move outside their own ethnic area—and because the emirate persists as a political, linguistic, and cultural entity, whose members feel a sense of unity, the Kanuri have of necessity become an effective pressure group in modern Nigeria.

NOTES

1. This material is covered in greater detail in Cohen 1966a, 1966b, 1967; Cohen and Brenner in press; Cohen in press [i].

2. See Barth, Vol. II: 337, for an account of Marghi incorporation in the 1850s.

3. See Chapelle 1957. Barth (Vol. III: 11) was told that Bornu would like to see the Turks conquer and pacify the Sahara as far south as Bilma and the Kanuri would then ensure the trade route between Bilma and Lake Chad.

4. Richardson (Vol. II: 224) notes that the Sultan of Zinder had power of

life and death over his subjects; that he could make war on his own, although with some advice from Bornu as to where he should direct his hostilities (p. 228); and he recently (1851) had been given adjudicative and punitive powers over Bornu citizens caught breaking the law in Zinder, because it had recently been recorded that some Bornu Kanuri were slave-raiding within the Zinder state (p. 269) Barth (Vol. III: 137) notes further that military assistance by tributary states to Bornu was not mandatory unless the warfare concerned was being conducted within the tributary state itself.

5. This account is taken from Richardson, Vol. II: 200-201; 182-183; 318-319.

6. In one case recorded of such action, a village headman refused this oath, because he claimed that he was on foreign soil and for the oath to be meaningful, the dirt had to be from his own home village. (Barth, Vol. III: 206)

7. Although my information on this area is very inadequate, I have reason to believe that even the emirate organization, although patterned on the model of the Bornu state, had a number of structural features that make it a much less centralized organization than its northern neighbor. Thus, local district heads today are elected and always have been, rather than just being centrally appointed. The source for this material is a Babur informant now studying at Ahmadu Bello University in Northern Nigeria.

8. For the sake of completeness in covering incorporation, the discussion to follow summarizes briefly the materials that are available elsewhere. (Cohen 1962; 1967; in press [i] ; in press [ii].

9. This paragraph was written before the death of the last Shehu. The nature and impact of the new succession is discussed in Cohen (in press [ii]).

REFERENCES

Barth, H. 1858. *Travels and discoveries in north and central Africa.* 5 vols. London, Longmans.

Bovill, E. W. (eds.). 1966. *Missions to the Niger: the Bornu mission 1822-25.* Cambridge, Published for the Hakluyt Society by Cambridge University Press.

Chapelle, J. 1957. Nomades noirs du Sahara. Paris, Plon.

Cohen, R. 1962a. "The analysis of conflict in hierarchial systems: an example from a Kanuri political organization," in R. Cohen (ed.). *Power in complex societies in Africa. Anthropologica* 4: 87-120. (Special Issue)

1962b. "The just-so so: a spurious tribal grouping in Western Sudanic culture." *Man* 62, article no. 239.

1965. "Some aspects of institutionalized exchange: a Kanuri example." *Cahiers d'Etudes Africaines.* (Ecole Pratique des Hautes Etudes, Sorbonne.) The Hague: Mouton, 5, no. 19: 353-369.

1966. "The Bornu king lists," in J. Butler (ed.). *Boston University Publications in African History.* Vol. 2: 41-83. Boston, Boston University Press.

1967. *The Kanuri of Bornu.* New York, Holt, Rinehart and Winston.

in press (i). "From empire to colony: Bornu in the nineteenth and twentieth centuries." Written for the Boston University Seminar on African History, discussed at Harvard University, March, 1965. To be published in V. Turner (ed.). *The Impact of Colonialism.* Stanford, Hoover Institute.

in press (ii). "The Kinship in Bornu," in M. Crowder (ed.), *West African Chiefs.* London, Faber.

———, and L. Brenner. 1969. "Bornu in the nineteenth century," in A. Ajayi, and M. Crowder (eds.). *The history of West Africa.* Oxford, Clarendon Press.

Richardson, J. 1853. *Mission to central Africa.* 2 vols. London, Chapman and Hall.

Smith, M. G. 1960. *Government in Zazzau.* London, Oxford University Press.

White, S. 1963. *Descent from the hills.* London, John Murray.

8

PROCESSES OF POLITICAL INCORPORATION IN MOSSI SOCIETY

Elliott P. Skinner

PROCESSES OF INCORPORATION

The attempt of contemporary Africans to create viable nation-states has led to a great deal of confusion among some scholars regarding the nature of traditional African societies and their capacity for large-scale organization. This confusion has been in part due to the fuzzy definitions of such concepts as: "lineage," "clan," "tribe," "nation," "empire," "state," and "nation-state." On the other hand, it is clear that part of the problem is a real ignorance among scholars of the integrative processes by which sociocultural groups merge into larger entities. This situation with respect to Africa is made much worse by the fact that most scholars writing about that continent lack an appreciation for the cultural and structural characteristics of the societies found and, furthermore, have little knowledge of Africa's past.

One classic example of what fuzzy thinking and ignorance about traditional African societies can produce is Rupert Emerson's comments about the problem of "nation-building" in Africa. He declares that:

Africa's problem is either that it has no clearly identifiable nations or that they are of such recent origin that they have only a tenuous hold on the popular imagination. The basic political pattern of other continents and regions has been determined primarily by their national make-up, even though the precise frontiers between states, often blurred by the interpenetration of people, may be pushed one way or the other as the fortunes of history dictate. The political pattern of Africa is one that was imposed by the imperial powers as they divided Africa among themselves . . . Everywhere in the world, nations have been shaped from diverse and hostile communities which have been brought into a common framework over the centuries, often through living together in a superimposed state. It may be that Africa is, belatedly, in the process of molding nations in the same way that they have been molded elsewhere, or, working with different ingredients at a different time, it may evolve new patterns of its own. (Deutsch and Foltz 1963: 96)

The attempt to unravel what Professor Emerson has in mind is a difficult task indeed. It is disturbing that he makes no distinction among the concepts: nation, state, and nation-state. Africa may have no nation-states, but the allegation that there are "no clearly identifiable nations" there, or that the nations have "only a tenuous hold on the popular imagination" confuses the issue when clear thinking is necessary. Secondly, it is not quite clear what Emerson means when he declares that the "basic political patterns" of Africa were "imposed by the imperial powers . . . " Most social scientists consider the concept "pattern" to mean the form of the institutions of a culture or society which are accepted by its people and give relative coherence and continuity to their way of life. One assumes that this is true for political patterns as well as other types of sociocultural patterns. However, it appears that Emerson has used the concept "political pattern" with respect to Africa to mean either "political boundaries" and/or "administrative units." If this is indeed his meaning, then he is certainly correct; but he has not said anything about political patterns. Thirdly, his declaration that Africa may be belatedly going through the process which took place "everywhere in the world" in which nations have been shaped from "diverse and hostile communities . . . brought into a superimposed state" shows a profound ignorance of, or disregard for, Africa's past. I dare say that there are few regions of the world where the frontiers between polities have not been "often blurred by the interpenetration of people, . . . pushed one way or the other by the fortunes of history." Professor Emerson's appreciation of Spiro's caution that Africans working at a different time with different ingredients may evolve their own patterns is worthy of attention. However, we are forced to ask whether the ingredients with which the Africans will work are the "basic political patterns" imposed by the Europeans, or something they had prior to the appearance of the Europeans in Africa.

The presence in Africa of some of the most complex political organizations outside of Asia and Europe has been recognized by anthropologists for a long time. Thus, Herskovits states, "Of the areas inhabited by nonliterate peoples, Africa exhibits the greatest incidence of complex governmental structures. Not even the kingdoms of Peru and Mexico could mobilize resources and concentrate power more effectively than could some of these African monarchies." (1948: 332) And Evans-Pritchard wrote, "It is particularly in Africa that relatively large-scale political societies can be studied." (1963: 134) Unfortunately, this has not been recognized and scholars go blithely on talking about the problems of "nation-building" in Africa as if similar processes had not taken place there in the past. Thus, in this paper I shall concern myself with identifying and delineating the processes used by African societies in the past to incorporate identifiably different groups so that these groups were able to live in the same society by submerging their social and cultural differences for a common end, or by accepting control of a superior political organization. Perhaps it might be, as some scholars, though not necessarily myself, are beginning to argue, that there are few structural differences between the processes of incorporation at work in "traditional," "modern," and "post-independent" Africa.

One of the most vexing problems confronting the scholar who is examining the traditional social and political organizations of Africa is the identification of the basic societal units found there. An understanding of the complexity of this problem is a *sine qua non* for dealing with the problem of political or other types of incorporation encountered on the continent. Anthropologists agree that the Bushmen of South Africa are organized in "bands"—that is, a group of usually related persons living together and having rights over the use of certain areas. Again, there is general agreement that the lineage, a corporate group of persons claiming descent from a known ancestor, is almost ubiquitous in African societies. However, confusion starts on this level because, while the "lineage" may be viewed as a corporation solely by its members and the other groups in the society, it is internally segmented. Its members often live in different settlements, and frequently distribute unequally among themselves, the strategic resources of the society over which the lineage has control. Moreover, there is no necessary equivalence between lineage segments since some segments grow to be much larger than others. As a result, it is often difficult to identify the genealogical equivalence of lineage segments in terms of distance removed from the founding ancestor because the more successful lineage segments fission more than the less fortunate ones. This is especially true of some "royal" or "noble" segments in the highly complex societies.

The "clan" in many African societies is also difficult to delineate because, while it is considered to be composed of a cluster of lineage groups claiming a common founding ancestor, the precise lines of genealogical descent from the founder are usually unknown. The result is that while some lineages of the clan remain lineages, others lose track of their genealogy, fuse together, and become "clans" within the clan, although genealogically they are equivalent to lineages within the clan. It should be pointed out that in some African societies, such as the Tiv of Nigeria, there are no clans since genealogical charters are maintained. In others, such as the Mossi, "clans" may be identified among the autochthonous Ninisi people conquered by the Mossi, and among Mossi groups which have lost access to political power, but they are not found among the people of noble status. Of course, many African "clans," like "lineages," are internally segmented, but the element of corporateness in clans is normally weaker than in lineages.

The "tribe," considered by most anthropologists to be the largest unit whose members may trace real or fictive descent from a common ancestor and feel a sense of exclusiveness, unity, and common destiny, is by far the most difficult entity to identify in traditional Africa. Sheer size may be a factor in the problem of identification, and thus, one reads about "subtribes," and about "sections" which are subdivisions of "subtribes." On the other hand, one reads of "tribal groups" among the Dinka and Sukuma, which are said to be a collection of "tribes." However, besides size and the problem of genealogical or population complexity, the factor of political organization apparently has created difficulties in identifying "tribes." Thus, Hilda Kuper defines the tribe in Africa as "a group composed predominantly of kin and under the leadership of the dominant kinship group." (1947: 11) And Isaac Schapera states that, "The nuclear stock of a tribe is generally composed of people all claiming descent from the same line of ancestors as the Chief. But even the smallest tribe contains many alien families or groups, while in the larger tribes only a small proportion of the people may belong to the original stock." (1937: 173) Schapera's very pertinent conclusion is that, "The tribe is not a closed group, like the clan. It is an association into which people may be born, or which they may voluntarily join, or into which they may be absorbed by conquest; and which they may, for one reason or another, leave again." (*ibid*.)

This juxtaposition of population complexity with political organization within the "tribe" has led some anthropologists to despair of there being any way of delineating the "tribe," and question the very use of the concept with respect to Africa. Herskovits declared quite frankly that "tribe," as a concept, is "difficult to define, and of little utility, whether for scientific or practical purposes." (1962: 70) Similarly, a rather confused young man in the former French Congo reportedly told a visiting American political scientist, "We anthropologists thought that tribes were small in this area . . . But the rise of local political organizations seems to have stimulated the re-emergence of larger associations than we had ever identified." (Carter 1960: 90)

A surprisingly large number of anthropologists confronted with the large sociocultural units found in Africa have deliberately eschewed the term "tribe." For example, Jean Buxton states quite specifically that, "The Mandari are not a tribe, but a people—a cultural and not a political group. There is no single Mandari founding ancestor, but certain groups consider they have a more rightful claim to Mandari country because they occupied their land prior to people of later advent." (Middleton and Tait 1958: 69) He adds that, "Historically, the Mandari regard themselves as being composed of different levels of incomers superimposed on earlier populations. This building up has been the result of immigration and absorption, which is clearly shown in the histories Mandari related about the orgins of their present-day clans and lineages." (*ibid.*) Kilda Kuper, faced with the same ethnic complexity among the Swazi, called them a "nation," explaining, "I use the word *nation* for a number of tribes owing allegiance to a central authority." (1947: 11) The difference between Kuper and Buxton apparently is due to the factor of political organization because, whereas the Mandari "never had any form of centralized political organization" (Middleton and Tait 1958: 71), the Swazi not only had a king but had a complex administrative organization within their polity. Similarly, Isaac Schapera found the sociocultural units among the Bantu-speaking populations of South Africa too complex to be referred to as "tribes." He tells us that, "From time to time there have arisen in South Africa large Bantu [*sic*] States, in which many different tribes were amalgamated into a single political unit . . . [and in some areas] the composite 'nations' still flourish." (1937: 174)

Historians, more so than anthropologists, have tended to refer to the very large territorial groupings of people that appeared in many areas of Africa as "empires." Thus, J. D. Fage states:

The history of the West African Sudan north of the forest between the fourth and the nineteenth century is largely one of a succession of great territorial empires . . . At their peak these empires were often of considerable extent, but their fall was apt to be as swift as their rise. The conquered peoples each retained their distinctive customs and language; they had little in common with each other except the fact of their subjection to the same conquering people. None of the great empires succeeded in constituting such diverse elements into a united nation, and their political relations with the subject peoples were for the most part determined by the maintenance of military rule and the levying of tribute. (1955: 16-17)

The apparent reason for this was, according to Fage, difficulty in administration:

Moreover, it presented the rulers with a dilemma which they could not easily resolve. By modern standards, communications were slow and defective. An able and active ruler might keep the reins of government in his own hands, and, by continually moving about his empire with his army, he might keep it intact and in good order. But if his successor were not as able and active, disorder and disintegration were likely to result. (*ibid.*)

Fage's comment on the inability of the African empires to create nations is a bit confusing if only because so few "empires" did or do. In time, they all retreat leaving chaos in their wake.

This brief survey of sociocultural units in precolonial Africa shows that they ranged all the way from "bands" to "empires." What needs to be examined now are the processes by which these units maintained their internal cohesion, interacted with other units, and incorporated them, thereby developing larger entities. Starting with the simpler sociocultural units found in Africa, the "bands," we find that no !Kung Bushman band lived in isolation. On the contrary, they were constantly interacting with other bands. Thomas states that fully one-third of the relatives of the kinsmen of band members lived in other bands, thus bands were tied together by means of cognatic, agnatic, and affinal links. In addition, all persons in !Kung bands having the same name (of which there was a limited number in Bushman society) were considered to be related. (1960: 24, 34, 86, 139) The Bushmen had no chiefs or strong political leaders, probably because of their limited resources and simple technology, but their *kinship* and *name* ties permitted them to adjust their social units to their ecology, expanding and contracting ties as conditions dictated. Bushmen traded with and were absorbed by their more highly organized Bantu-speaking neighbors. (Schapera 1937: 19 ff) The Bushmen even had myths linking them to non-Bushmen. "In the earliest days," one old man told Thomas, "the Bushmen and the non-Bushmen were all one nation . . . " (1960: 34)

The Pygmies, who, like the Bushmen, had "bands" were seldom isolated in small family groups. They lived in symbiotic or serf-like relations with their more powerful Negro neighbors, being tied to them by bonds of loyalty, fealty, kinship, marriage, and mutual convenience. These relationships permitted the Pygmies to take greater advantage of the resources of their environment. (Turnbull 1960)

The lineages and clans which formed the basic social units of more complex societies were linked to other units by numerous ties. In the so-called "stateless"[1] societies of Africa where these units formed the basis of corporate existence, we find them linked to each other throughout the society by a welter of crosscutting agnatic, cognatic, and uterine ties. In addition, in many of these societies, both lineages and clans were spread throughout their length and breadth, making for wider networks of relationships. Thus, Evans-Pritchard reported that among the Nuer, "In all these tribes and tribal sections there is much admixture of lineages in communities." (1940a: 209) Similarly, Ottenberg found that, in contrast to patrilineages, the "matriclans" among the Ibo by "spreading members through the different villages . . . serve as an important unifying factor among the Afikpo." (in Gibbs, 1965: 13) Of course, in the absence of overall political control, both Ibo and Nuer were unable to prevent fights and feuds within these societies, but it was true, at least for the Nuer, that the existence of lineages and clans permitted people to "marry and, to a small extent, trade across tribal boundaries, and pay visits to kinsmen living outside their own tribe." (Evans-Pritchard 1940b: 279) And Evans-Pritchard found that, "if there has been much intermarriage between two groups a feud is unlikely to develop" among them. (1940a: 146)

"Age" organizations were important integrating institutions crossing social units in the "stateless" African societies, as Tiv, Turkana, Masai, Kikuyu, and Dinka, and in some instances, across the larger societal boundaries. Evans-Pritchard reports that:

> Nuer age-sets are a tribal institution in the sense that, in the larger tribes at any rate, all the sections of a tribe have the same open and closed periods and call the sets by the same names. They are also the most characteristic of all Nuer national institutions . . . [A] djacent tribes co-ordinate their sets in periods and nomenclature, so that the Western Nuer, the Eastern Nuer, and the Central Nuer tend to fall into three divisons in this respect. But even when a man travels from one end of Nuerland to the other, he can always, and easily perceive the set which is equivalent to his own in each area. (1940b: 289)

Both Huntingford (1953: 1-2) and Peristiany (1939: 1,2,17,163,235) have shown how age-group organizations cut across the Nandi and Kipsigis permitting these two groups to intermarry and intermigrate. LeVine and Sangree have shown the same phenomena for the Tiriki and Terik of East Africa, adding, "The Tiriki-Terik alliance is a case of a bi-cultural society where both groups have, over a considerable period of time, continued to interact and view each other on a basis of social equality." (1962: 105).

A number of other nonpolitical institutions facilitated the creation of bonds within and between the several smaller and even larger units in Africa. For example, Bohannan reported that among the Tiv, "Age-sets, inter-locking market cycles, and peace ties . . . correlated with the higher degree of cohesion attained by relatively large populations in southern Tivland." (1958: 35) David Tait states that, "No market could exist solely for the use of members of a single group the size of Konkomba clans. Markets are therefore part of inter-clan, inter-tribal and inter-national relations . . . " (1958: 183) The markets and trade network controlled by the Aro traders are well known as integrating mechanisms for the precolonial Ibo. However, an important adjunct to these integrative economic institutions were the Aro Chucku oracles which were resorted to for judicial redress by people from many different Ibo groups. (Dike 1956: 37-41; Ottenberg 1958: 295-307)

The role of shrines as integrating and incorporating institutions in traditional African societies is of course well known. Middleton tells us that the elders among the Lugbara were able to prevent fighting among their people because they were all "linked by the tie of their having custodianship of their respective lineage shrines, which emphasizes that their relationship is one of 'brothers,' even if genealogically they are of different generations." (1958: 223) Gulliver states that, "At least twice a year the whole [Jie] tribe assembles at one of these [shrines] for rain-making ceremonies and general supplication to the High God." (1955: 10) And Fortes has reported how the great thanksgiving sacrifices at the shrines of the founding ancestors of Tallensi clans marked "the climax of one phase in the absorption of the accessory lineages by the authentic lineages of Tongo." (1945: 53) Among the Tiriki, "Circumcision rites and the traditional auguries and sacrifices at the sacred groves . . . are organized and conducted both on a multi-clan and on a multi-community sub-tribal" basis, and that they "serve not only to provide the traditional basis for social solidarity which cross-cuts clan loyalties, but also subordinate the community to a larger social collectivity." (LeVine and Sangree 1962: 105)

Similar to the role of shrines in group cohesion and integration in African societies has been the role of religious practitioners. Thus, Dinka prophet "in the past has drawn his followers from widely separated areas of Dinkaland, from hostile tribes and foreign groups. It is said of the greatest of these prophets, Arianhdit, who died some years ago, that he was great enough to influence members of hostile tribes to compose their differences." (Middleton and Tait 1958: 131) Among the northern Lugbara, "Rainmakers of different tribes are 'like brothers' and have important ritual and rudimentary political powers. The rainmaker calls people together after a lull in the fighting, wearing a cattle-skin, and forbids further strife." (1958: 224) The role of the Nuer leopard-skin chief in resolving disputes among Nuer communities is well known (Evans-Pritchard 1940a: 174ff), but there were also prophets in the country who "had a reputation among a number of neighboring tribes which united for raids at the direction of their spirits. They were not a mechanism of tribal structure like the leopard-skin chiefs, but were pivots of federation between adjacent tribes and personified the structural principle of opposition in its widest expression, the unity and homogeneity of Nuer against foreigners." (1940a: 189)

While in traditional African societies there existed a number of "nonpolitical" institutions and processes which made integration within groups and incorporation between neighboring groups possible, force and power were often used for incorporating small and distinct groups into larger entities. This use of force by one African group to incorporate foreign elements into larger entities was practiced by some weakly organized African societies. The stateless Nuer "broke from their homeland to the west of the Nile on to the Dinka lands to the east of that river and . . . they conquered and absorbed the inhabitants of what is now eastern Nuerland." (Evans-Pritchard 1940b: 280) The "Dinka who have been absorbed into Nuer society have been for the most part incorporated into their kinship system by adoption and marriage, and conquest has not led to the development of classes or cases." (1940b: 287) The Mandari, who had a little more highly developed political organization than the Nuer, have traditions recounting how their "dominant lines . . . founded or took over territories attracted and absorbed a non-related population of clients and settlers." (Middleton and Tait 1958: 72)

The use of force as an incorporating mechanism was more common in those societies which have been called "states" by Fortes and Evans-Pritchard.[2] Nevertheless, force was never the only mechanism used for the purpose of incorporation. Thus, Southall asserts that the "process of Alur domination consisted in the spread of the Alur concept of chiefship, by means of the natural increase and spatial dispersion of the persons through whom it could be expressed." (n.d.: 181) He tells us further that "Constantly recurring themes in the history of the absorption of non-Alur elements are: the kidnapping of chiefs' sons by clans of inferior status; the escape or banishment of chiefs' sons after committing offences or being worsted in feuds; the transference of allegiance by individuals and groups from chief to chief; and the rise and fall in the efficacy of chiefly power." (n.d.: 182-183) Apparently, the imperialist device by which people are incorporated because they asked to be is of long standing. However, among the Alur, as among other people who have used it, there was an ideological factor involved. "Chieflets all made rain, directly or indirectly," (n.d.: 196), thus bringing happiness to the conquered.

A widespread variant of this incorporating device occurred when the conquered population asked that they be given a ruler, but they received instead a son born of a member of the ruling group and a local woman. For example, there is the tradition that the people of Benin banished their ruler, and failing to make a nonmonarchical form of government work, sent a message to Oduduwa of the Yoruba at Ife, asking him

to give them one of his sons as their ruler. Although Oduduwa was not able to meet this request in his lifetime, his son and successor, Obalufon, sent his brother Oranmiyan to Benin. After living for some years at Usama, on the outskirts of present-day Benin City, Oranmiyan grew tired of the opposition he constantly met from the chiefs of Benin and decided to return to Ife, leaving in his place as Oba or king the son born to him by the daughter of a Benin chief. In his later years Oranmiyan founded the dynasty of Oyo and finally returned to Ife where he reigned as Oni. (Ryder 1965: 25)

Traditions of how larger sociopolitical groupings came about by means of outright conquest are common in Africa. They are especially numerous among the interlacustrine Bantu-speaking groups. Audrey Richards refused to become involved in the "pros and cons" of the "Hamitic" conquest theory of state-formation in this area, but believes that the "historical traditions [in this region] are important in so far as they account for the existence of a series of political structures formed by the conquest of indigenous inhabitants of the lake basin by a succession of ruling dynasties. . . . " (1960: 33) She feels that the "Hamitic invaders, together with other intruders who were Nilotic and probably Lwoo-speaking, such as the Bito, seem to have come in small bands without large armies or efficient administrative machinery and to have usurped 'thrones' rather than defeated whole peoples. The pattern of conquest evidently varied." (*ibid.*) However, a recurring theme among these societies was that after the initial conquest, the rulers sent their sons to govern conquered provinces and these sons often rebelled, forming new states in the process. (1960: 34, 132)

South African warrior groups who conquered local populations incorporated them by placing relatives of chiefs over them, but they also used many nonmilitary devices to incorporate the defeated peoples. Early Swazi kings, such as Sobhuza I, placed kinsmen as rulers over districts, but "he incorporated his subjects into the army to support him against attacks from rival relatives as well as from outside enemies." (Kuper 1947: 14) Later Swazi kings attempted to integrate the lower levels of their nation by "organizing all subjects into age groups that cut across local boundaries and kinship loyalties." (1947: 15) In this way, armies, which had been organized on a local basis with "each chief having authority to call up the men in his district," (*ibid.*) were reorganized on a national basis.

The Swazi rulers also used marriage to achieve national integration. When one especially prominent king, Mswati, came to power, "Diplomatic marriages continued to be made for national purposes. Wives were selected for Mswati from many subject groups, and marriage ties were created, not only with powerful chiefs, but with insignificant commoners." (1947: 17) This use of marriage for national integration carried down to lower levels. "Members of different stocks also intermarried, since the laws of exogamy forced them to seek wives outside the clan. Between conquered and conquerors, and between the conquered themselves, there was established a complex network of economic and social obligations, gifts and services in 'in-law' relationship." (*ibid*.) Kuper states that the result of this contact between the "diverse elements enriched the nation with new ideas, words, rituals and tools." (*ibid*.)

The Swazi rulers, like many others not only in South Africa but also in other parts of the continent, often found it necessary to institute a form of "indirect rule" over populations being incorporated because they had neither the resources nor the strength to govern them directly. Many groups conquered by the Swazi were permitted, "as long as they remained loyal, to retain their hereditary chiefs." (1947: 13) Schapera reports that Zulu, Ndebele, Sotho, and Ngwato rulers permitted conquered groups "a large measure of autonomy under their own hereditary leaders but often appointing subChiefs to watch over them." (1937: 174) Schapera, apparently fascinated by the implications of such organization, remarks that many of "these large States" which had this type of organization "have since broken up, mainly as a result of wars with the Europeans, and have reverted to the original system of small tribes. But in Basutoland, Swaziland, and Northern Bechuanaland (Ngwato) the composite 'nations' still flourish." (*ibid*.)

Similar types of political incorporation have been reported for the large kingdoms in the Congo region, but one of the most succinct reports of the incorporating mechanisms used by an African state is that of Evans-Pritchard on the Azande.

The Azande state resembled the classic conquest-state reported for other parts of Africa. According to Evans-Pritchard, at about the middle of the eighteenth century a considerable body of the Ambomu (sing. Mbomu) people under the leadership of their royal house, the Vongara, migrated from what is now the Central African Republic into the southern Sudan, conquering vast territories, driving before them or bringing under subjugation a number of foreign peoples. The descendants of these people were in varying degrees assimilated by their Ambomu conquerors, with the resultant amalgam forming the Zande people as they are known today. (1963: 136) Evans-Pritchard listed over "twenty foreign peoples" and many individuals representing yet other foreign stocks as having contributed to the Zande amalgam. These foreign elements were found "at all stages ranging from political absorption but cultural autonomy to total assimilation, both political and cultural," (*ibid.*) Evans-Pritchard declares that as the Azande went about incorporating foreign groups, there occurred "the growth of a colonial policy." (*ibid.*) Initially, the ruling house of the Azande remained aloof from the conquered people and permitted them to remain in their own territories and retain their own chiefs. The rulers only demanded of the local people that they acknowledge Azande paramountcy and provide tribute in labor and produce. Next, prominent Azande commoners or assimilated peoples were encouraged to settle in the conquered territory. "These colonists with their kinsmen . . . formed a nucleus from which disseminated their speech, manners and customs, and political institutions till in course of time, except where they formed large and in one way or another geographically isolated communities, the foreigners became indistinguishable from the Ambomu [Azande commoners] themselves and thought of themselves together with the Ambomu as Azande." (*ibid.*) It was only after this process was successful that "a scion of the royal house would set up his court in their midst." (*ibid.*) This made it possible for the local people to participate in Azande political affairs, and accelerated the process of assimilation. We are told that since the standards of living of the conquerors and the conquered were not too different, the lot of the common people "was by no means harsh." On their part, there were no attempts at rebellion and they finally ended up by taking part in the new conquests of the Azande armies. What class differences existed between the nobles and commoners of Azande origin and the population being assimilated manifested themselves in values, habits, speech, and more frequent visits to the court. However, we are told by Evans-Pritchard, that "there was so much movement from place to place, so much social mobility, and so much intermarriage that the class differentiation became less marked with each generation." (1963: 137) It is the opinion of Evans-Pritchard that, "Had it not been for the barriers presented by the Arabs and then the Europeans the processes of conquest, colonization, and absorption might have continued till ecological zones were reached which would have compelled the Azande to abandon their traditional way of life, for they had a political organization superior to that of most of their neighbors." (*ibid.*)

This is certainly not the place to describe in detail the organization of the several Zande kingdoms. Suffice it to say that they, like the others already encountered in East and South Africa, had commoner as well as noble governors over districts and provinces, administrative systems, armies, judicial machinery, the use of oracles, tax and tribute systems, diplomatic marriages, and dynastic rivalries.

THE CASE OF THE MOSSI

The political pattern of Mossi society, and the processes by which their distinct sociocultural entities were fused into one people are remarkably similar to those of the classic conquest-states in sub-Saharan Africa. Actually, Mossi society developed within the northwestern quadrant of what has been called the "Voltaic culture area," a region extending northward from Salaga in contemporary Ghana to Ouahigouya, and inhabited by people speaking Gur or Moshi-Grunshi languages. These people were and are primarily cereal cultivators growing several varieties of millet and sorghum. They also grow cotton, and herd horses, sheep, cattle, and goats. Most of the peoples in this area are patrilineal and consider the lineage, both in its segmental forms and as parts of clans, to be their basic social unit. Ancestor veneration lies at the core of the religious beliefs of the Mossi and most of the other Voltaic groups, but the existence of an otiose high god is also recognized, as are tutelary spirits, chief among whom is the earth deity, *Tenga* (also called *Teng, Tena,* and *Ten*). The *Tengsobadamba*, who are priests or custodians of the earth shrines, are found among all the Voltaic groups, and they often share leadership with more secular chiefs called *Naba, Na,* or *Nab*. Most of the ruling groups in the Voltaic area claim common ancestry and acknowledge the same totem.

The only glaring dissimilarity among the other Voltaic peoples and the ones with which this paper is primarily concerned lies in the realm of political organization and the incorporation of disparate smaller groups into larger ones. There were a number of large kingdoms in this area, surrounded by stateless groups. Delafosse makes the following generalization about the smaller groups:

It may be said of these people that, as a whole, they have remained quite primitive. With a few exceptions, they have not reached any significant level of political development; as a rule, they have not progressed beyond family unity. Although they neighbor on well-organized and powerful states such as the Mossi empires and the kingdoms of the Gourma and Bergo, which are inhabited by populations of the same ethnic group, they have derived little benefit from this proximity; some of them have been absorbed as subjects or vassals by these states, while others have remained on the outside, and seem to have but one purpose, the forceful preservation of their fierce but sterile independence . . . Attachment to the land seems to be the only solid and fecund institution in their chaotic society. (1931: 101)

Captain Rattray, who studied some of the societies in this region, believes that the development of such highly organized political systems as those of the Mossi, Dagomba, and Mamprusi may be traced to "small bands of strangers." He thinks that the outsiders were better armed, better clothed, and familiar with the rudiments of Islam, and that since they knew about the institution of kingship, they were able to "superimpose upon the primitive tribes among whom they settled a new and unheard-of political conception, namely the idea of territorial and secular leadership in place of the immemorial institution of a ruler who was the high priest of a totemic clan and dealt only in spiritual sanctions." Nevertheless, Rattray is not certain that the Voltaic groups would not have evolved complex political systems if they had been left to themselves. He makes the significant statement that if the subjugation by the bands of strangers had not taken place, the local earth-priest or priest-king "undoubtedly would have evolved into the type of native ruler . . . who was not only high priest and custodian of the land of his tribe and of the ancestral spirits but one who was a chief or king on a territorial basis, whose sanctions were secular and physical rather than spiritual; in other words, what the average European implies when he uses the word 'king' or 'chief.' " (I, xxii, xi; Skinner, 1964a: 5-6)

Rattray's supposition that small bands of conquering strangers might have been responsible for creating larger entities in the Voltaic area resembled other traditions in Africa, but is here supported by identical myths among the Mossi and neighboring Dagomba and Mamprusi peoples. According to this myth, some forty generations ago,[3] a king known as Naba Nedega, who ruled over the Dagomba, Mamprusi, and smaller groups, refused to permit his warrior daughter to marry. This young woman, Nyennega, fled north on horseback where she encountered and married a man named Riallé. According to some traditions, Riallé was a Busansi hunter and, according to others, a prince of the royal house of Mali. The couple subsequently had a son whom they named Ouedraogo in honor of the stallion which had taken Nyennega to freedom. They sent the boy back to live with his grandfather at Dagomba. When Ouedraogo grew up, he obtained permission from his grandfather to go north. Taking forty horsemen with him, he conquered the area from which his father had come. This region, Tengkodogo, became Ouedraogo's capital and from here he and his descendants completed the conquest of the country.

The myth that Ouedraogo was the son of a Dagomba woman and a local man became a theme in the mythical charter supporting the Mossi's incorporation of local groups. In fact, the Mossi themselves are considered to have been the descendants of Ouedraogo and his Dagomba warriors and their local wives. It was allegedly on the strength of this charter that Ouedraogo sent his, now Mossi, sons to rule in the region of Fada N'Gourma and in the region of Zondema inhabited by such stateless groups as: Busansi, Foulsé, Gurunsi, Kibissi, and Ninisi. This theme appears well developed in the charter for the Mossi's conquest of the Ouagadougou area. According to one tradition, a Ninisi earth priest in the Ouagadougou region sought to establish an alliance with Ouedraogo by giving him a daughter as wife. The king gave this woman to his son, Zoungrana. When, after several years, the Ninisi chiefs asked Ouedraogo's heir, this same Zoungrana, to restore law and order among warring factions in Ouagadougou, the king refused. However, he could not refuse to send his son, Oubri, to help the Ninisi, as it was the duty of a man to help his mother's relatives. Of course, Oubri went to Ouagadougou, conquered the region, and established the Ouagadougou Mossi kingdom linked to Tengkodogo but later to become independent of it.

A third theme used by the Mossi in their charter of political incorporation was in capturing the local *Tengsoba* or earth priest (who was often the only leader in the Voltaic area), settling him near the home of the warrior chief, and forcing him to make sacrifices to the earth shrines in the name of the conquerors. For example, in one district with which the writer is personally familiar, there is the tradition that the first district chief was a man called Biligo. Although an heir of Oubri, he did not wish to rule the kingdom of Ouagadougou. Biligo went hunting in the region and decided to remain in the sparsely settled Ninisi village of Nobere. The Ninisi ran away when they saw Biligo coming, but he persuaded them to return and live in peace under his command. The *Tengsoba* of the area refused to return. Biligo went into the bush and captured him so that he could continue to make sacrifices to the earth shrines, even though the district now had a secular sovereign. Biligo married a local woman and when she bore him sons, he sent these sons to rule over areas inhabited, not by the earth priest and his family, but by ordinary Ninisi. These sons and their families formed the noble classes in the district.

The consolidation of Mossi rule and conquest was made difficult because of lack of unity among the different rulers descended from Ouedraogo. Naba Oubri of Ouagadougou emerged as a rather strong ruler, but he was unable to completely conquer and pacify the country. Subsequent Ougadougou rulers spent most of their lives subjugating the rest of the country and the sites of their graves are markers along the road of Mossi conquests. It was only after the reign of Naba Niandfo (c. 1441-1511) that the rulers of Ouagadougou were able to confine their activities to the capital at Ouagadougou, and the elaboration of the administration of the kingdom did not take place until the time of Naba Warga (c. 1666-1681). However, by the time this occurred, the Mossi polity had divided into several kingdoms and principalities.

During the reign of Koumdimie, reputed to have been the fifth ruler after Oubri, several members of the royal house broke away from Ouagadougou's control. These men claimed that, as sons of Ouedraogo and Oubri, they shared in the power of the *nam*. (According to the Mossi, the *nam* was that "force of God which permitted one man to rule another"). Many of them took the title, *Dim* and vowed that they would "submit to God only." The Ouagadougou ruler was forced to recognize the independence of the kingdom of Yatenga, and the autonomy of such principalities as Mane, Tema, and Boussouma. The Ouagadougou rulers did not hesitate to interfere in the internal affairs of the principalities, but they tended to leave Yatenga alone. The kingdom of Tengkodogo, founded by Ouedraogo, was still considered senior to all, but as Ouagadougou became stronger, Tengkodogo fell within its orbit. More distant Fada N'Gourma was so far removed from the politics of the other three kingdoms that, except for the myth of the common origin of its royal house, the Gourmantches became separate from the Mossi.

The factors which have given the Mossi coherence as a people are not only the common myths of origin, common facial marks, common languages and customs, but, above all, common political institutions in all of the kingdoms and principalities. Moreover, all Mossi used similar institutions for maintaining internal cohesion and for incorporating foreign peoples within their various political units. Every Mossi ruling house attempted to legitimize its rights to rule by claiming the most direct line of descent from either Ouedraogo or Oubri. Even the ruler of the breakaway kingdom of Yatenga claimed that he, not the people of Ouagadougou, had the amulets of Ouedraogo's father, and thus, the ultimate symbol of authority. Again, the overall structures of all the Mossi kingdoms were quite similar. At the center was the *Mogho Naba* (literally, king of the world) in his capital, surrounded by medieval-like courtiers and retainers. Also at the capital, or in its vicinity, were provincial ministers of commoner status, responsible for governing the provinces into which the kingdom or principality was divided.

Scattered throughout the Mossi kingdom and principalities were members of the royal houses who were hereditary rulers of districts and who had been invested by their superiors. These district chiefs, known as *Kombemba*, had their capitals and miniature courts patterned on those of their superiors. And they, too, were surrounded by district ministers. These ministers were similarly not of noble status and were often related to the provincial ministers at the higher level. Below the district chiefs in the ruling hierarchy were village chiefs, the *Tense Nanamsé*, who were often, but not always, members of the royal house, and who were invested with the power to rule by the district chiefs. The *Tense Nanamsé* seldom could aspire to sumptuous living and had no ministers to help them administer the affairs of their villages. However, they were always surrounded by cronies and village elders who, having certain administrative skills and inclinations, took on the functions which, on the higher level, were performed by specific administrators or courtiers.

The Mossi always made a clear distinction between ruling houses and administrative houses, and interspersed the two for efficiency and stability. Thus, the *Mogho Nanmsé* ruled the district chiefs through the agency of provincial administrators; and the district chiefs ruled their villages through their own administrators. Only the village chiefs did not have administrators through which to rule but used pseudo administrators to the same effect. On the other hand, no subordinate ruler could approach his superior except through the responsible administrator. The hierarchy was always respected. Taxes, tribute, and presents for the rulers flowed up the hierarchy, and all orders came down the hierarchy. Similarly, the judicial machinery operated at each level of the hierarchy with cases moving up on appeal.

The Mossi had a number of institutions which made for national cohesion. One was the "Basgha," a New Year's festival of thanksgiving for new crops, as well as the annual Feast of the Dead. The *Mogho Nanamsé* and the *Dimdamba* (pl. of *Dim*) initiated the ceremony at their own court; later the district chiefs and their subordinates followed suit. Another national festival was the *Tense*, sometimes called *Naba Oubri ma koure* (the anniversary of the funeral of Mogho Naba Oubri's mother), celebrated all over the country on the same day. Curiously enough, Oubri's mother was not a central figure in the *Tense* celebration which laid great stress upon the fructifying powers of the earth and on the importance of the royal ancestors in Mossi life. There is indirect evidence, however, that the Mossi took over a fertility festival of the autochthonous Ninisi people and converted it into a memorial festival, "thus symbolically uniting the conquerors and the conquered." (Skinner 1964a: 130) Periodically, especially during times of drought or other national disasters, the *Mogho Nanamsé* authorized national prayers and sacrifices to local earth shrines for the health of the entire nation.

The Mossi placed such an emphasis on their political organization that almost all the other institutions they used for internal cohesion or to incorporate different sociocultural groups were consciously subordinate to it. This appears to be true of the capitals as well as the districts and villages in the provinces. The incorporating processes of the Mossi political organization are best observed at the borders of Mossi country. For example, the expansion of the Mossi people southward among the Busansi and so-called Gurunsi populations of the region now on the Upper Volta-Ghana border has still not stopped, and the Mossi generally consider all people south of them as "Gurunsi." Once, when the author took the chief of Nobéré district to visit a chief in the more northerly district of Béré, the Béré Naba jokingly saluted the Nobéré Naba with the words, "The Gurunsi chief has arrived." The Béré chief was not referring to the fact that the mother of the Nobéré chief was indeed a Gurunsi woman, but that he considered the Nobéré Naba to be "Chief of Gurunsi." As a matter of fact, in 1956 the *kourita* (the Mossi have the tradition of the "undying" ruler, and when a ruler dies his last son is nominated as *kourita*, the earthly representative of his father, and banished) of the last ruler of Nobéré was still living in Gurunsi country on the other side of the Red Volta River. Of course, the presence of the French prevented him from exercising authority over the Gurunsi. However, the presence of this man there confirms the tradition that the *kourit'damba* played an important role in Mossi expansion. (Skinner 1964a: 14)

More typical of the processes by which Mossi incorporated foreign people they had conquered were those by which the local Ninisi of Nobéré were absorbed. One was by the appointment of members of the royal houses to rule villages in which the Ninisi lived. This act did not result in any profound cultural change among the Ninisi, such as Evans-Pritchard reported for Azande, because both Mossi and Ninisi spoke the same language and shared most of the same customs. The primary change was the the Ninisi people were given a superior authority who had the right to judge certain cases among them as well as litigation between themselves and others.

Once the Ninisi had Mossi living among them in their villages, they were readily absorbed by intermarriage. Both Mossi and Ninisi are exogamous, but whereas the Ninisi could marry neighboring Ninisi whose relationship to them had been forgotten, the Mossi, because their political organizations encouraged the keeping of better genealogies and because they were newcomers and thus had fewer persons to marry, were forced to marry the Ninisi. The only problem was that since Ninisi were obliged to give their Mossi rulers more wives than they received in exchange, the conquerors expanded at the expense of the conquered. In addition, and often ignored by anthropologists, was the fact that very often the children of Mossi women and Ninisi men took advantage of ritual links with their more powerful mothers' brothers, moved into their compounds, and were frequently absorbed by these relatives. (Skinner 1946b, vol. 4: 467ff)

A second process by which the Mossi absorbed not only resident Ninisi in Nobéré district, but also Busansi families which had come seeking asylum in the district, was through politics and marriage. In the case of resident Ninisi who had not been given a Mossi chief, the change came through intermarriage between the Ninisi and the Mossi royal house. Any children of such marriages were known as *yagensé* (a kinship term given both to sister's sons and grand-children) of the Mossi royal house. Incorporation came when people lost track of whether or not the royal *yagensé* were sisters' sons or "grandchildren," when one of the *yagensé* was invested with the *nam*. The same process occurred when foreign groups such as the Busansi entered Mossi country. In many cases, the Mossi district chiefs gave the strangers land upon which to live, cautioned them not to "spoil the land" by repeating the behavior which was the cause of their expulsion from their homeland, and received the customary homage and tribute from them. Here, however, acculturation as well as intermarriage took place and in time the foreigners became the *yagensé* of the Mossi. Political incorporation was, however, much easier since few people realized when chiefs being invested with the *nam* ceased being the heirs of the immigrant Busansi chief and became another one of the *yagensé* of the Nobéré royal house.

The Mossi chiefs in the districts and villages also used an institution known as the *pughsiuré* (from *pugho*, the diminutive of *pagha* "woman" and *sioubo*, "to give with the hope of profitable return") to incorporate both Mossi refugees from other districts and foreigners. When outsiders visited Mossi districts they were taken to the chiefs who, if he allowed them to remain in the district, often gave them wives called *pughsiudsé*. In return for these wives, the men owed the chief both homage and tribute, and, in addition, their first daughters to serve as future *pughsiudsé* for the chiefs. That this was a purely political device is seen by the fact that the chief never regarded the *pughsiudsé* as being his own daughters. The man who received a *pughsiudga* from a chief had to establish his own affinal relationship with the woman's relatives.

The Mossi apparently deliberately refrained from absorbing a number of groups whose specialized functions were of importance in Mossi communities. Not absorbed, for example, were the Fulani herdsmen (known as Silimisé by the Mossi) who traveled in transhumance cycles throughout Mossi country, traded with the Mossi villagers in the markets, and often cared for the cattle of Mossi cultivators. They were relatively free to come and go as they pleased, provided their headmen paid tribute to the chiefs in whose districts they were traveling. However, throughout Mossi country there are groups of people said to be descended from Fulani who, either through misfortune or volition, chose to become sedentary. They were given Mossi wives to cultivate for them—since it is universally believed that Fulani women cannot cultivate—and, in time, their descendants became indistinguishable from the Mossi. Interestingly enough, these mixed cultivators and herders are called *Silimi-Mossi* because of their mixed origin.

The requirements of the more complex political and administrative systems at the Mossi capitals influenced the way in which the conquered population and foreign groups there were treated by the Mossi. Of course, the Mossi in the capitals assimilated most of the local Ninisi people and many foreigners through such institutions as marriage and the *pughsiuré*. However, the fact that there was a greater need for specialized groups to perform particular activities for the ruler and his administration resulted in what gives the appearance of being greater ethnic complexity in the capital than elsewhere in Mossi society. The fact is, however, that this made for greater national integration since it supported the Mossi political, administrative, and economic systems. For example, all the chiefs and administrators in the capital and in the district had families of retainers known severally as *Daporé (Dapobi)*, who performed all sorts of chores for their masters, and *Baglré (Bangaré)*, retainers who herded their masters' cattle. The origins of both groups are obscure. Dim Delobson maintains that the Dapobi "are wrongly considered (even by themselves) to be captives." (1933: 89) He believes that they were of Kibissi origin and came to Ouagadougou "of their own volition." (*ibid.*) Baglré, on the other hand, are said to have been "Peulh [Fulani] captives who have gradually cast off the authority of their masters and who have submitted voluntarily to the authority of the Mogho Naba." (Dim Delobson 1933: 90) Dim Delobson adds, however, that not all the Baglré are "former Peulh slaves since a free individual who has committed a serious crime in his native village and fears reprisal comes to join the 'herd.' " (*ibid.*)

The problem of both the Dapobi and Bangaré is not their origin, since "true" Mossi were permitted to join them, but that in them the rulers and administrators of Mossi country had a necessary class of retainers. Dim Delobson believes that ordinary Mossi did not give their daughters to these retainers, but, given the small size of these groups, nonintermarriage would have made them all related; thus, they would have had to intermarry or commit incest. There is no doubt that the Mossi chiefs took the daughters of these retainers as wives. These acts tied the retainers to the Mossi chiefs by kinship but, in contrast to other groups so linked, the Dapobi and Bangaré were not absorbed, remaining apart as necessary serfs. The same was apparently true of another group of retainers in the capital, the *Kamboinsé*, who were the gunners of the Mogho Naba. These people are believed to have originally come from Ashanti, but, according to Dim Delobson, "While the first-mentioned Kamboinsé are voluntary slaves, the others are true slaves captured in war or bought by the emperor." (1933: 91) However, like the Dapobi and Bangaré, the Kamboinsé were not absorbed as was customary with other slaves captured by the Mossi. They remained sociologically apart but became indistinguishable from the Mossi in race and language, as well as culture.

The Yarsé (Dioula) and Hausa (Zanguete) traders who lived in special wards in the Mossi capitals for several centuries were likewise incorporated by the Mossi but not absorbed by them. These two groups had their own chiefs and headmen and paid homage to the Mogho Naba as part of the cortege of the Baloum Naba, the Chief Steward of the Palace and "Mayor" of Ouagadougou. They are distinguished from the local Mossi population partly by language (all are polyglot) and religion (Islam), but especially by occupation since they remained traders. However, as one examines the genealogies of these Hausa and Yarsé, it quickly becomes evident that they are part Mossi. A very large percentage of them had Mossi mothers, including daughters and sisters of former Mogho Nanamsé, and, of course, their sisters and daughters married Mossi men including the Mogho Nanamsé. For example, Mogho Naba Zombre (1681-1744) reportedly married a Yarsé woman named Habo whose son became Mogho Nabe Kom I (1744-1762). Thus, both the Hausa and the Yarsé, like the retainers already discussed, were in fact the *yagensé* not only of ordinary Mossi, but of the Mossi royal house. They were not absorbed because they had the important role of conducting the trade with people of their original homelands who visited Ouagadougou. The visiting traders lived with their fellows in Ouagadougou and were represented by them at court if and when there were problems to be resolved. It was, therefore, in the interest of both the Mossi political hierarchy and the resident trader populations that the linguistic and other skills necessary for dealing with foreign traders were retained. As a matter of fact, contemporary Yarsé and Hausa in Ouagadougou still maintain that their retention of the languages of their ancestors is important for trade. However, they admit that in almost every other aspect of their social life and culture they have become Mossi.

The Mossi faced a number of other problems of incorporation when dealing with the Hausa and, especially, the Yarsé. These traders were Moslems and the Mossi had had reason to fear the influx of Moslems into their country. The Mossi fought the Moslems of Mali in 1328 A.D. (1333 A.D., according to the Mossi) and had resisted three attempts of the Songhay to convert them to Islam by means of the *jihad*. Thus, when during the seventeenth century Yarsé traders and emigrants from such Mandingo cities as Timbuctu and Djenne began to enter Mossi country in large numbers, Islam became a potential threat to the local population. It is not known how the Mossi rulers viewed Islam in the eighteenth century, but apparently they welcomed the traders and had few qualms about permitting them to establish communities.

About 1780, Mogho Naba Kom I gave his mother's Yarsé countrymen permission to establish communities in such important trading areas as Dakay (Sagabtenga) near what is now the Ghanaian border, and during the subsequent reigns of Sagha I and Doulougou, the Yarsé traded and built mosques in Ouagadougou and the outlying districts. Naba Doulougou, "imitating his kingly relative, the Gambaga Naba, ruler of the Dagomba" finally appointed the first Muslim Imam at court. (Dim Delobson 1933: 205)

On the other hand, in Islam, Doulougou apparently saw a threat to the religious support of the Mossi kingdom and expressly forbade his eldest son and heir, Sawadogo (1802-1834) to become a Moslem. Still, the young man persisted in his adopted religion even though he ruled as Mogho Naba. However, subsequent Mogho Nanamsé abandoned Islam until the time of Koutou (1850-1871) who, in the words of Dim Delobson, "was a truly a Muslim." (1933: 210) Nevertheless, even Koutou tried to avoid placing the traditional religious support of the Mossi kingdom in too great jeopardy. "All [his children] except his eldest son, who succeeded him as Naba Sanum, were sent to Koranic schools, although none did any serious work there since they were more interested in becoming *naba*." (*ibid.*) And, of course, being a Moslem was believed to jeopardize a Mossi ruler's relationship with his royal ancestors.

After Naba Koutou, Islam declined among members of the royal house, but Mossi rulers continued to maintain mosques at their courts for the use of visiting Muslims and were in regular attendance at Muslim celebrations within their commands. Captain Binger, who had the good fortune to be at Sagabatenga (Dakay at the end of Ramadan in 1888, reported that "Moslem or not, all the blacks celebrate this feast." (1888: vol. I, 452) What really surprised Binger, however, was that although the chief in that area (the future Mogho Naba) encouraged him to attend the ceremony, he was convinced that the chief was "a Moslem in outward appearance only. When the prayers were about to begin, he [the chief] asked me whether I was going to worship. I told him that this festival was not in accord with those of the Christians. He seemed to be delighted by the idea that the whites are not Moslems." (*ibid.*) Binger did notice that the chief was respectful to the Imams, gave them gifts, and held them in high esteem. He concluded that the Imam and his aides were "old and wise men who cannot but give" the chief "excellent counsel." (*ibid.*)

French conquest weakened the power of the Mossi chief; made possible the introduction of new institutions; exposed the Mossi people to forced and voluntary labor outside of their villages, districts, and kingdom; and drafted many to die in the name of "ancestors with blond hair and blue eyes." The vicissitudes of colonial history and administrative policy resulted in the merging of the Mossi people with non-Mossi populations into a territory known as the Upper Volta. In 1932, when the Upper Volta was suppressed, the Ouagadougou and Tengkodogo kingdoms were incorporated into the Ivory Coast and the kingdom of Yatenga into the French Soudan. Nevertheless, the Mossi still felt their national unity and made several appeals to the French to be placed in the same administrative unit. In order to sit around a conference table and deliver a joint appeal to the French, the Mogho Nanamsé of Tengkodogo, Ouagadougou, and Yatenga had to discard the myth that if they ever came face to face they would die. And when, in 1947, the desire to curb the power of Houphouet-Boigny of the Ivory Coast made the French more responsive to the Mossi appeals, the three Mossi kingdoms were again united into a recreated Upper Volta. Later, when faced with political activities in other parts of the Upper Volta as well as other territorial units, the Mossi chiefs and young men formed political parties to defend their interests. But, when it appeared to Mogho Naba Kougri, in 1958, that the parliamentarians from all of the Upper Volta would jeopardize the status of three million Mossi in a territory of only four million people, he summoned his army and tried to take over the Territorial Assembly. The attempt failed, and many young Mossi, whose political orientation was antichief, joined the resurgent allies of Houphouet-Boigny and gained control of the Territorial Assembly. Nevertheless, when the Upper Volta became an independent republic, the man named to be its first president, was Mossi.

CONCLUSION

It should now be quite clear that the peoples of Africa, like the peoples on other continents and at other times, have been continuously bringing "hostile communities" into a "common framework," often "through living together in a superimposed state." The frontiers between the polities that existed in the past were, in fact, "often blurred by the interpenetration of people . . . pushed one way or the other as the fortunes of history dictate." The political patterns which arose in Africa are quite clear and permit scholars working in different parts of the continent to recognize the similarities and, what is more important, to try to account for the differences. There are few known techniques for political and cultural incorporation found anywhere in the world which have not been tried at some time by some African society. Almost all of them were, at one time or another, tried by the more complex ones.

It is quite clear that attempts at political incorporation have appeared historically in Africa as almost anywhere in the world. And while all of these polities have apparently headed toward some form of ecumenical entity, they have always been stopped and reversed—that is, up to now. Citizens or subjects of the great empires in the past (whether these empires, like Rome, lasted a thousand years, or like that of Mali, just three hundred) subsequently found themselves paying allegiance to petty rulers and squabbling among themselves. It often took a red-shirted "patriot" to give some kind of coherence to the politics of peoples whose ancestors had "worldwide" empires.

The people who have been welded into such entities as Mossi, Zulu, Yoruba, and Baganda nations still have primary loyalties to them, and (here I agree completely with Professor Emerson) not yet to such newer entities as Upper Volta, Nigeria, and Uganda. However, in this they are only slightly different from the nations of Switzerland with respect to the Swiss nation-state; the English, Welsh, Irish, and Scots to Great Britain; the Protestants and Catholics to Northern Ireland; the Walloons and the Flemish to Belgium; and the French and English in Canada to that nation-state. And even given the longer history of these nation-states one is left to wonder whether or not they will survive the pull of their respective nationalities or break up.

Africa's contemporary problem is not that its peoples have failed to go through the crucible of "nation-building," but that the sociocultural entities which existed there before the colonial epoch have been pushed together or pulled apart by the colonial powers. The integrative mechanisms which the colonial powers left in these newly created nation-states were, in many cases, "brand-new," having never been tried out, even by the colonizers themselves before departing. Whether it will work or not is another question. Times have changed, and, as Spiro pointed out, the Africans may evolve new patterns of political incorporation specific to their type of nation-state or to newer political entities.

NOTES

---

1. By "stateless" Fortes and Evans-Pritchard mean, "those societies which lack centralized authority, administrative machinery, and constituted judicial institutions—in short which lack government—and in which there are no sharp divisions of rank, status, or wealth." (1940: 5)

2. Fortes and Evans-Pritchard consider "states" to be, "those societies which have centralized authority, administrative machinery, and judicial institutions—in short, a government—and in which cleavages of wealth, privilege, and status correspond to the distribution of power and authority." (1940: 5)

3. The chronology of Mossi is not well worked out at present. The first historical account for this population comes from the *Tarikh es Sudan* with the report that the Mossi attacked Timbuctu during the reign of Mansa Musa sometime between 1328 and 1333 A.D.

REFERENCES

Binger, L. G. 1892. *Du Niger au golfe de Guinée par le pays Kong et le Mossi.* Paris, Librairie Hachette.

Carter, G. M. 1960. *Independence for Africa.* New York, Praeger.

Delafasse, M. 1913. *Haut-Senegal-Niger.* 3 vols. Paris, Larose.

Deutsch, K., and W. J. Foltz (eds.). 1963. *Nation-building.* New York, Atherton Press.

Dike, K. 1956. *Trade and politics in the Niger Delta.* Oxford, Clarendon Press.

Dim Delobson, A. A. 1933. *L'empire du Mogho Naba.* Paris, Loviton.

Evans-Pritchard, E. E. 1940. *The Nuer.* Oxford, Clarendon Press.

——— 1963. "The Zande state." *J.R.A.I.* vol. 93, Part I: 134-154.

Fage, J. D. 1955. *An introduction to the history of West Africa.* Cambridge, Cambridge University Press.

Fortes, M. 1945. *The dynamics of clanship among the Tallensi.* London, Oxford University Press.

———, and E. E. Evans-Pritchard (eds.). 1940. *African political systems.* Oxford University Press.

Gibbs, J. (ed.) 1965. *Peoples of Africa.* New York: Holt, Rinehart and Winston.

Gulliver, P. H. 1955. *The family herds.* London, Routledge and Kegan Paul.

Herskovits, M. J. 1962. *The human factor in changing Africa.* New York, Knopf.

——— 1950. *Man and his works.* New York, Knopf.

Huntingford, G. W. B. 1953. *The Nandi of Kenya*. London, Oxford University Press.

Kuper, H. 1947. *An African aristocracy*. London, Oxford University Press.

Levine, Robert A., and W. H. Sangree. 1962. "The diffusion of age-group organization in East Africa." *Africa* vol. xxxii, no. 2: 97-109.

Middleton, J., and D. Tait. 1958. *Tribes without rulers*. London, Routledge and Kegan Paul.

Ottenberg, S. 1958. "Ibo oracles and inter-group relations." *Southwestern Journal of Anthropology*. vol. 14, no. 3: 295-307.

Peristiany, J. G. 1939. *The social institutions of the Kipsigis*. London: Routledge and Kegan Paul.

Rattray, R. S. 1932. *Tribes of the Ashanti hinterland*. Oxford, Clarendon Press.

Richards, A. I. (ed.). 1960. *East African chiefs*. London, Faber and Faber.

Ryder, A. F. C. 1965. "A reconsideration of the Ife-Benin relationship." *Journal of African History*. vol. vi, no. 1: 25-37.

Schapera, I. 1937. *The Bantu-speaking tribes of South Africa*. London, Routledge and Kegan Paul.

Skinner, E. P. 1964. *The Mossi of the Upper Volta*. Stanford, Stanford University Press.

1964a. *The Mossi of the Upper Volta*. Stanford, Stanford University Press.

1964b. "The effect of co-residence of sisters, sons of African corporate patrilineal descent groups." *Cahiers d'Etudes Africaines*. vol. iv, no. 4: 467-478.

Southall, A. W. 1956. *Alur society*. Cambridge, Heffers & Sons.

Spiro, H. J. 1962. *Politics in Africa*. Englewood Cliffs, Prentice Hall.

Thomas, E. M. 1960. *The harmless people*. London, Readers Union Secker & Warburg.

Turnbull, C. M. 1961. *The forest people*. New York, Doubleday.

9

SOCIETAL AND CULTURAL INCORPORATION IN RWANDA

Jacques Maquet

INTRODUCTION: SOCIETAL CONTINUITY FROM TRADITION TO INDEPENDENCE

In the formation of the Rwanda global society, incorporation processes have been crucial from the sixteenth to the nineteenth century. There has been what we may call a vertical incorporation: some cultural differences between pastoral and agricultural groups (which were at the origin of the hierarchized strata of Rwanda) were replaced by common features, and new institutions were substituted for *some* former pastoral and agricultural organizations. There has been also a horizontal incorporation: when the Rwanda kingdom expanded territorially, formerly independent political units were incorporated into a larger administrative structure. Both types of processes have been active during the four centuries preceding the colonial era (which, for Rwanda, began rather late, in 1899). Of course, they were more intense at certain periods than at other ones.

But the incorporation mechanism played a very small part at a time when it has been most operative almost anywhere in Africa: at the birth of the independent states. The year 1956 marks the beginning of the decolonization period in Africa south of the Sahara; that year Sudan became independent and in the following one, Ghana; the movement culminated in 1960, the year of seventeen independences, and it went on at a slower pace. Rwanda became the Republic of Rwanda on July 1, 1962. At that time, its situation was exceptional.

New African states were indeed the successors of other political entities which were not the traditional global societies, but the colonies. (By that term, we refer to the European dependencies in sub-Saharan Africa, whatever their juridical status: protectorate, colony, crown colony, United Nations trust territory, overseas "province" or "department." As is well known, colonial territories were delimited on application of the Treaty of Berlin (1885) and no attention was paid to the boundaries of the tradtional kingdoms and tribes. It is safe to say that a colony's borders always encompassed several traditional societies and often cut across the territories of a few of them. Thus, during about seventy to eighty years (taking 1885 as the starting point of the colonial period and 1960 as its end) several global societies traditionally alien to each other coexisted and interacted within the framework of a single political unit, the colony. Living together produced only a small measure of incorporation as the colonial situation was a serious setback to the formation of a collective identification. Consequently incorporative processes became important and gathered momentum only at the end of the colonial period when it appeared that the new states about to be born were in search of corresponding nations. (Maquet 1962a: 172-173, 183-186)

Rwanda did not follow that common pattern. When Captain von Bethe, a German officer, obtained from the King of Rwanda, in 1899, acceptance of the Imperial Government's protection, Rwanda was a densely populated centralized state. Bethe estimated the Rwanda population at approximately 2,000,000 and the *mwami* (king) had achieved a large measure of effective sovereignty over his country. (Louis 1963: 114; Maquet 1961a: 13) In 1965 the population was estimated as about 3,000,000. Rwanda entered the German East African empire as a global society. The Germans referred to it as a sultanate and to the king as a sultan. During the Belgian period (1916-1962), Rwanda was included in the Ruanda-Urundi Territory in which it kept its identity. In spite of the fact that the Territory was under the authority of a single colonial officer, the governor, and had a single capital, Usumbura, Rwanda and Burundi remained distinct, each with its own colonial hierarchy, with a resident at the top. At the level of the "native administration" the separation was complete: having adopted a policy of indirect rule, the Belgians had made the Rwanda king and the Burundi king head of the African hierarchy of his own country (with a few tens of chiefs and a few hundreds of subchiefs).

The traditional Rwanda society has thus remained a unit throughout the sixty-three years of colonial regime: its territory has always corresponded to an important colonial subdivision, its African hierarchy was direct heir to the traditional rulers. It was part of a larger unit, the Ruanda-Urundi Territory, yet it was not lost in it as it included about half the population and half the area. The vitality of Rwanda and Burundi were such that when the colonial regime was near its end, both countries refused to remain associated in independence, in spite of the advice of the United Nations General Assembly which recommended the formation of a single independent state. (Nkundapagenzi 1961: 363) Rwanda and Burundi are, to my knowledge, the only traditional global societies of sub-Saharan Africa which became, as such, independent modern states. Consequently they were also the only states in which the incorporation of several traditional units (tribes or kingdoms) into a single new nation was not required. Some problem of vertical incorporation arose, as we shall see later on, but not horizontal ones.

CONSTITUENT SOCIETIES: HERDSMEN AND PEASANTS

At the very beginning of Rwanda, it is certain that there were several societally and culturally different groups and that the kingdom of Rwanda is the result of their incorporation.

The lakes of Central Eastern Africa delimit a privileged region. Its borders are, in the west, Lakes Albert, Edward, Kivu, Tanganyika; in the south, a line running eastwards from Malagarasi River to Mwanza Bay (Lake Victoria); in the east and north, Lakes Victoria and Kyoga. It is a highland area covered with savannah and occasional forest (except in the high altitudes of the Congo-Nile divide where the forest is thick and dense). This environment, neither too humid (because of the elevation which is above 3000 feet), nor too dry (because of the latitude which is between about 3 degrees north and 5 degrees south), is suitable for cattle-rearing as well as for cultivation and its openness permits easy population movement. Attracted by the favorable conditions, many groups migrated into the interlacustrine area during the last two, or perhaps three, millenia. There were Pygmy hunters as in the other forests of the equatorial region, and Ethiopid nomadic pastoralists coming from the north and entering the uplands by crossing the Victoria Nile between Lakes Albert and Kyoga, Bantu-speaking hoe-cultivators emigrating from the Congo basin.

Rwanda is somewhat peripheral in the interlacustrine region. It is situated in the southwestern part, on both sides of the chain of mountains which separate the Congo and Nile drainage basins. It has certainly been reached by agriculturalists who had perhaps assimilated early Ethiopid waves before the thirteenth century. The nomad Hima or Tutsi pastoralists who are of the original Rwanda dynasty (the Nyiginya) belong certainly to late Ethiopid waves which entered the Rwanda Plateau from the thirteenth up to the fifteenth century. The Nilotic Lwoo invaders who destroyed the Kitara empire of Chwezi and established the Nyoro kingdom, in the northern part of the interlacustrine region, did not reach Rwanda. (Fage 1958: 21-22; Oliver 1963: 180-191)

The late Ethiopid waves were very likely composed of small groups of warriors moving slowly with their cattle (up to now, Hima nomads have maintained their nomadic patterns in the northeastern region of Rwanda). A human group may live entirely on cattle which, if properly cared for, provide milk, meat, blood, and leather. As, with a minimum of human work, a herd will subsist forever and even increase, it is a very useful instrument for the production of goods: because of these characteristics, it has been said to be very similar to a capital good. It is a "natural" capital in the sense that its returns are produced by its inherent qualities and not by an economic organization as is the case with the interests of a money capital. As cattle are mobile and precious, there is always a danger of raiding (they have to be defended): pastoral nomadic societies are usually warlike. They are also made up of small-scale units of people living together: when there is no stalling and cattle-feeding and when the vegetation is scarce, the cattle have to be scattered over large areas, and this prevents any kind of human concentration. Within the warrior band there was no political authority in the sense that there were no relations of physical coercion: among the warriors, one had certainly more authority than the others because of his ancestry, his ability, his intelligence; consequently, his opinions were usually followed. Leadership based on influence is not to be confused with political power founded on the possibility of the use of coercion. As in any small human group in which there is no significant difference in wealth and weapons, social equality was the prevalent pattern among the pastoral invaders.

The population they met in the region that was to become Rwanda was living by agriculture. Possibly they also had some cattle, but it is very likely that they maintained the same kind of life up to the twentieth century in the small peasant communities of northern Rwanda. In the villages in which all the inhabitants belonged to a few patrilineages, and in which the economy was not very much above the subsistence level, these small groups were autonomous. Inside the village, social order was maintained and conflicts were solved by the kinship heads whose authority was based mainly on their position in the lineage: they were closer to the ancestors than the younger generations and they represented the collective force of past forefathers on their living descendants. Here again, there was no coercive power.

PLURALITY OF GLOBAL SOCIETIES

Rwanda was born by vertical incorporation of two global societies: a pastoral-nomadic and an agricultural-sedentary one. This is of course an abstract view, as there were more than two global societies concerned. A societal unit may be called global when its members' activities are organized in such a way that the survival and the development of the group does not require permanent relations with other groups. A global society provides for the needs of the individual from birth to death and encompasses the networks of social relations in which individuals interact with each other. When the techniques of production are very simple and when there are no specialized activities (when each familial productive unit consumes directly what it produces), a global society may be very small. For food, shelter, ritual, social control, and magical protection a village or a pastoral band are self-sufficient; usually matrimonial relations require a larger horizon. Even taking this into account, there were certainly many pastoral and many agricultural global societal units in the southwest of the interlacustrine area around the fifteenth century. As several pastoral Tutsi bands wanted to settle among the peasant Hutu villages, many incorporative processes occurred, very probably according to the same pattern.

THE NEW SOCIETY: STRATIFIED, FEUDAL, POLITICAL

The two former global societies became one new global society very different from its original components. Whereas there was no social stratification in the warrior bands and in the peasant villages, the new society was made of two hierarchized layers: the Tutsi group became the superior stratum, and the Hutu one the inferior. The phenomenon of social stratification, when distinguished from other kinds of nonsymmetrical social relations such as the political one, is not easy to grasp. It is defined only by the ranking of the two groups: one is *before* the other, one is *above* the other, as we are compelled to use space images. It results from the ranking that any member of the global society is socially situated with respect to any other member of the same society as either an inferior, or a superior, or an equal. Each of these social roles is defined by a set of duties and rights, irrespective of the personal characteristics of each individual.

The members of the superior layer, the Tutsi, had privileges: they could exert pressure on an inferior to oblige him to provide services and goods; they were the only ones who could become warriors or be appointed to serve in the government structure. As is usual in stratified societies, the advantages of the aristocrats cannot be listed: they are diffused, but very real. It may be summarized by saying that they commanded an amount of social power much greater than the peasants; their opportunities to obtain what they wanted or to get things done were much better than those of the Hutu.

A second new feature of the Rwanda global society was the feudal institution called *ubuhake*. As it has often been described (see Maquet 1961a: 129-133), it is sufficient to indicate here that it was a relationship created when an individual with low social power (usually a Hutu) offered his services to and asked protection from a person with great social power (practically always a Tutsi). If the latter accepted, a permanent link was created between himself (called *shebuja*, lord) and the other (called *garagu*, dependent). Both roles were socially defined. When, as it was usually the case, the feudal link connected a Hutu and a Tutsi, its function was to strengthen the incorporation of the two strata in a single global society: by the personal protection of his lord, the Hutu dependent was somewhat identified with him and consequently enjoyed some security; another Tutsi could not exert pressure on him without risking trouble with his Tutsi lord. On the other hand, the system was very favorable for the Tutsi, as it organized the exchange of protection—a non-economic value—for goods (beans, peas, and other agricultural produce) and services. It should be added that the protection's bond was symbolized by one or a few head of cattle granted by the lord to his dependent; but the latter had only usufruct rights to those cattle (he could use the milk), not ownership. These goods were not equivalent to the ones provided by the Hutu dependent; this is why the *ubuhake* relationship cannot be considered economic in spite of the cattle provided by the Tutsi lord.

A third difference between the Hutu and Tutsi societies and the Rwanda mixed society is the political organization which emerged with the incorporation. A political organization is certainly more than a coercive system, but it can be identified by it. And there was a very strong one in Rwanda. Rwanda society was divided into rulers and subjects; the authority of the former on the latter was sanctioned by the possibility of the use of physical force. Of course, the other sanctions of authority (the sacredness of the kings, their legitimacy based on the uninterrupted patrilineal direct succession, the mythical tales of the divine origin of the rulers, and so forth) validated the political power, but if they were not effective in obtaining obedience to the rulers' decisions, coercion was a last resort. This did not exist in the peasants' villages or in the pastoral bands: if a deviant was not willing to comply with the elders' or with the leader's decisions, collective pressure could be used against him, from ridicule to ostracism, and finally he could be obliged either to submit or to leave, but he was not threatened by coercion.

In Rwanda, the political structure as it existed in the nineteenth century was a powerful and complex one. At the top, there was a sacred king who was mystically identified with Rwanda itself (when he was growing old and weak, the vitality of the country itself was impaired) and who had theoretically unlimited power; the queen-mother shared the royal prerogatives with him and if the mother of the king died before he did, another woman was chosen to play the part of the queen-mother. The king was the supreme ruler, but he was nor the only one. He was assisted by a group of people living near his residence, the court which functioned as a central government; in the regions of Rwanda too far from his capital to be directly ruled, he was represented by appointed officers whose main duty was to collect tribute; he had at his disposal several armies that could implement his orders inside the country and deal with his enemies outside.

The court, the administration, and the armies were complex organizations that have been described elsewhere. (Maquet 1961a: 101-128) Each was a pyramidal structure with officers at different levels; all those who belonged to these political structures could to some extent command the use of coercion and benefit from the taxes paid by the population. Of course, for petty officials the participation in both privileges was not very important; yet it was sufficient to put them in the ruling group, as distinguished from the mass of subjects. The barrier between the Tutsi stratum and the Hutu layer did not coincide with the line separating rulers and subjects: if all the rulers were Tutsi, all the Tutsi were not rulers—in other words some were subjects.

Vertical incorporation of Tutsi bands and Hutu villages has thus produced a new society with marked differences in social organization—social stratification, feudal institution, political power. In the other fields of social organization, important changes do not seem to have occurred. Hutu and Tutsi kinship groups remained apparently what they were. However there must have been some leveling of differences, as there are very strong parallels between the Tutsi and the Hutu kinship models: for both strata, the names of the descent groups, *inzu* (primary patrilineage), *umulyango* (secondary patrilineage), and *ubwoko* (patriclan) are the same and have the same meaning; the terminology used to designate kinship and affinity roles is the same; matrimonial institutions follow the same pattern. The few differences are related to the occupational particularities of Hutu and Tutsi and are accounted for very easily (for instance, the bride-wealth was rendered in cows among the Tutsi and goats and hoes among the Hutu).

CULTURAL CONSEQUENCES OF
VERTICAL INCORPORATION

Societal incorporation set in motion acculturative processes in Rwanda. The "continuous first-hand contact (of two) groups of individuals having different cultures" of the famous Herskovits definition was certainly realized

when Hutu and Tutsi began to live together within the same society. (Herskovits 1948: 523) After three or four centuries, it seems that acculturation has
produced a cultural uniformity. There is a Rwanda culture with, of course,
differences. But the differences could be adjustments of each stratum to its
own situation rather than survivals of the original different cultures.

Nevertheless, on the level of techniques for obtaining food from the environment, the differences may be interpreted as survivals. Cattle-herding and
agriculture subsisted up to the twentieth century as distinctive pursuits for
Tutsi and Hutu. Tutsi did not learn to till the soil and remained experts in
cattle-rearing. However, they were interested in agricultural products for con-
sumption and their diet changed considerably: they ate sorghum, sweet bananas (as food and beer), peas and beans, though milk and meat remained their
typical prestige articles of diet. Hutu, on the other hand, appreciated dairy
products (which were very scarce for them); as Tutsi did not object to using
them for taking care of the cattle, the Hutu learned herding.

In the religious field, the beliefs concerning the high-god, *Imana*, were
shared by all Rwanda people. The ancestor's cult was also common. Even the
more particular *Ryangombe* cult is not restricted to a single social group.
Ryangombe is said to have been the leader of a small group of friends and
dependents. Accidentally killed by a buffalo during a hunting party, Ryangombe was not deserted by his friends. They threw themselves on the bull's
horns and went to live with Ryangombe in the spirit world on the slopes of
the Karisimbi, a former volcano, which is a notably more agreeable place than
the underworld where the ordinary spirits of the dead reside. To have the
privilege of joining them in the afterlife, living people have to be initiated into
Ryangombe's cult. Hutu and Tutsi may become initiates, but it does not
imply a participation in the same rituals. Initiation is a lineage affair: the
person who receives the new initiates is a member of the lineage who, for the
occasion, impersonates Ryangombe. If the ceremony takes place in a Hutu
lineage, all the audience is Hutu and vice versa.

A study of Rwanda cultural values conducted several years ago, concluded
that for the Tutsi the ultimate values were power and reputation; children
and cattle were their main instrumental values in the sense that they were the
almost indispensable means for achieving these ends. The Hutu were seen as
seeking security through the production of agricultural goods and the protection of a powerful patron. (Maquet 1954: 176-182) The difference reflects
the situation of a hierarchial society; power and fame are highly valued everywhere, but in a stratified society only the upper level has access to these
values. Ambition for power is proper for people who do not have to worry

about fundamental human needs such as food, shelter, and so forth. For them, security comes first. There is no basis for asserting that the difference of values is a survival of the original cultures of the peasants and of the herdsmen. The Rwanda language, very similar to the neighboring Rundi and Ha, belongs to the Bantu family. The agriculturalists who invaded the interlacustrine area before the Tutsi pastoralists did are said to be Bantu because they were carriers of Bantu languages. It is thus certain that the Ethiopid conquerors adopted a language which originated among agricultural populations (of course it does not mean that Tutsi acquired a Bantu language only after they had settled in Rwanda: their ancestors could have adopted it previously from other agricultural groups with whom they could have been in contact). It is certain also that Hutu and Tutsi spoke the same language in the nineteenth century. Linguistic differences between Hutu and Tutsi are the kind that arise when the same tongue is spoken by two distinct social strata.

HYPOTHESIS 1: THE CULTURE OF INCORPORATED SOCIETIES

Acculturative consequences of the vertical incorporation of two global societies into a new one have resulted in the formation of a fundamentally homogeneous culture. When there were differences, they appeared to be variations on a single theme rather than pieces belonging to cultural universes alien to one another. They appeared also to be intelligible as expressions of the duality of a stratified society rather than as survivals of separate cultures that have existed in the past. If this interpretation is correct, we may tentatively propound an hypothesis: when two global societies merge and constitute a new one, the resulting culture reflects the new society more than it preserves parts of the parent cultures. Expressed in general terms as an hypothesis, this assertion should be tested; as a statement about Rwanda society, this analysis emphasizes the paramount importance of its stratification.

Rwanda culture is one: the two strata live separately but are in close contact. Separation and closeness—almost contradictory attributes of Rwanda society—made castes rather than classes out of the Rwanda strata. Segregation was the rule (Tutsi and Hutu did not intermarry, did not eat together, did not amuse themselves in common festivities, did not fight in the same military units against Rwanda enemies). Social interaction took place only when it was required by the necessities of work or exploitation (Hutu were given orders and were watched by their Tutsi masters). There was no social mobility: to be a Tutsi, one had to be born a Tutsi, that is to say, have a father and a mother who were Tutsi. The caste system resulting from societal incorporation was the focal point of Rwanda society. Its characteristic features (unity of the global society, separation of its layers) were reflected in its culture: basic homogeneity interpreted by each caste according to its situation in the hierarchy.

TERRITORIAL EXPANSION BY HORIZONTAL INCORPORATION

If Rwanda was born by vertical incorporation, it grew by horizontal incorporation. Oral traditions are numerous, and from what has been collected, an historical picture emerges. (Pages 1933; Kagame 1959: d'Hertefelt 1962; Vansina 1962) It permits us to retrace the main stages of the territorial expansion of Rwanda.

At the beginning of the sixteenth century Rwanda was a small kingdom whose rulers belonged to a Tutsi lineage, the Nyiginya. They recognized the paramount authority of the neighboring Bugesera kingdom, which was another small political unit dominated by a Tutsi dynasty. The Rwanda kings lived in the vicinity of Lake Mohasi (in the eastern part of the present-day Republic of Rwanda), and the first monarch whom historians consider to have "really" existed (as opposed to the previous ones who were perhaps mythical) is Ruganzu Bwimba who, according to the Vansina chronology, died at the end of the fifteenth century, precisely in 1482 (with a margin of plus or minus twelve years). (Vansina 1962: 56)

During the sixteenth century, the Nyiginya kings succeeded in becoming independent from Bugesera and began their territorial enlargement by incorporating other small Tutsi chiefdoms: Nduga, Bumbogo, Buriza, Rukoma. All these units were two-storied societies made up of Tutsi and Hutu, following the pattern described for Rwanda; but these societies, being much smaller than the nineteenth-century Rwanda we have analyzed, had institutions which were not so complex. For instance, as the territory on which the ruler had authority did not exceed the possibility of direct administration, he did not delegate his power to officers; for that reason, the term chiefdom seems more appropriate than the term kingdom which should be reserved for political units requiring the representation of the ruler in "provinces."

These conquests were made by military means. There were at first rapid raids near the frontiers aimed at capturing cattle. After several skirmishes, an important expedition was organized inside the enemy territory; there was resistance from the invaded Tutsi warriors which culminated in a decisive battle. The Rwanda Tutsi were either driven off and forced to flee; or they overcame the invaded ones—the chief was killed, his genitals cut off, his drum taken away. There was a military occupation, and after some time the former independent chiefdom was incorporated into Rwanda. Assimilation was eased by the cultural similarities between the conquering society and the conquered one; in both cases there was the same social organization, the same economic system, the same idea of authority, the same language. The Hutu peasants were not much concerned. As in the European Middle Ages, wars were mainly power struggles among aristocrats. They affected the peasants when they happened to be in the way of the warriors' bands, but the results were rather indifferent. The Hutu-exploited condition remained the same in any case.

During the following centuries, the territorial expansion of Rwanda continued according to the same patterns. Other Tutsi kingdoms or chiefdoms were conquered, then incorporated: Bwishaza and Mvejuru (seventeenth century), Mubari and Ndorwa (eighteenth century), Bugesera and Gisaka (nineteenth century) are the most important territories assimilated by the kingdom of Rwanda. Meanwhile inside Rwanda there was a parallel development of the political institutions in the direction of a growth of the royal power: the central government was consolidated by the creation of high-rank officers responsible for the ritual knowledge concerning the life of the society (see d'Hertefelt and Coupez, 1964) and by the organization of armies in the sixteenth century. In the following century, the theory of the sacred kingship was enriched by the affirmation of the divine character of the monarch and the establishment of the cycles of royal names. Finally, under the reign of Rwabugiri (1860-1895), the Rwanda monarchy became absolute in theory and despotic in fact. (see Maquet 1961b, 1962b)

Tutsi states were not the only units that Rwanda incorporated. Up to the twentieth century, small Hutu units remained independent in the mountains of the northern and western part of present-day Rwanda. If the Tutsi domination were not already firmly established there, all of the autonomous Hutu communities—which were certainly numerous throughout the region in the sixteenth century—would have been incorporated by Rwanda in the course of time. The process seems to have been indirect and peaceful: it was not military conquest. Rwanda Tutsi who were settled near a Hutu village lent them some cattle, received some sorghum or bananas, were asked to arbitrate disputes, and finally were in position to establish the caste system in which they stabilized their privileged status. (Maquet and Naigiziki 1957)

HYPOTHESIS 2: THE IMPACT OF POLITICAL POWER
ON CULTURAL UNIFORMITY

Acculturative consequences of the horizontal incorporation have not been studied exhaustively. Regional variations were more important than it appears at first sight (d'Hertefelt 1962: 23), but d'Hertefelt seems to restrict cultural differences to the Hutu layer. According to him regional variations were not apparent because they were masked by the homogeneous Tutsi culture which covered the whole Rwanda territory. This is certainly true in that the ratio between the two castes was not the same everywhere. At the end of the traditional period, let us say, during the first decade of the twentieth century, the percentage of Tutsi for the whole Rwanda was estimated to be around 15 percent, but it was far from being uniform in the several provinces as the more precise figures obtained fifty years later prove. (see tables in Maquet and d'Hertefelt 1959) A region in which Tutsi constitutes 25 percent of the population is obviously different from one in which they constitute only 2 or 3 percent. As in any territorial administration, there was much mobility among Tutsi officers representing the king's authority; they moved frequently from one region to another, from the court to the provinces; they were thus agents of cultural uniformity.

We may conclude this section with another tentative hypothesis: when there is incorporation of several groups by territorial expansion, the cultural uniformity of the whole is a function of the political strength of the central government manifested by its appointed officers.

THE TWA MINORITY

In this discussion of the incorporative processes in operation in traditional Rwanda, we have not mentioned up to now the Twa, usually thought to constitute the third caste of the society. Twa are the descendants of the Pygmy hunters who were probably the first inhabitants of the country. In historic times, Pygmoid Twa were either hunters wandering in the high forests of the Congo-Nile divide, or potters and dancers settled among other Rwanda people. They were few, probably less than one percent of the population.

Vertically incorporated in the Rwanda society, they certainly were situated on the lowest level, on the margin of humanity (often said to be similar to apes). This status had advantages: considered irresponsible, a free behavior was admitted from them more easily than from other people. However almost any Twa familial unit was linked to an important Tutsi household; as hunters, they provided their masters with skins and furs; as servants, they entertained them by singing, dancing, and mimicking, and they were sometimes used as faithful personal guards. (In the 1959 Hutu revolt, Twa protected their Tutsi masters and even killed for them.) Thus the social integration of the Twa was in fact accomplished through the mediation of the Tutsi.

Culturally, they had a distinct subculture within the Rwanda one. They were not subjected to the common food taboos—or repulsions—concerning mutton, for instance; the language they spoke was the Rwanda one, but with many peculiarities. Again, the distance between their own cultural variety and the Rwanda common heritage reflected very closely the social distance between their minority caste and the other two, much above them.

COLLAPSE OF THE STRATIFIED SOCIETY

At the end of the nineteenth century, just prior to the colonial period, Rwanda was a large kingdom, not a tribe. Its strong and complex permanent political organization deserved the qualification of state, and its common culture, slowly developed by people who had acquired the habit of working together, indicated the existence of a nation. Both processes of incorporation, vertical and horizontal, had made a new social and cultural reality out of three main cultural units (the pastoralists' way of life, the agriculturalists', and the hunters') and out of numerous small societal units (the bands of herdsmen, the villages of peasants, the groups of hunters). Yet, within three years (1959-1962) the vertical structure collapsed entirely (but the horizontal integration was maintained).

During the colonial period, the Rwanda caste system persisted in the sense that a Tutsi was offered more opportunities for personal promotion than a Hutu. Opportunities were different: to go to school, to be appointed clerk in a government office, to work as an overseer in a plantation, to become a chief or a subchief in the "native" administration, to be ordained as a Catholic priest. These were the highest situations an ambitious young Rwanda man could hope to obtain during the half-century of colonial rule. Young Tutsi had better chances to achieve these ends than young Hutu for several reasons, the main one being the policy of moderate indirect rule applied first by the Germans, then by the Belgians. The traditional political hierarchy with the king at the top was used by the colonial authorities to administer the *résidence du Ruanda* within the Ruanda-Urundi Territory. Obviously the traditional system was, in the course of the colonial period, modified several times in order to convert former rulers, "chiefs" whose legitimacy rested on traditional grounds, into officials appointed by the colonial authorities and accountable to them. Transformed in a subordinate administrative setup, the network of Rwanda political relations mantained a large degree of its influence on the population, and the Tutsi succeeded in keeping a complete control over the "native administration." In 1956, there was not a single Hutu "chief" (out of 46) and not a single Hutu "subchief" (out of 603). From this exclusive position in administration there resulted many other privileges for Tutsi. In the last decade of the colonial regime, Tutsi still had a notably higher social power than Hutu. This has been described and analyzed elsewhere. (Maquet 1964)

This situation of inequality was resented by Hutu to an extent that most observers did not perceive. (Codere 1962) The suddenness and the violence of the Hutu reaction to that situation when they were convinced that they had the opportunity to change it indicate that they were perfectly aware of their exploited condition, and that they endured it only because they did not think that they were strong enough to reverse it. Awareness and impatience have certainly been made more acute during the colonial period which, in spite of the many limitations of the education system, brought new ideas and opened up new vistas, but they certainly existed already in traditional times: proverbs, tales, and some tentative revolts are indications of deep dissatisfaction. The 1956 elections were not significant (electing people who would elect members of the subchief's council which was only an advisory body), but they were the first elections organized in Rwanda and they gave Hutu a realization of the power of their sheer number. The following year Hutu political parties were created, and in November, 1959, a general uprising ended definitively the Tutsi supremacy. When Rwanda became independent in 1962, it was as a republic (the last king having been deposed and the monarchy suppressed after a United Nations supervised referendum on these questions). (Nkundabagenzi 1961) The government and the high administration of the Rwanda republic are entirely Hutu; many Tutsi live as refugees in neighboring countries and on several occasions there have been social disorders and massacres of Tutsi.

HYPOTHESIS 3: THE STABILITY
OF A CASTE SOCIETY

The Rwanda stratified society, constituted by vertical incorporation with its typical political and feudal institutions, was not so solid as would be expected from a unity slowly developing over four centuries and presenting an homogeneous cultural facade. In fact, what kept the castes together was Tutsi force, which they apparently did not have to use often. The mere existence of Tutsi armies was a sufficient deterrent. (The same is true for most African colonial territories: the obvious military superiority of the colonial authorities prevented attempts to revolt.) It has been said that Tutsi domination collapsed because Rwanda had been subjected to the Western impact during the colonial regime. This is probably true, not so much because the knowledge of the modern world made their condition less bearable for the Hutu, but mainly because Tutsi could no longer threaten Hutu with the use of physical force. They attempted to do so during the 1959 Hutu insurrection, and they would have succeeded perhaps if the Belgian authorities had not prevented them.

Let us conclude with a third tentative hypothesis: when a society is constituted by vertical incorporation, the inferior—thus exploited—stratum is kept in its place in the social hierarchy only by the threat of potential use of force. People seem never to resign themselves to social inequality.

REFERENCES

Codere, H. 1962. "Power in Rwanda." R. Cohen (ed.). *Power in complex societies in Africa. Anthropologica* 4: 45-85.

d'Hertefelt, M. 1962. "Le Rwanda," in A. A. Trouwborst, M. d'Hertefelt, J. Scherer. *Les anciens royaumes de la zone interlacustre méridionale.* pp. 15-112. Tervuren, Musée royale d'Afrique centrale. (Another edition of this book is published by Oxford University Press, London.)

―――, and A. Coupez. 1964. *La royauté sacrée de l'ancien Rwanda, texte, traduction et commentaire de son rituel.* Tervuren, Musée royal d'Afrique centrale.

Fage, J. D. 1958. *An atlas of African history.* London, Edward Arnold.

Herskovits, M. J. 1948. *Man and his works.* New York, Knopf.

Kagame, A. 1959. *La notion de génération appliquée à la généalogie dynastique et á l'histoire du Rwanda des Xe-XIe siècles á nos jours.* Bruxelles, Académie royale des sciences coloniales.

Louis, W. R. 1963. *Ruanda-Urundi 1884-1919.* London, Oxford University Press.

Maquet, J. 1954. "The kingdom of Rwanda," in D. Forde (ed.). *African Worlds.* London, Oxford University Press.

1961a. *The premise of inequality in Rwanda.* London, Oxford University Press.

1961b. "Une hypothèse pour l'étude des féodalités africaines." *Cahiers d'études africaines* 2(6): 292-314.

1962a. "L'integration culturelle dans les sociétés en croissance." *Transactions of the Fifth World Congress of Sociology, Washington, D. C. 1962* 2: 171-195.

1962b. "A research definition of African feudality." *Journal of African History* 3(2): 307-310.

1964. "La participation de la classe paysanne au mouvement d'indépendence du Rwanda." *Cahiers d'études africaines* 4(16): 552-568.

–––, and M. d'Hertefelt. 1959. *Elections en société féodale, une étude sur l'introduction du vote populaire au Ruanda-Urundi.* Bruxelles, Académie royale des sciences coloniales.

–––, and S. Naigiziki. 1957. "Les droits fonciers dans le Ruanda ancien." *Zaire* 11(4): 339-359.

Nkundabagenzi, F. 1961. *Rwanda politique 1958-60.* Bruxelles centre de récherche et d'information socio-politique.

Oliver, R. 1963. "Discernible developments in the Interior c. 1500-1840," in R. Oliver, G. Mathew (eds.). *History of East Africa.* Oxford, Clarendon Press.

Pages, A. 1933. *Un royaume hamité au centre de l'Afrique.* Bruxelles, Institut royal colonial belge.

Vansina, J. 1962. *L'évolution du royaume rwanda des origines à 1900.* Bruxelles, Academie royale des sciences d'outre-mer.

10

TRIBAL COHESION AND THE INCORPORATIVE PROCESS IN THE TRANSKEI, SOUTH AFRICA

David Hammond-Tooke

INTRODUCTION

The Transkei, situated on the eastern seaboard of the Republic of South Africa and the largest consolidated area of "native reserve" in the country, became in 1962 the center of world-wide interest when the Prime Minister announced that it was to become the first Bantu "Homeland" to achieve a limited form of self-government. It was a logical choice for this experiment as, apart from its size and compactness, it has had a long history of experience in local government through a system of local councils which, although largely advisory, controlled auxiliary departments of agriculture and engineering and, with the bureaucratic hierarchy of white magistrates and their staffs, integrated the whole area into a common structure, at least on some levels.

Political incorporation is not a new phenomenon in the Transkei. The process of annexation from 1879 to 1894 merged the numerous small-scale political units into the wider framework of the Transkeian administration, a branch of the then Department of Native Affairs, imposed radical changes on the nature of the political units themselves, and involved chiefs and lesser political officers in a drastic redefinition of their roles. In 1955 a new system of local government, that of Bantu Authorities, was introduced which attempted to revive the old chiefdoms after sixty years of a policy designed to break down their integrity and, in 1963, elections for a new Legislative Assembly placed much of the administration of the area in the hands of the sixty-four tribal chiefs and forty-five elected members. In strong contrast to most of former colonial Africa, therefore, we have the phenomenon of the introduction of an electoral system, with its full paraphernalia of ballot box and political parties, on the one hand; on the other, an explicit attempt to revive chieftainship and make the old chiefdoms the basis of local govern-

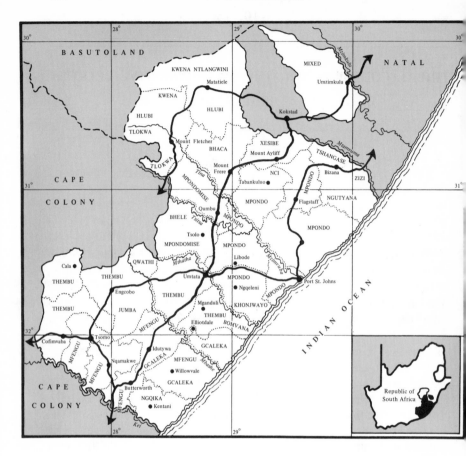

MAP 3. THE TRANSKEIAN TERRITORIES: SHOWING DISTRICT BOUNDARIES AND APPROXIMATE DISTRIBUTION OF MAIN TRIBES AFTER 1879-1894 ANNEXATION

ment. This disparity between universalistic and particularistic norms leads inevitably to conflict and strain. (Hammond-Tooke 1964)

Incorporation in the Transkei must be seen as only one local instance of a wider process that affected all the nonwhite peoples of South Africa, drawing them irrevocably into the orbit of the emerging state, but its strongly marked historical, geographical, and cultural identity makes it possible to treat the Transkei as a relatively self-contained entity for purposes of analysis. The patterns of the incorporative process and the problems that arise from it will apply *mutatis mutandis* to other reserves in the Republic, where similar administrative developments are envisaged or have already begun.

THE SETTING

The Transkei, lying between the Kei and Mzimkhulu Rivers (the latter, the border of Natal province), came into being as the result of successive annexations, beginning with the proclamations relating to Fingoland and East Griqualand in 1877 and culminating in the incorporation of Pondoland in 1894.[1] Its 16,554 square miles fall into four main physical regions, running southwest to northeast parallel with the coast—the coastal belt, a central corridor, the highlands, and the Great Escarpment. (Nel 1957) The coastal strip is extremely broken as the "grain" of the country lies towards the sea. Precipitous promontories jut into the Indian Ocean, particularly in the central region, and much of the area is a tumble of hills and bluffs bisected by the five main rivers. The coastal dunes are clothed in semitropical bush backed by savannah thorn scrub. The central corridor, between 2,000 and 4,000 feet, is undulating grassland, punctuated by mesas and peaks and scored by the upper reaches of the perennial rivers, but with a few fairly extensive flats. The highlands are in reality the foothills of the Drakensberg range which lies in a majestic curve from the eastern Cape through Natal to the eastern Transvaal, like the backbone of the dragon from which it gets its name.

The climate is fairly equable with brilliant dry winters and hot wet summers, with precipitation mainly in the form of thunder storms. The average annual rainfall is between 20 and 30 inches, but is uncertain and droughts are frequent.

These ecological features have had their effect on the patterns of migration into the area. The Transkei was settled by waves of Nguni-speaking Bantu migrants from the northeast, their advance funneled down the 100-mile corridor between the Drakensberg and the sea. The earliest immigration was that of the Xhosa, Thembu, Bomvana, Mpondomise, and Mpondo, who moved slowly down from what is now Natal with their herds of cattle and practiced a form of shifting agriculture. Portuguese records show that by at least 1554 there were Bantu-speakers south of the Mthatha River (see Map 3) but, as Wilson emphasizes (Wilson 1959: 178), there is nothing to show that they were not there centuries before.

Another wave of immigration began in the early decades of the nineteenth century, triggered by the expansion of the Zulu state under Tshaka. His ruthless subjugation of neighboring chiefdoms (an atypical example of indigenous political incorporation) set up a chain reaction which precipitated a number of tribes (for example the Ngwane under Matiwane, the Hlubi under Mpangazitha, the Ndebele under Mzilikazi, and the Bhaca under Madzikane) to undertake careers of rapine and plunder which shook not only the Nguni tribes already in the Transkei but also Sotho-speakers in what is now Basutoland and the Orange Free State. Between c. 1818 and 1840 a number of fleeing tribes penetrated the Transkeian area and settled among the long-established Xhosa and others. Such were the Bhaca, Ntlangwini, Zizi, Bhele and Hlubi, and some Sotho groups (Kwena and Tlôkwa) from over the Drakensberg.

The early migrations were channeled along the two main "corridors," the highlands and the inland corridor, especially the latter, and early travelers speak of areas of dense settlement in these zones. (Bird 1888: 42-46; Wilson 1959: 172) Bird quotes the report of a party from the shipwrecked *Stavenisse* (1686), which had gone some way inland, that the country was "extremely fertile and incredibly populous and full of cattle." Generally speaking the sourveld of the coastal strip was avoided. Later the incursions of Bhaca, Ngwane, and Zulu led to the concentration of settlement in the broken country along the river valleys and the open flats were avoided. The Thembu, due to Mpondo and Bhaca raids, withdrew to the Mbashe and upper reaches of the Kei River (Hammond-Tooke 1957: 14-15) and in the 1830s Faku's Mpondo sought refuge from Zulu foraging expeditions in the broken country of the Mngazi. With the removal of external threat from other tribes, however, mainly due to the presence of colonies of whites in the north (Natal) and south (Cape Colony), particularly the defeat of the Zulu in 1836, the tribes moved back into the plains and into the coastal belt until today the whole area is overpopulated and overstocked.

The relevance of this settlement pattern to problems of incorporation is mainly in regard to communications. It is a striking fact that patterns of christianization (and westernization in general) have been determined to some extent by proximity to the main routes that traverse the two main corridors. It is the tribes in the coastal belt, Xhosa, Bomvana, and Mpondo, which tend to be more conservative and have not participated to the same extent in the social, economic, and religious development of the area, as Pauw (Pauw 1965: 246-247) has also noted. Increasingly efficient road transport is today breaking down the isolation of these areas and is permitting much more frequent contact among all parts of the Transkei.

CULTURAL UNIFORMITY AND STRUCTURAL DIVERSITY

The tribes inhabiting the Transkei, apart from a few Sotho chiefdoms along the Basutoland border, all belong to the Cape Nguni group of patrilineal pastoralists practicing hoe culture and speaking dialects of *isiXhosa*. Culturally they exhibit extraordinary uniformity. The settlement pattern was one of scattered homesteads consisting of a number of beehive-shaped huts grouped round a cattle byre of stone, brushwood, or planted aloe, each the residence of a family which was ideally polygynous. Households tended to cluster in well-defined, named areas settled by a dominant lineage or lineage segment. Contiguity, patrikinship, and mutual economic interests imparted a strong feeling of solidarity to this neighborhood grouping which, in places, today approximates the true village found in other African areas. A number of neighborhoods formed the area of a ward headman, usually a man of wealth and often the head of the dominant lineage in the area. Wards themselves were grouped into larger areas (districts) under a subchief (*inkosi*) who was usually a close agnate of the chief, and finally the chiefdom or tribe[2] itself, under the chief (*inkosi enkulu*). The tribes were grouped genealogically into clusters (see below).

Parallel to and partly interlocked with this territorial distribution was the kinship and descent system. Most basic was the family, ideally polygynous, although probably not more than twenty percent achieved this ideal. Polygyny, where it occurred, gave rise to a special structuring of the family into greathouse and righthand house with their supporting houses, which, as we shall see, had important consequences for the stability of chiefdoms. Families were embedded in the wider structure of the patrilineage, of five to six generations depth, which mediated succession to status, inheritance of lineage property, and participation in ritual matters. Lineage segments, and to a lesser extent lineages, were local groups and formed the cores of neighborhoods. Clans too, in the early days, tended to be local units, but intertribal movements soon meant that clan members were scattered throughout a number of tribes, an important factor in intertribal relations. Each chiefdom, however, had its core of "true" clansmen.

Basically similar rituals took place at the crises in the life cycle. Female initiation is found throughout and male initiation, involving circumcision, seems to have been universal formerly but is no longer performed by Bhaca, Xesibe, and Mpondo. Where performed, the canon of these rites is almost identical, with only slight variations in detail. Systems of religion and magic, similar for all tribes, were characterized by the ancestor cult and an all-pervasive system of witch-beliefs and sorcery. All tribes practiced subsistence agriculture, with stock-keeping the dominant interest, amounting to a cattle cult.[3]

Yet this cultural homogeneity must not be overstressed. There were diacritical elements that distinguished the tribal clusters (see below) from one another, but most were of a comparatively minor order. Chief of these were slight dialectal variations and differences in the details of law, ceremonial dances, and dress.[4] Perhaps the most significant was the absence of the levirate among Xhosa and Thembu and of the greathouse-righthandhouse dichotomy among Bhaca commoners.

Structurally, however, there was considerable diversity. The Transkei was settled by a number of independent chiefdoms, each with considerable structural integration achieved through a hierarchy of administrative offices. These chiefdoms were grouped into a number of mainly unrelated tribal clusters, each with its own history, variety of custom, and strong sense of distinctiveness. There are twelve of these clusters: Xhosa, Thembu, Mpondo, Mpondomise, Bomvana, Bhaca, Hlubi, Xesibe, Bhele, Zizi, Mfengu (Fingo),[5] and Ntlangwini; and the chiefs within each cluster are related to one another through membership in a royal patrilineage. Thus the Xhosa cluster comprises the independent chiefdoms of Gcaleka, Ngqika, Ndlambe, Dushane, Qhayi, Dange, Gasela, Ntinde, and Hleke; the Thembu cluster contains the three independent Hala tribes and the related Jumba, Hlanga, Tshatshu, and Ndungwana. In some cases the cluster also contains unrelated tribes which have become tributary to the paramount chief, for example, the chief of the (often theoretically) genealogically senior chiefdom. Among the Xhosa, the Gqunukhwebe fall into this category, as do the Hegebe and Qwathi among the Thembu and the imiZizi, Ngutyana, and Tshangase among the Mpondo.[6]

Nguni political units were inherently segmentary and tended to split into two groups of coordinate status politically, a process which was greatly facilitated by the typically Nguni dualism of the great house and right-hand house. (Hammond-Tooke 1965: 152-166) There was a preemptive right for the heir in the right-hand house of a chief to establish his own independent chiefdom separate from that of his father so that, theoretically, royal-lineage segmentation could lead to fission in each generation. In effect, there was an institutionalized *expectation* of fission. Tribal histories show, however, that this seldom operated with such precision and whether or not it occurred depended on a number of factors, chief of which was perhaps the personality of the chief and his heirs, pressure on tribal lands, and external pressure from other tribes. The relationship of the chiefs to the paramount chief of the cluster must be stressed. All chiefs were related and ranked on the basis of genealogical connection, according the paramount chief ritual deference, in particular the right to initiate the annual first-fruit rituals. In all other respects, however, they enjoyed equal status, were entirely independent of one another and free to manage their internal affairs without outside interference.

The chiefdoms, then, were a divisive factor imposed on a pattern of considerable cultural uniformity. We must now discuss the nature of the chiefdoms themselves, with particular reference to internal cohesion and external relations.

THE DYNAMICS OF TRIBAL COHESION

We have, unfortunately, little direct evidence of the nature of the seceding group which formed a new chiefdom as the imposition of white control inhibited the waging of war between rival segments (the usual immediately precipitating cause of fission) and, by limiting the tribe to well-defined areas, made it almost impossible for breakaway segments to find territory in which to settle. It thus also eliminated one of the most important sanctions against chiefly despotism by removing the threat of secession. It is probable, though, that a newly independent chief of, say, the right-hand house would be accompanied by his uterine brothers and also those of the supporting houses so that the new chiefdom had a core of royal kinsmen, but it is certain that the bulk would be made up of nonrelated personal followers. In any event such a group would soon be joined by individuals and groups that had broken away from other chiefdoms. As Schapera has pointed out for the South African Bantu generally: "To Bantu, indeed, the tribe is essentially a body of people all paying allegiance to a common chief. They certainly do not visualize it as a group of kin, not even in terms of residence." (Schapera 1956: 28) The crucial desideratum of independence was a clear spatial separation from the parent chiefdom involving the occupation of a separate territory, although from the evidence it is unlikely that mere residence in a tribal area conferred citizenship.

The focus of integration of the new chiefdom was the chieftainship, a political office around which the hierarchy of subsidiary offices was locked. In the old days of slow migration southwards, before the Nguni were confined to their present-day reserves, the territorial aspect does not appear to have been of prime importance. Civic rights stemmed from an act of personal allegiance to the chief. This relationship was basically contractual despite the fact that, for most, recruitment to citizenship was by birth. In return for protection, not only from external enemies but also from offenses perpetrated by fellow tribesmen (as well as assistance in time of need), a tribesman contracted, merely by remaining under a chief's jurisdiction, to support his overlord against his enemies, to perform communal labor when called upon to do so, and to defend the chiefdom with his life. The relationship was symbolized by the obligation of the subject's heir to pay the *isizi* death dues to the chief on his demise. Here the redistributive aspect of the concentration of wealth in the hands of the chief played a vital role.

But political integration in Nguni chiefdoms was achieved by mechanisms other than the purely political. There are at least three other levels of integration: the kinship, religious, and what might perhaps be called the ideological or conceptual.

On the kinship level the structuring of the society into exogamous unilineal descent groups, the lineages (including the nuclear, compound, and extended families embedded within them), and clans achieved an organic solidarity, in the Durkheimian sense, through a "division of labor" that proscribed self-sufficiency in the reproductive function of the group. None of the groups could be allowed to be sufficient unto themselves in this matter and wives had to be sought from other, unrelated groups, thereby forging affinal bonds that ramified throughout the chiefdom. Tsolo Mpondomise material indicates that, for this tribe at least, over 80 percent of marriages today are within the chiefdom (see Table 1), and the percentage was probably higher in the past, when intertribal relations were often strained. From an analysis of 429 marriages in Zingcuka Location,[7] Tsolo district, it was found that 28 (9 percent) had occurred between members of the same location section (neighborhood), 118 (27 percent) within the location itself, while by far the greatest number, 349 (80 percent), had been contracted within the chiefdom. At this point a critical sociospatial threshold is reached and the rate of intermarriage drops sharply. In the sample there were 32 (7 percent) marriages with non-Mpondomise but within the district of Tsolo, and 58 wives (13 percent) came from outside the district, from such places as Umtata, Qumbu, Libode, Mqanduli, Mount Fletcher, and Ngqeleni. All these are Transkeian districts lying fairly close to Tsolo, but some wives came from areas much further afield such as Herschel, Lady Grey, Queenstown, and even Port Elizabeth, all in the Cape Province proper.[8]

It will be seen from the above that, although the neighborhood tends to be exogamous, well over a quarter of all marriages occur within the location, an area of perhaps six or seven square miles. This ability to marry locally reflects the essentially nonkinship character of present-day locations and has implications for Professor Wilson's thesis that the highly sexual nature of Cape Nguni witch beliefs is correlated with limits on marriage choice due to the local concentration of exogamous kinship groups. (Wilson 1951) In fact, today the composition of locations is so heterogeneous that there seems little difficulty in finding a wife nearby.

TABLE 1. SPATIAL DISTRIBUTION OF AFFINAL LINKS:
PROVENANCE OF WIVES
(ZINGCUKA, TSOLO, 1963)

	Same Section	*Same Location*	*Same Chiefdom*	*Same District*	*Extra-District*	*Total*
All Marriages	28 (6%)	90 (23%)	221 (51%)	32 (7%)	58 (13%)	429 (100%)
Marriages of Household Heads Only	16 (7%)	50 (22%)	114 (50%)	17 (7%)	33 (14%)	230 (100%)

On the other hand, marriage into families too closely situated is regarded by the folk culture as undesirable. The proverb: *Induku igawulwa ezizweni* ("A good stick is gathered from another tribe") points up the possible tensions which can arise between in-laws. The close interaction between neighbors, with all its latent possibilities of conflict and rivalry (the other side of the coin from relations of cooperation and solidarity), does not accord well with the mutual respect demanded between affines. "It is embarrassing to live too close to your in-laws. They will see all that goes on at your home. If you meet at beerdrinks you may quarrel, or your cattle stray into their lands. The major relationship may be spoilt by petty quarrels." In view of these clearly expressed objections it is interesting that, in fact, so many men take wives from their own location.

From the figures quoted the chiefdom itself emerges as an almost endogamous grouping, statistically if not ideally. Only 7 percent of marriages are with non-Mpondomise groups in Tsolo district. The 13 percent of marriages with women from further afield reflects the greater mobility of workers, for example agricultural and forestry laborers, throughout the Transkei today.

Agnatic ties do not seem to have had the same integrative significance. Although it is likely that formerly chiefdoms were composed predominantly of kinsmen, the essentially contractual nature of political ties, and the aggregation of individuals and groups that had seceded from other chiefdoms, gave the tribe a basically nonkinship composition. Apart from creating what Fortes calls the "agnatic fence," bonds of unilineal descent tended to create extratribal ties as clansmen soon became scattered throughout the chiefdoms, creating networks of personal relations that ramified through the entire area.

Among the Mpondomise, but not the other Cape Nguni, there is a further interlocking mechanism. This is the institution of the quasikinship hospitality groups which cut across neighborhood boundaries and unite otherwise unrelated tribesmen in associational groups which have important functions at feasts and serve also as labor units. (Hammond-Tooke 1963) The organic solidarity they create does not extend to the chiefdom as a whole, however.

At the religious level the numerous discrete ritual communities centering on the lineage, each worshiping its own ancestral shades through the priestly office of the lineage head, reflected the importance of descent-group segmentation. But on the tribal level all members of the chiefdom were subject to the power of the royal ancestors, the shades of past chiefs who were believed to watch closely over the well-being of the tribe as a whole, especially in relation to alien and perhaps hostile tribes. The chief-centered communal rituals of the doctoring of the crops, the strengthening of the army, and the first fruits emphasized tribal solidarity by restating, often in dramatic ceremonials, the mystical value of chieftainship and citizenship, the involvement of each member in the tribe as a whole and its essential unity.

On the conceptual or ideological level the cohesion of the chiefdom was expressed by allegiance to the chief (tribesmen referred to themselves as the "People of So-and-So"), the possession of a common name (invariably, unlike the Natal Nguni, the eponym of the founding royal ancestor), the occupation of a certain territory, however vaguely defined, and other cultural diacritic marks such as a dialectal variety of *isiXhosa*, idiosyncracies of dress and custom and, occasionally, specific tribal marks. Examples of the latter are the *inchaza* face cuts of Bhaca, Xesibe, and some Mfengu, the body scarification of the Thembu, finger-joint amputation of the Xhosa and Mpondo, and the tattooing of Mpondo and Mpondomise. All these factors, strengthened by the continual threats of external aggression, served to make the Cape Nguni chiefdom a clearly defined unit with fairly discrete social boundaries.

RELATIONS BETWEEN POLITICAL UNITS

Authority structures were coterminous with the chiefdom: it was the moral and jural community. It was only within the chiefdom that the rule of law operated, that disputes were settled by due process in the courts, and that the obligations of cooperation and loyalty were laid on members.

Beyond the chiefdom lay other chiefdoms with which relations were based on naked power. This meant that what might perhaps be termed "international law" hardly existed. Distance between the chiefdoms varied along two coordinates, the geographical and the social. Geographical distance meant, in most cases, that chiefdoms situated far apart from one another seldom entered into relations with one another. On the other hand, there was a tendency for neighboring chiefdoms to be in a perpetual state of mutual enmity. Fighting between the contiguous Thembu and Xhosa was so frequent that a strip of land along the right bank of the Mthatha River was granted to certain white settlers in c. 1869 by the Thembu chief Ngagelizwe, against the payment of an annual quitrent of six pounds sterling, as a defense against Mpondo raids. The Mpondo chief, Nqwiliso, made similar allotments on the left bank. (Hammond-Tooke 1957: 15-16) Bransby Key, the first missionary among the Mpondomise, speaks of wide strips of open veld that divided some tribes. He writes that between the territory of the Mpondomise and Mpondo there was "a belt of unoccupied country some twenty miles across waving with grass, intersected by no roads. There were only one or two little narrow footpaths, hardly visible in the long grass, worn by the few travellers who passed from tribe to tribe. . . ." This neutral zone was the haunt of game and was said still to be tenanted by lions. As Key observes: "In those days [c. 1865] such a belt of unoccupied country between tribe and tribe was felt to be necessary as a protection. It would have been quite impossible for the Mpondomise to have built their kraals within measurable distance of the kraals of the Tembus. At any moment the war-cry might be shouted from hill to hill, and the cattle swept away by raiders." (Callaway 1911: 28) That this neutral zone was not always present, however, is indicated by the Rev. H. H. Dugmore's comment: "One general remark is applicable to the whole of the above tribes [Thembu, Mpondo, and Bhaca]. The limits of their respective territories are not clearly defined, and hence their 'Borderers' are frequently intermingled; which has been the occasion of many feuds, and in some instances has involved whole tribes." (Maclean 1858: 8) In the latter half of the nineteenth century the administration also found it necessary to settle displaced Mfengu between the Gcaleka and Bomvana as a buffer strip.

On the other hand, there was some tendency for tribes belonging to the same cluster to cooperate. Although politically independent of one another, segments tended to merge when one of their number was attacked. But this process was not inevitable and there are many cases in the tribal histories of intracluster feuds. There was little or no trade between these small-scale subsistence economies, apart from limited barter in salt, iron, and ochre, and the only diplomatic links between chiefdoms, apart from cluster ties, were those forged by royal intermarriage. It was expected that the marriage of a chief's great wife should be a political alliance, through marriage with the daughter of a foreign royal dynasty. Among the Xhosa there is a tradition that their chiefs should obtain wives from the Thembu royal house. Of thirty-seven instances of royal marriages collected from the histories of Xhosa, Thembu, Bhaca, and Mpondomise, well over half were contracted with other royal families, as indicated in Table 2. The comparatively large number of

TABLE 2. SOME INTERDYNASTIC MARRIAGES

Between	Xhosa	Thembu	Bhaca	Mpondomise	Mpondo	Xesibe	Bomvana	Commoner
Xhosa	1*	7	–	–	–	–	2	8
Thembu	2	–	1	1	2	–	–	–
Bhaca	–	–	–	–	1	1	–	3
Mpondomise	1	1	–	–	1	1	–	4

*With Gqunukhwebe part of Xhosa cluster but chiefs not of royal lineage. (see Soga 1931: 11-12)

commoner marriages among the Xhosa is due to the fact that these figures include the relatively small Ciskeian tribes of the Xhosa cluster (for example, Ntinde, Gasela), among whom the chieftainship does not have the prestige it enjoys in the Transkei.

These dynastic marriages tended to forge bonds between the chiefdoms, but they do not seem to have been an inhibiting factor if war broke out. In fact, on more than one occasion, they have been the cause of war. In c. 1786 the Thembu chief Ndaba contracted to marry the daughter of the Xhosa chief Rarabe, and sent only one hundred head of cattle as bridewealth. Rarabe considered this an insult and invaded Tembuland, routing the Tembu and capturing large numbers of cattle. (Soga 1930: 131-132) History repeated itself in 1870 when conflict again broke between Xhosa and Thembu, provoked by the Thembu chief, Ngangelizwe's, treatment of his Gcaleka great wife. If marriage relations are amicable, affinal bonds reinforce political *ententes*; if not they can cause friction.

Intertribal relations in preannexation Transkei, at least during the nineteenth century, appear to have been characterized by constant conflict. We have discussed the frequent factional disputes that resulted in the hiving off of dissident sections to form the present-day clusters, but interchiefdom disputes over land or stock-lifting were even more frequent. An almost constant state of enmity existed between Xhosa and Thembu despite the tradition of royal intermarriage, and the same can be said for Thembu and Mpondo. There was the ever-present danger of border quarrels between Mpondo and Mpondomise, Bhaca and Mpondo, Mpondo and Xesibe—and even the constituent tribes of a cluster warred between themselves. Marais quotes a letter written in 1795 by Marthinus Pretorius in which he states that "Captain Sambe [Ndlambe], and his son Dyka [Ngqika], and the Madanges [imiDange, all of the Xhosa cluster]" were at war with one another. (Marais 1944: 80) This was not unique.

This, then, was the state of political relations in preannexation Transkei. There does not appear to have been any indigenous incorporative tendency, rather a continuing process of increasing diversification through the segmentation and fission of the political units. The only exceptions were the six cases of tributary chiefdoms mentioned above. As the process of annexation took its course the chiefdoms were drawn into a wider political structure, lost their freedom of self-determination, and became, in effect, local governmental units within an overarching bureaucratic structure. Indeed, it was rather the subdivision of the chiefdom, the administratively demarcated "location" under an officially appointed headman, which became the building block of local administration. And yet the chiefdoms have retained their essential integrity and have recently been made the basis of a new system of Bantu Authorities. What has this meant in terms of political incorporation? What is the function of tribalism, in this sense, in the emerging Transkeian state? The rest of this essay will be an attempt to answer this question.

FROM SELF-GOVERNMENT TO LOCAL GOVERNMENT:
THE PROCESS OF INCORPORATION

Notwithstanding the fact that the chieftainship had been dealt a death-blow, it was at the time of annexation still very much alive. Although deprived of their powers to try criminal cases and forbidden to wage war or "eat up" recalcitrant tribesmen, the chiefs still retained much of their former power, and some began to chafe under the new conditions—despite the fact that many of the tribes had themselves asked to be taken over by the government, due mainly to the confusion and dissension in the area caused by the influx of new tribal groups. Thembu, Mfengu, Bhaca, Xesibe, Hlubi, Sotho, and Mpondomise had all made specific representations for British protection. Some, like Cetywayo of the Zulu (1879) and Mhlontlo of the Mpondomise (1880), made active attempts to throw off the British yoke. It was obvious that the chiefs were dangerous and were possible focuses of resistance, and their influence had to be drastically curtailed in the interests of good government.

This was effected by imposing an administrative system that cut across tribal boundaries. The Transkeian Territories were divided into twenty-seven magisterial districts that paid scant regard to the old political units. Eastern Pondoland was apportioned between five districts, Western Pondoland between three. Some districts included more than one chiefdom. In Qumbu there were Sotho, Hlubi and Mpondomise chiefs; in Mount Frere, two Bhaca chiefs; in Mqanduli there were Thembu, Bomvana, Mpondo, and Hegebe. (Van Warmelo 1935; Hammond-Tooke 1965) Occasionally a district boundary cut through a chief's domain. The districts themselves were subdivided into "locations," based more or less on the old wards, approximately thirty to a district, and over each was placed a government-appointed headman. In the majority of cases the appointee was a district chief or ward headman, but in some areas, notably Fingoland, former interpreters, clerks, policemen, and others singled out for their leadership and loyalty were appointed. Although, in fact, succession to office was almost invariably inherited, in law the headman was appointed by the government and was subject to bureaucratic rules of censure and dismissal. The chiefs, as such, were all but ignored. Appeals now went from the courts of the headmen to that of the Resident Magistrate (later styled Native Commissioner) and could bypass the chiefs' courts entirely.

The main reduction of authority was in the judicial sphere. No chief or headman was permitted to decide any criminal case, and even in civil cases their role was merely one of arbitration. Most important, they had no power to enforce their decisions, and any litigant not satisfied could bring his case to the magistrate's court where it was heard *de novo*. Magistrates had full jurisdiction in all civil cases, and appeals in cases either between whites or between whites and blacks went from their courts to the superior courts of the colony (later the Cape Province) or, in cases between Africans, to the Appeal Court of the Territories, composed of the Chief Magistrate sitting with two magistrates and five Bantu assessors. In civil cases indigenous custom was administered wherever not repugnant to, or inconsistent with, the common law. All cases of a serious nature, beyond the competency of the magistrate, were dealt with by way of preliminary examination and forwarded to the circuit court.

An important development was the passing of the Glen Grey Act in 1894, which introduced a system of local councils. By 1931 all districts had adopted the system and they were federated into the United Transkeian Territories General Council (UTTGC). Each district was divided into four electoral wards, the landowners and taxpayers in each electing one member to the district council. An additional two members were nominated by the magistrate, who acted as chairman. The UTTGC, or *Bunga*, met annually at Umtata the capital, under the chairmanship of the Chief Magistrate of the Transkei and, although its functions were purely advisory, it did provide a forum for African opinion from all over the Transkei. Tribalism, as such, was irrelevant and, although a majority of chiefs and headmen were in fact elected, the General Council contained a fair number of the more progressive and educated commoners.[9]

A third development took place in 1951 with the passing of the Bantu Authorities Act. Under the new system administration was to be based not, as formerly, on the location headmen, but on the chief. The building block of the system was, and is, the *tribal authority*, which governs a group of locations owing allegiance to a chief. Tribal authorities belonging to the same tribal cluster or (where an area has a mixed population) in the same general area are grouped together in a *regional authority*, and the nine regional authorities together made up the Transkeian Territorial Authority, the legal successor to the Bunga. Between the tribal and regional authority has been interposed the (probably temporary) *district authority* to facilitate the transfer from the previous system of district administration. Bantu Authorities can be seen as an attempt to effect a synthesis between the three "strands" of local governmental structures that existed side by side in the Transkei. Despite the establishment of the white bureaucracy, the informal moots and courts of headman and chief continued to function, and at the same time the Council system, based on popular elections, provided a third mechanism for local government. The new system envisaged the integration of these three structures into one. (Hammond-Tooke 1964)

An important development was the passing of the Glen Grey Act in 1894, which introduced a system of local councils. By 1931 all districts had adopted the system and they were federated into the United Transkeian Territories General Council (UTTGC). Each district was divided into four electoral wards, the landowners and taxpayers in each electing one member to the district council. An additional two members were nominated by the magistrate, who acted as chairman. The UTTGC, or Bunga, met annually at Umtata the capital, under the chairmanship of the Chief Magistrate of the Transkei and, although its functions were purely advisory, it did provide a forum for African opinion from all over the Transkei. Tribalism, as such, was irrelevant and, although a majority of chiefs and headmen were in fact elected, the General Council contained a fair number of the more progressive and educated commoners.[9]

A third development took place in 1951 with the passing of the Bantu Authorities Act. Under the new system administration was to be based not, as formerly, on the location headmen, but on the chief. The building block of the system was, and is, the tribal authority, which governs a group of locations owing allegiance to a chief. Tribal authorities belonging to the same tribal cluster or (where an area has a mixed population) in the same general area are grouped together in a regional authority, and the nine regional authorities together made up the Transkeian Territorial Authority, the legal successor to the Bunga. Between the tribal and regional authority has been interposed the (probably temporary) district authority to facilitate the transfer from the previous system of district administration. Bantu Authorities can be seen as an attempt to effect a synthesis between the three "strands" of local governmental structures that existed side by side in the Transkei. Despite the establishment of the white bureaucracy, the informal moots and courts of headman and chief continued to function, and at the same time the Council system, based on popular elections, provided a third mechanism for local government. The new system envisaged the integration of these three structures into one. (Hammond-Tooke 1964)

Finally, in 1963, elections were held in the Transkei and in the main urban areas for a Legislative Assembly which thus supplanted the short-lived Territorial Authority. All sixty-four tribal chiefs are ex-officio members of this body, outnumbering the forty-five elected members, and the Chief Magistrate has been superseded by the Chief Minister and his Cabinet.

This, then, has been the formal process of political incorporation in the Transkei. The atomism of the traditional structures has been countered all along the line by administrative action that has sought to weld the chiefdoms into a common system. Even the Bantu Authority system, despite its anachronistic emphasis on the chiefdoms, envisages the whole area as a common political unit and, indeed, was only accepted by the General Council on the understanding that it would not interfere with the "solidarity of the Transkei." (Terms of Reference, 1955 Recess Committee)

THE INCORPORATIVE PROCESS AND THE ROLE OF TRIBALISM

Political incorporation in the Transkei, then, had little if any indigenous pattern which could provide a model, unlike the expanding conquest states of Zulu and Ndebele or the assimilative "diplomatic" state of Moshesh's Sotho. There *was* incorporation on the level of individuals, groups, and even whole tribes (in fact confined to the aforementioned Hegebe, Gqunukhwebe, Tshangase, Ngutyana, Zizi, and Qwathi), who achieved citizenship by acknowledging the authority of an alien chief—particularly since annexation, when the demarcation of tribal land gave a *territorial* dimension to citizenship—but there was no tendency for the large-scale coalescence of chiefdoms. As in many new African states, wider-scale interaction within a larger territorial framework was the result of explicit, self-conscious administrative action on the part of the colonial power. The impetus for incorporation was external and, in a sense, artificial. What have been the implications of the process in terms of acceptance by the peoples of the Transkei? More specifically, what is the role of tribalism[10] as a category of interaction, in the present administrative and political system, and to what extent have these changes been followed by structural and cultural incorporative processes?

Generally speaking imposed political incorporation has stimulated incorporation on all other levels. As we have seen, the imposition of the *Pax Capensis* put an end to intertribal wars and permitted free movement between the chiefdoms. This has resulted in the increasingly heterogeneous compositon of these groups (in one Mpondomise location no less than thirty-four different clans, many non-Mpondomise, were represented) and the development of the aforementioned network of agnatic links that give most people relatives in other tribes. Visiting throughout the Transkei is becoming increasingly common, not only for purely social but for ritual reasons also, as when a lineage head travels to another district to officiate at a piacular sacrifice for a member of his scattered lineage. A network of bus routes throughout the Transkei has today made most areas rather easily accessible. Affinal links are also becoming increasingly important, although, as we have seen, they are not as significant due to the tendency to chiefdom endogamy.

The breakdown of the self-sufficiency of the small-scale subsistence units was the inevitable result of limitation on land and fast-growing human and stock population. In the period 1904-1961 the population of the Transkei increased from 801,330 persons to almost 1.5 million, and population density averages 89 persons per square mile. (Umtata 100; Willowvale 134; Mount Frere 82) Overstocking for these three districts is 40 percent, 83 percent, and 25 percent respectively. The net result of this is that most able-bodied men are forced to seek work at the labor centers, where they come into contact with other Transkeians. The importance of tribal categories varies with the urban area in which they meet and interact. In Johannesburg and the towns of the Transvaal, where there is considerable tribal diversity, the main cleavage is between Nguni- and Sotho-speakers, but in East London (Mayer 1961) and Cape Town (Wilson 1963: 34-37; 113-131) the vast majority are Cape Nguni. Wilson states (1963: 34) that tribalism among workers in Cape Town is of little significance, although tribal names are used. "But tribal names from within the same linguistic group are rapidly being reduced to the same level as clan names. In town they are being overshadowed by the country-town cleavage." (1963: 35) Even the traditional "tribal days" (the Mfengu Emancipation Day on May 14, the Xhosa Ntsikana Day on March 14, and Moshesh Day on March 12) have always been a rather self-conscious innovation of the westernized "school people" which is being increasingly criticized as sectional. More and more Transkeian expatriates are thinking of themselves as Transkeian citizens and less as members of tribes.

On the more specifically economic level there is also greater interaction between tribes. Farmers' Associations bring together a limited number in pursuit of a common interest. In 1961 the four zones into which the Transkei is divided for this purpose had 255 associations for men with a membership of 4,340, and 302 for women with 5,911 members, and 17 district shows were held with a total attendance of nearly 12,000 people. (TTA 1962: xvii) This type of interaction breaks down tribal exclusiveness, at least within the zones. All are involved in a unified monetary system and the widespread incidence of trade goods is obliterating tribal diacritical signs of dress and details of material culture. African traders do not necessarily set up their stores in their home areas and the recent move to form a Traders' Association will create further interaction on the intertribal level. The same can be said for other occupational groupings, particularly the civil servants. Clerks, interpreters, teachers, police, dipping foremen, forest guards, and agricultural demonstrators are appointed irrespective of tribe and district of domicile, and they and their families form pockets of settlement throughout the Transkei. In June 1964 there were approximately 2,500 permanent posts in the Transkeian Civil Service, plus some 10,000 other posts for laborers. (Horrell 1965: 148)

Clerks, teachers, and interpreters are particularly significant in this respect, as they tend to form a reference group in a cultural sense to which the "school" peasant aspires and, therefore, constitute an important stimulus for the incorporation of Western wants and values. The schools that are found throughout the Transkei (there were 1,637 in 1964, employing about 5,000 teachers—Horell 1965: 147) are, of course, the chief agents for the diffusion of Western skills and attitudes. Standard *isiXhosa* is taught, tending to iron out dialectal variations. Borders from all over the Transkei attend the five secondary institutions, and interschool competitions, particularly by choirs, tend to break down parochialism. After a brief experiment in mother-tongue education until Standard VI, the Legislative Assembly has ruled that from Standard III on English or Afrikaans should be gradually substituted as a medium of instruction, thus providing for wider intellectual and communicative horizons.

In the religious sphere the introduction of Christianity in the nineteenth century has established associations which cut across tribal boundaries and has created a far-reaching dichotomy between "believers" (*amakholwa, amagqoboko*) and pagans (*amaqaba*). This cleavage between what Mayer has called "Red" and "School" has been well documented. (Hunter 1936, Mayer 1961, Hammond-Tooke 1962, Pauw 1965) There is some tendency for Christians to stand aloof from active participation in tribal government, although this is more true of participation in the tribal rituals of rainmaking and first fruits. (Hammond-Tooke 1962: 312) Although local congregations cater to local needs, the Church, with its emphasis on Christian brotherhood, stresses universal rather than tribal loyalties. It is significant that the sectional Zionist sects are not, generally speaking, characteristic of the Transkei (Pauw: personal communication) and the only example of tribalism in this context is the short-lived Thembu Church founded by Nehemiah Tile in 1884, with the chief Ngangelizwe at its head. (Sundkler 1948: 38) Most Transkeians belong to one or another of the white mission churches and, for example, Umtata Cathedral was packed with Africans from all over the Diocese of St. John at its reconsecration in 1963. The tribal or communal religion, that is, rituals involving the propitiation of chiefly ancestors, is dying, but on the other hand, the strength of the lineage-based ritual communities appears to have remarkable vitality. Both Dr. Pauw and the author have been struck by the constant reference to ancestral shades by committed Christians to whom, as among pagans, the shades appear in dreams. Frequently they act as a moral force, for example, by warning against drunkenness and immorality, and not a few religious conversions have been due to their intervention. In a sense the shades themselves have become christianized!

Finally, what of incorporation on the political level? Intertribal cooperation has been built, as it were, into the various administrative systems that have functioned in the Transkei since annexation. The General Council system ignored tribalism as such and relied heavily on the services of the more progressive "school people." Of the 84 African members present at the Special Session of the UTTGC in November 1955, 13 were chiefs (4 Paramount Chiefs *ex-officio*), 51 headmen and 20 commoners, but commoner representation was much higher at the district-council level. Little if any indication of tribal rivalries emerged in the proceedings of this Council, apart from a frequent plea, particularly from Pondoland representatives, for greater powers for the chiefs. (Hunter 1936: 430 and UTTGC Proceedings) Local interests were of course put forward, but there appears to have been a clear conception of the Transkei as a single administrative unit with well-defined common interests. In fact, the most pronounced example of sectional loyalties was found at the location level. In view of their comparatively recent origin, a quite remarkable location loyalty has developed and the faction fights, which still break out sporadically, are almost invariably interlocation rather than intertribal. This is particularly the case at weddings, where visiting youths arrive in location-based gangs and compete in dancing and for the favors of girls. Trespassing on location boundaries is also a frequent source of litigation.[11]

While it is true that the Bantu Authority system is explicitly based on the original chiefdoms, it, too, is incorporative, as tribalism operates only at the level of the individual tribal authorities. They are merely units within the wider structure of the Transkei and are themselves grouped into district and regional authorities. Where a district contains more than one chiefdom, the chiefs take the chairmanship of the district authority in rotation and the same goes for the regional authority, except where it consists of a tribal cluster with its well-defined paramountcy. The short-lived Transkeian Territorial Authority consisted of 64 chiefs (many newly appointed), 39 headmen, and 17 commoners.

It is true that when the demarcation of tribal authorities in preparation for the establishment of the new system was first begun, there was a period of heightened tribal consciousness. It became necessary to appoint chiefs, wherever possible, to head these authorities, and extensive research was undertaken to establish legitimate claims. The Chief Magistrate's office was inun-

dated with letters from obscure headmen, invariably accompanied by genealogies, claiming chieftainship over some small groups that had entered the
Transkei during the post-Tshakan migrations. More particularly, alien tribal
segments that had become incorporated into larger chiefdoms now saw their
opportunity to achieve independence and there was a general "shake up" of
political alignments that had, over the years, achieved a certain equilibrium.
In the great majority of cases these claims were resisted, on good historical
grounds, and, in fact, few if any chiefs lost supporters. There were exceptions. One source of tension was the promotion of Chief Kaizer Mathanzima
of the Hala (Thembu) tribe of St. Marks (and present Chief Minister) to
regional chief of Emigrant Tembuland. It was considered that Tembuland was
too large to form one regional authority and, as Kaizer was the senior cluster
chief in the St. Mark's-Xalanga area, he was appointed its head. The resent-
ment of the Paramount Chief, Sabata Dalindyebo, at this imagined threat to
his status (Kaizer persistently styled himself "Paramount Chief of Emigrant
Tembuland") was the initial cause of the antagonism between these two
leaders, which thus stems from intracluster politics. (Hammond-Tooke 1964:
521; Carter 1967) By 1957 the number of chiefs in the Transkei had more
than doubled (from 30 to 64), among the most important appointments
being three Mfengu chiefs in Fingoland: for the Hlubi, Zizi, and Bhele tribes
respectively. In effect the demarcation of the tribal authorities was achieved
with little, if any, dislocation of the *de facto* tribal distribution: the main
change was the status-raising of legitimate heirs of defunct or latent chieftainships.

The introduction of the Legislative Assembly in 1963, with its 64 chiefs
and 45 elected members, who now interact on a political rather than administrative level, would seem to provide ample scope for tribal rivalries. In fact,
political cleavages have not, to any great extent, followed tribal lines.

The first indication of emerging political alignment occurred within the
Thembu tribal cluster when Chief Mathanzima, a graduate and qualified law-
yer, emerged as a strong supporter of separate development. His Paramount,
probably originally from personal motives (see above), immediately joined
forces with Paramount Chief Victor Poto of Western Pondoland to form the
Transkei Democratic Party, dedicated to so-called "multiracialism," the other
chiefs aligning themselves in terms of this party and Mathanzima's Transkei
Independence Party. The election on November 20, 1963 was fought on the
issue of separate development versus multiracialism. Poto won between 35
and 38 of the 45 elected seats, but Mathanzima was elected Chief Minister by
54 votes to 49 in the combined Assembly. It is clear that up to now tribal
affiliations have not determined political alignments, and the distribution of

tribes between government and opposition does not, by any means, follow cluster allegiances. An analysis of the voting in the No Confidence debate at the second session of the Legislative Assembly in 1964 shows that both government and opposition include chiefs from Thembu, Bhele, and Mpondo clusters. (Transkei Hansard 1964: 45-46)

What of the future? The above analysis has shown that the Transkei has achieved a remarkable homogeneity of outlook and a strong sense of corporate identity. Strong forces operate to merge tribal differences within a wider political framework and the particularism of the small-scale chiefdoms is increasingly giving way to wide-scale relations in the social, economic, religious, and political sectors. There has not, as yet, occurred the resurgence of tribalism characteristic of some other African states after independence. Conceivably this is due to the fact that the Transkei is still in a dependency situation. White control is retained over defense, external affairs, police, telecommunications, roads, immigration, currency, and finance, and it is possible that divisive tendencies are being repressed during these crucial formative years of the new state.

Political incorporation was something new to the Cape Nguni, whose pre-annexation political systems were atomistic and shot through with conflict. Yet, probably due to cultural uniformity, the emasculation of the chieftainships, and the black-white cleavage that dominates South Africa, the administrative, economic, and religious changes of the last seventy years have achieved a remarkably homogeneous structure in which intergroup conflict flows from differing political goals rather than from the traditional categories of tribalism.

NOTES

1. For further details of this process see Hammond-Tooke 1966, Campbell 1959, and Brownlee 1923.

2. I use the terms "tribe" and "chiefdom" interchangeably.

3. See the following for further details of specific tribes: Hunter 1936 (Mpondo); Soga 1931 (Xhosa); Cook 1931 (Bomvana); Hammond-Tooke 1962 (Bhaca).

4. *Mfengu.* This is a residual category which excludes the Hlubi, Zizi, and Bhele, who are also classed as Mfengu.

5. This is particularly so today, as with the introduction of trade cloth, different tribal styles, especially in women's dress, have become traditional. Married women of the Xhosa, Thembu, Mpondomise, and Khonjwayo wear blankets ochred to a terra cotta, edged with black braid; Mfengu ochre is deep red; and beads and mother-of-pearl buttons are favored as trimming. Bhaca and Xesibe women dress in fat-smeared goatskins and the Mpondo effect white blankets. Formerly the men of all these tribes went naked but for a penis sheath.

6. A full discussion of the composition of these tribal clusters and the formation of new chiefdoms will be found in Hammond-Tooke 1965.

7. I retain the South African term "location" for this modern territorial unit and use "ward" for the area under the traditional headman. A location averages six or seven square miles and includes four or more neighborhoods (location sections), each under a subheadman appointed (unofficially) by the headman. Despite considerable heterogeneity, neighborhoods still tend to be settled by a dominant lineage or lineage segment.

8. It is interesting, in this connection, that two French demographers, J. Sutter and L. Tabah, have succeeded in computing the average size of what they call marriage "isolates" in all French *départments*, and have found that they have an average size varying from less than 1,000 to over 2,800 individuals, *irrespective of the size of the area involved*. This is quoted in Levi-Strauss 1963: 294.

9. For a more detailed description of the General Council system see Rodgers 1933, Hammond-Tooke 1964, 1968, Hailey 1938, Hunter 1936: 430-433, Brookes 1927.

10. I here use the term "tribalism" as Mitchell (1956, 1960) uses it in his Copperbelt studies—a concept that determines relations between persons interacting within a wider social field (for example, an urban area, the Transkei as a whole) in terms of their membership in small-scale cultural and/or political units.

11. It will be interesting to see the effect of the Bantu Authority system on location solidarity, with its merging of locations into the tribal authority.

REFERENCES

Bird, J. 1888. *Annals of Natal*. vol. 1: 27-56.

Brookes, E. H. 1927. *History of native policy in South Africa*. Pretoria.

Brownles, F. 1923. *The Transkeian native territories: historical records*. Lovedale, Lovedale Press.

Callaway, G. 1911. *A shepherd of the veld*. London.

Campbell, W. B. 1959. "The South African frontier, 1865-1885: a study in expansion." *Archives Yearbook for South African History* 1, esp. Chapter 2.

Carter, G., T. Karis, and N. Stultz. 1966. *South Africa's Transkei: The politics of domestic colonialism*. Evanston, Northwestern University Press.

Cook, P. A. W. 1931. *The social organization and ceremonial institutions of the Bomvana*. Cape Town.

Hailey, Lord. 1938. *An African survey*. London, Oxford University Press.

Hammond-Tooke, D. 1957. *The tribes of the Umtata District*. Pretoria.

1962. *Bhaca society*. Cape Town, Oxford University Press.

1963. "Kinship, locality and association: hospitality groups among the Cape Nguni." *Ethnology* 2(3): 302-319.

1964. "Chieftainship in Transkeian political development." *Journal of Modern African Studies* 2(4): 513-529.

1965. "Segmentation and fission in Cape Nguni political units." *Africa* 35(2): 143-166.

1966. Chapter 4 in G. Carter, T. Karis, and N. Stultz. *South Africa's Transkei*.

1968. "The Transkeian council system 1845-1955: an appraisal." *Journal of African History* 9(3): 455-477.

Hobart Houghton, D., and E. M. Walton. 1952. *The economy of a native reserve*. Pietermaritzburg.

Horrell, M. 1965. *A survey of race relations in South Africa*. Johannesburg.

Hunter, M. 1936. *Reaction to conquest*. London, Oxford University Press.

Levi-Strauss, C. 1963. *Structural anthropology*. New York, Basic Books.

MacLean, J. 1858. *A compendium of Kafir laws and customs*. (1906 edition).

Marais, J. S. 1944. *Maynier and the First Boer Republic*. Cape Town.

Mayer, P. 1961. *Townsmen or tribesmen*. Cape Town, Oxford University Press.

Mitchell, J. C. 1956. *The Kalela dance*. Manchester, Manchester University Press.

1960. *Tribalism and the plural society*. London, Oxford University Press.

Nel, D. E. 1957. "A geographical outline of the Transkeian territories." *Journal for Geography* 1(1): 51-61.

Pauw, B. A. 1965. "Patterns of Christianization among the Tswana and the Xhosa-speaking peoples," in M. Fortes and G. Dieterlen (eds.). *African systems of thought*. London, Oxford University Press.

Rodgers, H. 1933. *Native administration in the Union of South Africa*. Johannesburg.

Schapera, I. 1956. *Government and politics in tribal society*. London, Watts.

Soga, J. H. 1930. *The south-eastern Bantu*. Johannesburg.

1931. *The Ama-Xosa: life and customs*. Lovedale.

Sundkler, B. 1948. *Bantu prophets in South Africa*. London, Lutterworth.

Transkei Government. 1964. *Hansard*. Umtata.

Transkeian Territorial Authority. 1962. *Proceedings and reports of select committees at session of 1962*. Umtata.

Van Warmelo, N. J. 1936. *Preliminary survey of the Bantu tribes of South Africa*. Pretoria, Government Printer.

Wilson, M. 1951. "Witch beliefs and social structure," *American Journal of Sociology* 56: 307-313.

1959. "The early history of the Transkei and Ciskei." *African Studies* 18(4): 167-179.

1963. *Langa*. Cape Town.

11

URBAN PLURALISM, INTEGRATION, AND ADAPTATION OF COMMUNAL IDENTITY IN KANO, NIGERIA

John N. Paden

INTRODUCTION

The Kano urban context in Northern Nigeria may contribute to the understanding of ethnic incorporation in several respects. While Kano has been an urban "melting pot" for at least nine centuries, it has also exhibited some of the classic characteristics of a plural society. Even in the mid-twentieth century, when interethnic integration within Kano City has progressed to a high degree, the residue of residential segregation is a reminder of past ethnic diversity. Since Kano City has never been destroyed or dislocated physically, the settlement patterns of today give clear clues to the ethnic migrations of past centuries.

The argument of this essay is as follows: Because of the considerable experience of Kano urban people with migrants, a complex of categories had arisen to accommodate the various types of communal identity. However, in the twentieth century, new pressures developed which resulted in an unprecedented degree of migration into Kano City. The most important of these pressures was the introduction of groundnuts as a cash crop during the 1920s and the establishment of the Kano urban area as the groundnut capital of Northern Nigeria. The dramatic increase in urban migration from the rural areas pushed traditional incorporation mechanisms, mainly the family or clan structures, beyond their capacity to function effectively. Partly to fill this breach, the Islamic religious brotherhoods expanded considerably. They became major mechanisms of incorporation into the urban system. During the 1930s these brotherhoods extended themselves to a trans-ethnic base for the first time in Kano history.

Partly as a result of this religious contact, a greater degree of social integration occurred during the 1940s. Intermarriage became common between

Hausa and Fulani sectors. During the 1950s, political structures were developed for the first time to link these two sectors into a common framework. The resultant product in the 1960s has been a Kano city-state nationalism, which goes well beyond structural integration to the point of a new urban-communal identity. For various reasons, this essay will not assess in detail the impact of unassimilated southern migrant communities on the integration of northern ethnic groups.

After delimiting the patterns and development of urban pluralism and ethnic integration, this essay will examine the extent to which the conceptual *categories* of communal identity in Kano have been functional or dysfunctional to the process of integration. The process of integration will be considered as consisting of three stages: interactions and transactions, functional interdependency, and value congruence. The units to be linked by this process could be any specified group, class, or organization but in this essay will include only ethnic groups. As a preliminary, however, it is useful to summarize some of the conceptual dimensions of urban ethnicity, in contradistinction to rural ethnicity.

CONCEPTS OF URBAN ETHNICITY

ETHNICITY AND ETHNIC GROUP FORMATION

A number of processes seem to result in ethnic group formation. Within the broadest context, ethnicity is a combination of in-group and out-group ascriptions as to the boundaries which significantly distinguish communities. The process of *fusion* may occur when a new and larger reference system develops significant additions to the group of external perceivers. Gellner suggests that this external source of classification may be arbitrary, but we may conclude from his example of the Kabyles that they did not "become" an ethnic unit as a result of external political pressure. (Gellner 1965: 116)

The reverse process may occur with a constricting of the sociopolitical system. Internal cleavages may develop into boundaries which have the effect of turning subsystems into fully functioning ethnic units. A major source of such division has been the introduction of a universalistic religion which is accepted by only a portion of the original ethnic group. Those who do not convert become known as one ethnic unit, and the converts come to act as a separate unit.

An additional type of ethnic group formation is related to ethnic assimilation and restratification. Within a given system, the upward mobility of a certain group may result either in assimilation, or in creating a new mode-of-

intricate ethnic mosaic of the country-side becomes simplified to a manage-able number of ethnic categories. A sense of membership in a group signifi-cantly expanded in scale from the clan and lineage system of the very local-ized rural "tribal" community develops. (1967: 30)

An example of reduction and ethnic emergence cited by Anderson, von der Mehden, and Young (1967: 31) is the case of the so-called Bangala of Kin-shasa. No rural ethnic counterpart exists to the urban category of Bangala.

One final observation should be made regarding emergent urban ethnicity. The external criteria of communal identity may or may not be similar to rural ethnicity. New types of communal groups may emerge in an urban context, which have no counterpart in the rural context. One example of this might be occupational communality. Audrey Richards (1966: 361) has suggested that occupational groups with strong sociocultural perimeters, such as the civil service community, may come to be regarded as ethnic groups. She attributes such a development to the replacement of European urban officials by Afri-cans who have no strong personal identification with any of the more tradi-tional ethnic groups. Other examples of communal identity based on occupa-tion might include the university communities and the prostitute communi-ties. In all cases, the criteria of ethnicity would be whether the occupational roles are essentially "communal" or "associational." If communal, the group tends toward a separate cultural identity; if associational, the group is inter-acting, but members are maintatining cultural membership in other groups.

URBAN PLURALISM IN KANO

THE KANO URBAN AREA

The Kano urban area consisted of one-quarter million persons in 1963. This urban area has been divided into three parts: Kano City (*Birni*), the "Outside" migrant area (*Waje*), and the former European quarter or township (*Nassarawa*). The city itself is divided into four districts (*fuska*) and one hundred twenty-seven wards (*unguwa*).

Prior to the twentieth century Kano City was not formally subdivided into administrative units. However, there were "sections" of the town, consisting primarily of ethnic, descent, and/or occupational groups. These sections have become the contemporary wards. At the turn of the century there were ten major sections in Kano City: Zungwo, Goran Dama, Madabo, Chediya, Jun-gau, Sheshe, Dalma, Makama, Shetima, and Chigari. Within these broad ward-sections were subsections with distinctive ethnic characteristics. Thus, the Madabo section included Hausa descent groups and migrant groups such as

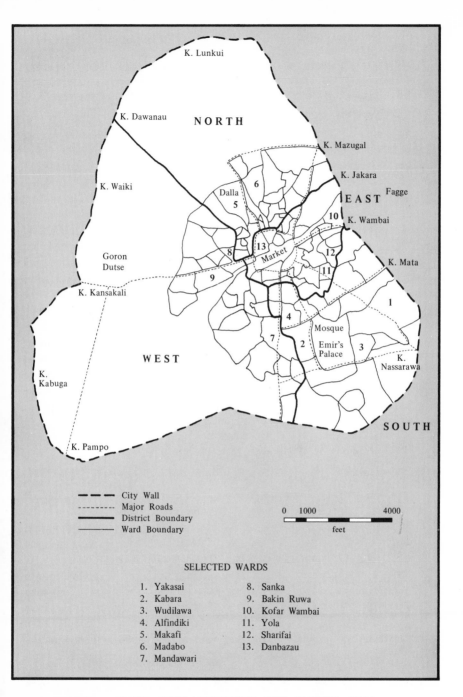

K. Lunkui

K. Dawanau   **N O R T H**

K. Mazugal

K. Jakara

K. Waiki   Dalla   **6**   Fagge
            5   **E A S T**

            10   K. Wambai

Goron   **8**   **13**   **12**   K. Mata
Dutse   Market

K. Kansakali   **9**   **11**

                1

        4

    WEST   **7**   **2**   Mosque   **3**
                Emir's   K.
K.   Palace   Nassarawa
Kabuga

                    SOUTH

K. Pampo

- - - City Wall
.... Major Roads
━━━ District Boundary
─── Ward Boundary

0   1000   4000
        feet

SELECTED WARDS

1. Yakasai   8. Sanka
2. Kabara   9. Bakin Ruwa
3. Wudilawa   10. Kofar Wambai
4. Alfindiki   11. Yola
5. Makafi   12. Sharifai
6. Madabo   13. Danbazau
7. Mandawari

MAP 4. KANO CITY DISTRICTS AND WARDS, 1964

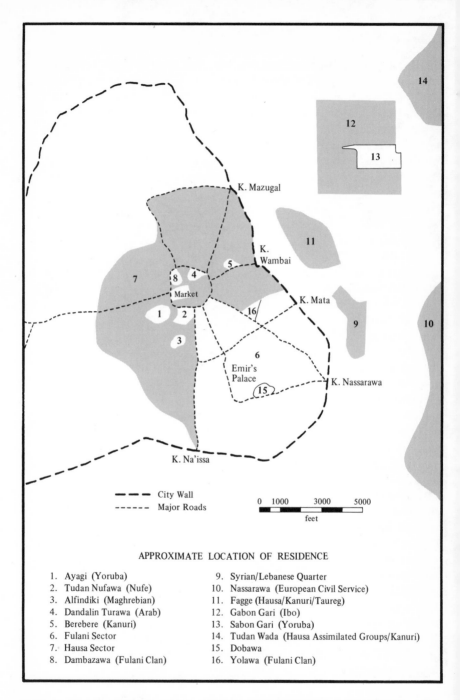

- - - City Wall
----- Major Roads

0 1000   3000   5000
feet

APPROXIMATE LOCATION OF RESIDENCE

1. Ayagi (Yoruba)
2. Tudan Nufawa (Nufe)
3. Alfindiki (Maghrebian)
4. Dandalin Turawa (Arab)
5. Berebere (Kanuri)
6. Fulani Sector
7. Hausa Sector
8. Dambazawa (Fulani Clan)

9. Syrian/Lebanese Quarter
10. Nassarawa (European Civil Service)
11. Fagge (Hausa/Kanuri/Taureg)
12. Gabon Gari (Ibo)
13. Sabon Gari (Yoruba)
14. Tudan Wada (Hausa Assimilated Groups/Kanuri)
15. Dobawa
16. Yolawa (Fulani Clan)

MAP 5. KANO URBAN AREA ETHNIC-RESIDENTIAL LOCATIONS, 1960

the Zeitawa, Dururawa, and Sankawa, who had come to Kano before the Jihad from "Wangara." The Chediya section included the important Hausa ward of Bakin Ruwa, a triangle stretching west from the market toward Goron Dutse and containing some of the original Hausa peoples of Kano. Chediya also contained most of the Arab quarter, and especially those Arabs who had left Katsina for Kano after the Fulani Jihad. Sheshe was identified with a pre-Jihad migrant group from Birnin Shem, reputedly of Arab origins. Dalma included many Fulani descent groups, as well as the Sharifai area containing those identified with al-Maghili, who claimed descent from the Prophet Muhammad. This area also contained migrant groups of Nupe (Nufa-wa ward) and Tuareg (Agadasawa ward), plus such Fulani groups as the Kurawa and Yolawa.

The division of the original ten sections into one hundred twenty-seven wards was largely for purposes of colonial administrative convenience. These wards were grouped in four "districts": South (*Fuskar Kudu*), East (*Fuskar Gabas*), North (*Fuskar Arewa*), and West (*Fuskar Yamma*). Within these four districts, there has been a clear pattern of Hausa ethnic group residence in Kano West and North, and Fulani group residence in Kano South and East. The characteristics and population distribution of each district would include the following: (1) *Kano South* (52,098) is the main area of Fulani settlement, and the seat of Native Authority government and housing. (2) *Kano East* (40,596) is the location of the central market and is inhabited by laborers and traders. (3) *Kano North* (32,060) is the most recently settled of the districts, and was formerly used for cattle grazing. Much of this unoccupied land was given by Kano Emirs to the new class of Hausa businessmen in the past fifty years. (4) *Kano West* (40,383), center of the original Hausa settlement, is inhabited today by craftsmen and traders.

The walled city of Kano serves as the seat of urban government, yet the twentieth century has seen the growth of important migrant communities to the east of the walled city. Thus the total urban area has come to include: (1) *Kano City* (165,455), the traditional walled city, which, with certain exceptions, was restricted to Muslim Hausa-Fulani inhabitants. (2) *The "Out-side" migrant area* (83,584), which was comprised of four subsections—*Fagge*, originally a camping site for Niger caravans in the nineteenth century, but later a modern Hausa district and commercial center; *Sabon Gari*, consisting mainly of Ibo and Yoruba immigrants and including a large market; *Tudun Wada* and *Gwagwara*, both recently settled areas of Northern (Muslim) immi-grants. (3) *Township* (9,246) formerly the Government Residential Area and later populated by civil servants and expatriate commercial residents.

In the twentieth century, Kano has evidenced an extremely high rate of urban migration. On the basis of census figures over a fifty-year period (1911-1962) the Kano urban area has increased in population by 650 percent. Furthermore, this increase was from a significant starting point, since Kano City was probably the largest urban center in Sudanic West Africa in the nineteenth century.

The ethnic pluralism of twentieth-century urban Kano can be best understood through longitudinal examination. Kano people regard their precolonial history as falling into four categories. The Abagayawa and Maguzawa periods are felt to be characterized by ethnic dominance patterns. The Hausa Islamic and Fulani Islamic periods are based on a combination of ethnic and religious patterns. Ethnic dominance, religious, and migration patterns may be summarized as follows:

The Abagayawa Period (c. 850-1000 A.D.). According to legend, a blacksmith and his clan migrated from the area of Gaya (present-day Kano Emirate) to the area surrounding Dalla Hill in what is now Kano City. Because of their original location (Gaya), these people came to be known as the Abagayawa. There were no apparent ethnic migrations into the settlement of the Abagayawa, and presumably the community was relatively isolated. Very little is known about this period, and most accounts draw heavily on a manuscript entitled the "Kano Chronicle." (Palmer 1928: 92-132) The descendants of the Abagayawa still dwell in Kano near Dalla Hill, and, although Muslim-Hausa, they are still termed "Abagayawa" in certain situations. The blacksmith guild in Kano is said to have derived from this group.

The Abagayawa Period is a reference point for communal identities of later peoples in Kano, including elements of the contemporary population. There are racial and religious overtones to certain symbols of community ascribed to this period. Thus the "pagan" blacksmith kings of Dalla, the sacred place of "black water" (Bakin Ruwa), the ascribed "blackness" of the Abagayawa have blended into an image of "primitiveness" and "darkness," which set a standard in Kano literature and attitudes by which later Islamic "progress" and "civilization" could be measured.

The Maguzawa Period (1000-1500). The term "Maguzawa" refers to non-Muslim Hausa, and in the sense of "common origins" there is no difference between Hausa and Maguzawa. The Magazawa Period in Kano history is reputed to have begun in about 999 A.D., when Bagauda, who had been living with his people about halfway between Kano and Daura, conquered the Abagayawa and became the first Hausa king of Kano. The descendants of Bagauda continued to rule Kano until the Fulani Jihad in 1806. The legends as to the origin of the Hausa people are important both as indicators of migration movements and ethnic pluralism, and as a reservoir for later mythology which has been significant in the process of ethnic integration.

The Hausa legend of origins is centered around the figure of Bayajidda, who is said to have been a refugee from the internecine religious wars of Baghdad. In his migration he had passed through the kingdom of Bornu and finally arrived at Daura, where he married the Queen of Daura. The progeny of this union formed the first generation of Hausa people.

An alternative explanation assumes that Bayajidda (or "Ba-Yazid") was an individual or clan of Berber stock which migrated south from North Africa under the pressure of Arab conquests. Palmer (1928: 95-96) has suggested that the word "Hausa" was employed by these Berber migrants, although more recent linguistic evidence tends to suggest that "Hausa" was a later Songhai word for "peoples of the East." (Neil Skinner, private conversation, April 1967) The Palmer analysis remains of interest for his distinction between "Habe" and "Hausa." He recognized Hausa as a linguistic category, while Habe, he notes, was a Fulani word which referred to "any Negro race." In both explanations of Hausa origins, it is interesting that the founding patron of the Hausa people was of Arab or North African descent. According to tradition, the first Hausa Emir of Kano, Bagauda, was the grandson of Bayajidda and the Queen of Daura.

During this period a high degree of ethnic migration began to occur, and to some extent a "plural" society existed in Kano. A recently translated pre-Fulani poem in Hausa tells of peoples migrating to Kano from every direction. (Hiskett 1965: 115) During this time of growing heterogeneity many of the original Abagayawa continued to live near Dalla, although under Maguzawa authority. The Maguzawa themselves began to mix with the migrant groups.

The major transformation of Kano into a "plural" society is said to have occurred during the latter part of the Maguzawa period. The various Fulani groups, under pressure from kingdoms to the West, began migrating into the Kano area. The Fulani were nominally Muslim. At the same time, Arab and Berber Muslim "scholars," in some cases retreating from the same political pressures which affected the Fulani, began to visit Kano. According to the "Kano Chronicle," the Hausa King of Kano (Yaji) was persuaded to adopt Islam in about 1350, although recent evidence tends to place the date somewhat later. (Last and Al-Hajj 1965: 231-240) His son, however, reverted, and not until the time of Muhammad Rumfa (c. 1463-1499) did the Kano Hausa kings begin to effectively impose Islam as the official state religion. Since Rumfa, all kings of Kano have been officially "Muslim."

The Hausa Period (c. 1500-1800). With the spread of Islam in the Western Sudan, trade routes were opened up, both on a North-South and an East-West axis. Kano became a primary focal point on both of these axes. A division of labor occurred between farming and trade. Hausa commercial processes became centralized through the Kano City market. The Fulani groups were primarily pastoralists. The Hausa farmers in the rural areas around Kano continued to follow many of the Maguzawa religious and cultural patterns.

The development of Kano as a trade center established both commercial and cultural contact over a broad geographical area, including much of North Africa. The impact of such culture contact resulted in the growth of Kano as an "urban" area in all of the relevant dimensions, especially in the division of labor.

The most important consequence of the establishment of contact over a broader area was a rapid intensification of warfare; this affected ethnicity by creating "prisoners of war" from different ethnic groups, who were subsequently incorporated through concubinage into the host society. It also brought Kano under a succession of foreign conquerors, and hence Kano became part of larger systems, which were to some extent able to improve their own definitions of group identity into the "Kano" people. In 1512, Kano became a tributary to Askia of Songhai; this was followed by the successful Kebbawa conquest of Kano. In the late sixteenth century, Kano began a series of wars with Katsina which were to last from about 1570 to 1706. During the seventeenth century, the city-state was conquered by the "pagan" Jukun (Hausa: *Kwararafa*) from the South. In 1734 Kano was conquered by Bornu from the East. In all of these cases, a tributary relationship was established and trade continued as usual. Much of the necessary taxation for the tribute (which in some cases amounted to one-third of all Kano revenue), began to fall on the rural Hausa peasant. Perhaps as a partial means of "legitimizing" increased exercise of power over the "semi-Muslim" peasant, the Hausa rulers of Kano began to incorporate Maguzawa religious and cultural practices into official religious practices of the state.

Partly as a response to this de-Islamization, and partly as a response to the heavy hand of Kano central authority, many of the Fulani clans in the late eighteenth century began to agitate against the Hausa rulers in several of the Hausa city-states. Finally, a Fulani mallam of the Toronke clan declared civil war against the rulers of Gobir. The "Jihad" of Usman dan Fodio spread to other city-states, and in 1806, the Fulani forces defeated Muhammad Alwali, the Hausa emir of Kano, and brought to an end the Hausa dynasty which had ruled since the time of Bagauda.

The Fulani Period (c. 1806-1903). Establishment of the Fulani government marked the beginning of an ethnic stratification pattern which continued essentially unchanged into the colonial period. During the nineteenth century threats of invasion and various wars seemed to dominate the Kano political scene, but were not able to fuse the Hausa and Fulani groups except in some of the border areas where the non-Muslim Ningi were in a constant state of attack. The first European traveler had visited Kano in 1826, followed in the second half of the century by a number of explorers from Europe. Later still, the British declared the Northern Provinces a protectorate in 1900, and in 1903 they enforced this proclamation by conquering Kano. Twentieth-century migrations and system changes will be mentioned below.

ETHNIC-UNIT CHARACTERISTICS IN URBAN KANO

The traditionally relevant ethnic groups in and around Kano City are, and have been for many years, the Hausa, Fulani, Kanuri, Arab, Tuareg, Nupe, and Yoruba. A brief description of each will provide a basis for understanding their similarities and differences as well as the relations between them.

The *Hausa* may be regarded either as an ethnic group or as a language group. The reason for different criteria between these two categories has been the strong assimilationist tendencies of the Hausa "ethnic group," and the widespread use of Hausa as a *lingua franca.* These processes have been so extensive that the "official" position in recent years has been to regard the Hausa as a language group and no longer as an ethnic group. According to the Northern Nigerian Census of 1921, "Under Hausa are included the Hausa-speaking Agalawa, Gimbanawa, Maguzawa, Shirawa, Teschinawa, and Wangarawa, in addition to the well-recognized Hausa groups such as the Hausa speaking peoples of Kano, Katsina, Gobir, Zamfara, Kebbi, Daura, Hadejia, etc." (Meek 1925: II, 174) And this same criteria was used thirty years later in the census of 1952: "The Hausa are simply a linguistic group consisting of those who speak the Hausa language as their mother tongue and do not claim Fulani descent, and including a wide variety of stocks and physical types . . ." (Department of Statistics 1953: 10)

In this essay the term "Hausa" will be used in the narrower sense of perceived kinship, unless otherwise stated. The original scope of Hausaland was an area of about 200 square miles which included seven city-states: Daura, Kano, Rano, Katsina, Zazzau, Gobir, and Garun Gabas. These city-states shared a common myth of origin, common cultural patterns, and a common language. In general, Hausa society was bilateral tending towards patrilineal descent among the upper-class political leadership and the Muslim religious leaders; it was also hierarchical in most of its functionally important social relations.

Hausa dialects developed in all of the city-states, but those of major importance were Kananci (Kano), Gobirci (Gobir), Katsinanci (Katsina), Zazzaganci (Zaria), Adrarci (Adrar), and Sakkwatanci (Sokoto). These are all mutually intelligible. During the colonial period, the Kano dialect became widespread in Northern Nigeria as an administrative and commercial language.

The non-Muslim Hausa (Maguzawa) have been regarded for census purposes as a separate ethnic unit and were estimated to number only 49,659 within Kano Province. (Department of Statistics 1953: Table II) They are concentrated in the rural districts of Gwarzo, Karaye, Sumaila, Tudun, Wada, Dawakin Tofa, and Bici. Within Kano City, they have been connected historically with the wards of Darma, Sharifai, Yakasai, Girki, and Shasha.

The *Fulani* ethnic groups regard themselves as having a common ancestor, who was the product of a marriage between an Arab Muslim military commander and a Jewish woman from Palestine. This group is said to have migrated to Morocco, and at some unspecified time migrated further to Senegal, acquiring in the process their distinctive features and language. The Fulani practice patrilineal descent, and in their role as pastoralists have been characterized as having a segmentary clan structure. A range of dialects exists to the extent that a Fulani from Senegal would have difficulty understanding a Cameroon Fulani.

With the settlement of Fulani in villages and later in towns, the distinctions based on lineage cleavages became less important than distinctions based on "mode of life." By the beginning of the twentieth century, the Fulani themselves distinguished three different groups: the nomadic cattle pastoralists (*Bororo*), the settled villagers (*Fulanin Kauye*), and the urban dwellers (*Fulanin Gida*). Each of these three groups can be described as having different culture patterns and even different languages (since urban dwellers increasingly spoke Hausa rather than Fulfulde). It was the urban Fulani who supplied the administrative class both in the nineteenth and twentieth centuries. The urban Fulani social structures have become hierarchical. With the assimilation of Fulani urban groups into Hausa urban culture, the identity "Fulani" is used only situationally.

The major Fulani subgroups in Kano at the time of the Jihad included the Sullubawa (who lived in Kuri ward and near Kofar Na Isa), the Dambazawa (of Dambazawa ward and Dambatta district), the Yolawa (or Yola ward), the Mundabawa (of Dawakin Tofa ward), the Danejawa ward and Bici district), and the Ginawa, a nonruling group from which most of the judicial appointees were later recruited. In addition Palmer (NAK/SNP 15 no. 367, 1907: 16) mentions four clans of wealthy Kano Fulani who did not join the Jihad, and were consequently not included in the ruling class: Bebedawa, Sankarawa, Gerimawa (of Dambatta), and Japhunawa. Since the time of Dabo, the royal family has been Sullubawa.

During the nineteenth century, the various Fulani groups that had participated in the Jihad gradually consolidated their elite structure into a ruling class which could be referred to as "urban Fulani."

The third major ethnic group in Kano has been the *Kanuri*, or to use the Hausa term, "beriberi," which refers to persons (including Kanembu) from Bornu, who speak a dialect of Kanuri.[2]

Within Kano Province, certain Kanuri-speaking ethnic units are regarded as Kanuri-related: for example, Mangawa, Ngisimawa, Lerewa, Koyamawa.[3] They are located mainly in the rural districts of Babura, Birnin Kudu, Dutse, Gaya, Gwarzo, Ringim, and Rano. Within Kano City, many live in Berebere ward, but others are distributed evenly in Kano West. The Kanuri settlement in Fagge has always been strong and the Galidima of Fagge has been Kanuri by tradition. Prior to the British conquest, Kanuri entered Kano Province in three periods: during the eighteenth century when Bornu had conquered Kano; after the Fulani Jihad; during the wars under Rabeh (1890s). Originally there was an antagonism between the Hausa and Kanuri. The Kanuri word for Hausa is *Afuno*, which is believed in Kano to mean "people of the loin cloth." With the Fulani wars against the Hausa and Kanuri, there was a rapprochement between the two defensive groups. Certainly, there has been intermarriage between Hausa and Kanuri, and since the nineteenth century their mallam classes have studied together. This rapprochement is slightly mitigated by the traditional rivalry between Kano and Zinder (which has had a Kanuri ruling class).

The Kanuri are bilateral and have a myth of origin which identifies a common ancestor from somewhere on the Arabian peninsula. Cohen places their actual origins in the Sahara to the northeast of Lake Chad. (1967: passim)

The Kano urban ethnic group of next importance are the *Arabs*. Based on oral history data, the earliest claim to Arab migrant group location in Kano seems to have been in Madabo ward (Kano West).[4] It is claimed by contemporary descendants that, before the coming of Bayajidda, a certain Muslim Arab clan settled near the Dalla Hill. The area came to be known as "madabo" from the Arabic *madd al-islam wa aba al-kufra* ("Islam is founded and idolatry is gone"). Over time, especially after the Hausa accepted Islam, intermarriage produced in Madabo ward a distinct Hausa-Arab group known as Madabawa. The ward became a center of Islamic learning and after the Fulani Jihad the leader of the Madabawa, the *Babban Mallamai*, became a primary religious adviser to the Fulani emirs, representing all of the non-Fulani Muslims in Kano. At present the Madabawa are regarded by Hausa-speaking people as a Hausa subgroup, and are physically and culturally indistinguishable from other Hausa. The primary mechanism of incorporation has been intermarriage.

The second Arab group to claim early settlement in Kano are the descendants of Shaikh al-Maghili, who established Sharifai ward.[5] Although al-Maghili eventually left Kano, three of his sons remained.[6] Through intermarriage with Hausa, a large group of descendants has developed in Kano,[7] who are considered *sharifai* in certain situations although they are physically and culturally indistinguishable from other Hausa.

The third group of Arab migrants came to Kano with the establishment of the trans-Saharan trade. These Arabs were from Ghadames or Tripoli. By the nineteenth century, the Maghrebian Arabs in Kano lived in two wards: the Tripolitanian Arabs lived in Dandalin Turawa ward, and the Ghadames Arabs lived in Jingau ward (which was later divided to create Alfindiki ward).

Finally it is apparent that Fatimid Arabs were to be found in Darma ward, Egyptian Arabs in Zaitawa ward, and Shuwa Arabs ("black Arabs") in Sudawa and Dandali wards. The "spokesman" (*Mallamin Turawa*) for all Arabs in Kano was, by tradition, from Ghadames. Most of the Arabs were engaged in trade of one sort or another and had a distinctive social and legal status. Many took Hausa wives.

The Hausa term for "Arabs" (*Larabawa*) is a linguistic classification. The Hausa also have a locational-cum-racial reference for Arabs (*turawa* or *turabusawa*) which was used to describe persons from North Africa who were regarded as having "lighter" skin color than other Arabs.

In the twentieth century, contact in Kano was established with three new groups of Arabs: those from North Africa in general (not just Tripoli or Ghadames); those from the Sudan, especially from Khartoum; Syrians or Lebanese from the Middle East. All were referred to as *larabawa*, but in the vernacular, distinctions have been made on the basis of location. Thus, the North Africans, who were identifiable by their white caps were called *yan Kwara* ("white caps"). The Sudanese, who tended to wear the long cloak or *jallaba* were called *jallabiyya*. They were also called *yar-Khartoum* ("sons of Khartoum") or *Kartumawa* (singular: *Bakhartume*). The Syrians who settled outside the old city in Kwari district were called *Larabawa Asali* ("original

Arabs"). In most cases, the basic structures of migrant urban Arab culture have been similar to urban Hausa culture. In fact migrant Arabs have probably exerted a disproportional influence on Hausa culture in matters of patrilineality and hierarchy.

Of the remaining northern ethnic groups, the *Nupe* probably settled in Tudan Nufawa ward during and after the time of the Jukun conquest of Kano. Yoruba migration must have occurred at about the same time, although the circumstances are not clear. They have been settled in Ayagi ward for approximately three hundred years and have been completely assimilated into Hausa culture. Yet in certain situations they identify themselves as Yoruba. Likewise, the Wangarawa from Melle, who settled in Mandawari ward, have also been assimilated to the point where it is difficult to distinguish them from the Hausa-Fulani. Tuareg (Buzaye) from Agades settled in Agadazawa ward during the nineteenth century and through intermarriage became assimilated.

The statistical distribution of ethnic groups in Kano City has become difficult to assess due to the multiple systems of ethnic classification and the high degree of inter-ethnic assimilation. Table 1 gives some general idea of the distribution in 1931. (Brooke 1933: II, 45)

TABLE 1. KANO OLD CITY ETHNIC COMPOSITION, 1931

	Ethnic Classification	Percent Total	Language Classification	Percent Total
Hausa	68,515	77.15	87,194	97.79
Fulani	10,014	11.67	250	—
Kanuri	6,168	6.61	846	—
Arab	399	.49	195	—
Tuareg	1,741	1.62	384	—
Shuwa Arab	281	.27	—	—
Nupe	1,190	1.43	50	—
Yoruba	854	.76	243	—

All of the above ethnic groups have myths of origin which focus on the Middle East. All have acquired similar culture patterns in Kano on matters of descent-reckoning and authority organization. All would profess to be Mus-

TABLE 2. KANO NEW CITY ETHNIC COMPOSITION, 1954-1955

Ethnic Classification	Men	Women	Boys	Girls	Total	Percent
Ibo	3,670	3,758	2,844	2,496	12,770	59.05
Yoruba	1,484	1,710	928	1,046	5,174	23.92
Urhobo & Itsekiri	360	400	108	67	935	4.32
Efik & Ibibio	279	530	48	49	906	4.18
Benin, Ishan & Kukuruku (Edo)	168	144	74	60	446	2.06
Ijaw (Okirika & Kalabari)	195	101	33	20	349	1.61
Gold Coast Togoland & Dahomean	48	34	20	15	117	.54
Nupe & Igala	105	210	40	24	379	1.75
Idoma & Allies	80	131	16	8	235	1.08
Hausa & Fulani	16	74	8	6	104	.48
Cameroonian	20	30	15	8	73	.37
Sierra Leonean	10	20	10	8	48	.22
Tripolitan & Sudanese Arab	12	3	21	5	41	.18
Chadian	18	10	6	4	38	.17
Kanuri	3	4	–	–	7	.03
West Indian	2	–	–	–	2	.01
Total	6,470	7,165	4,171	3,814	21,624	100.00

lim. All would now speak Hausa. These are the groups that have been welded into the larger corporate entity of "people of Kano" (*Kanawa*).

Since part of this integration process entailed a reaction formation *vis-à-vis* "outside" groups, the non-northern ethnic groups in the Kano urban area should be mentioned at this point. After World War I, two distinctive groups came to occupy locations "outside" of the Old City: Southern Nigerians and Europeans. Both groups were forbidden by law to reside in the Old City. Southern Nigerian migrants resided in the Sabon Gari and to a large extent retained their separate cultural identities. The heterogeneity of this group can be seen in Table 2. (N.A.K. 5908) The major period of migration to Kano occurred from 1950-1960.

The European population in Kano was located primarily in the restricted Government Residential Area ("G.R.A."). The term for European (*turawa*) referred to light skin color and was originally applied to the Tripolitanian Arabs. A second term for European was *Nasara*, or "Christians." Within both of these categories, locational identifications were distinguished: Italians were known as *mutanen Rum* ("men of Rome"); English as *mutanen Ingila*; Germans as *mutanen Jamus*, Americans as *mutanen Amirka*. The number of Europeans in Kano has never been great. Of these about two-thirds have been British.

CONCEPTS OF COMMUNAL IDENTITY IN KANO

The standard Hausa term for "community" is *umma*. The term *umma* is also used for "mother," and the implication of blood linkage is not entirely coincidental to the notion of community. *Umma* has not been used traditionally to connote "associational" or "affiliational" linkages. It refers to any group which is a primary reference system. In the Islamic sense, it is a religious community. However, in Hausa usage it may indicate any primary-group reference system on the spectrum from "humanity" to "family." The Hausa expression *al-ummar dan Adamu* ("the community of the sons of Adam") refers to all human beings and would be used in contradistinction to certain categories in the spirit world. The Hausa expression *al-ummar gidammu* ("the community of our household") would refer to the immediate extended family.

There have been at least eight major categories of communal identity in Kano. These have included religion, birthplace, ancestral home, clan or family, country, language, urban location, and race. It is of considerably importance to note how these categories have facilitated expansion and/or contraction of ethnic boundaries.

Religion (Addini): Religious communities were divided into three categories: Muslim *(Musulmi)*; people of the book (Jews *[Yahudawa]* and Christians *[Nasara]*); and pagans *(kafirai* or *arna)*. Since Kano Emirate was relatively homogeneous in this respect (98 percent Muslim), the matter of group identity arose primarily in connection with alleged backsliding or apostacy. With the settlement of Southern Nigerians and Europeans in urban Kano (both groups being non-Muslim), religious identity increased in importance. The standard manner of inquiring whether a person is Muslim or not is to ask whether "he prays" *(yana salla?)*. If a person does *salla*, he is regarded as a part of the Muslim community. Traditionally, the major non-Muslim community in Kano has been the *Maguzawa* (non-Muslim Hausa).

Birthplace (garin haifuwa): Place of birth has been extremely important in Hausaland in determining political, legal, and ethnic identification. The term *Yan kasa* ("sons of the land") referred to persons born in a given place. It could also refer to the original people of a locality. Place of birth was an important indication of maternal identity, since it was (and is) customary to go to the mother's home for childbirth. In addition, place of birth determines which of the four Muslim legal schools a child would follow.

Ancestral home (asali): This locational identity has come to be included in census surveys as representing a type of ethnicity. The classification partly reflects the importance of migration patterns and the need to fit "original" groups into a framework of communal identity. People who came to Kano from Shiri were called *Shirawa*; those who came from the village of Auyo were called *Auyokawa*; the earliest settlers of Kano, who came from Gaya, were called *Abagayawa*. In more recent years the concept of *asali* has continued to be an important ethnic criterion. This is particularly appropriate if the person in question has acquired an urban identification at some later date.

Family or clan: The concept of "family" identification may be appropriate both in the narrow sense of household *(gida)* or in the broader sense of common, but not genealogically traced, descent *(jama'a)*. The term *jama'a* may be used also in certain circumstances to suggest any sense of common identity. Thus, when the concept of "northerner" was introduced in Nigeria, one of the terms used by its proponents was *jama'ar arewa* ("community of the north"). In the technical sense, the Kano Hausa term for a genealogically traced descent group is *zuriya*. The nuclear family or immediate dependents is usually referred to as *iyali* and the extended family as *dangi*. The concept of *dangi* is perhaps the most important of the restricted kinship concepts since it is used to indicate three- or four-generation bilateral relationships (with complementary adjectives to refer to matrilateral or patrilateral kin). These have considerable bearing on ethnic identities which are appropriate at times of marriage.

Country (*kasa*): In the absence of a Hausa term for "nation" the concept of "land" or "country" (*kasa*) has been used to imply inhabitants of a defined political area. Thus Arabic-speaking countries were called *kasashen musulmi*. The modern Hausa word for "nationalism" is taken from this concept and is translated, "jealousy of the land" (*kishin kasa*). The relatively modern (and perhaps short-lived) communal identification attached to the northern region of Nigeria (*Arewa*) illustrates the idea of *kasa*.

Language (*kabila*): *Kabila* is the normal Hausa word for "tribe," and *kabilanci* refers to "tribalism." Yet this term connotes a *linguistic* category, and is theoretically unrelated to political identification. There is some question as to whether *kabila* is an *umma* type of identity. Such language groups as Hausa, Arab, and Yoruba would be considered to be *kabila*.

Urban (*birni*): Urban place of residence usually entails identification with one of the major Hausa city-states. Thus, persons from Kano are known as *Kanawa*. The identification by urban center rather than "first language" was probably necessitated historically by the assimilation processes which have occurred in the urban centers.

Skin color (*fata*): Most Kano Hausa believe there to be two racial groups in the world: white and black. Indians, Arabs, Chinese, and Europeans are considered to be white. Yet even within Hausa society, a distinction is made between light and dark skin. A person with an unrecognizable amount of Arab "blood" would claim to be Arab for status reasons. The Fulani are regarded as being a mixture of white and black. Within Islamic society, such skin-color distinctions are theoretically regarded as irrelevant. However, the historical Arab identification of West Africans as *tukrur* (black persons from Western Sudan) may have reinforced racial categories of identification among those Hausa who had traveled in Arab lands. The Hausa term *bakin mutum* is used specifically as the equivalent of "Negro," and is relevant only in a biracial bicultural situation. The concept is infrequently used as an ethnic identification, mainly because more precise criteria of differentiation are usually required, and because there are few recognizable culture/value concomitants to skin-color identities.

In partial reaction to the Arab pejorative use of *tukrur*, certain modern Kano Hausa have come to consider the prophet Muhammad as having been dark skinned. Many of the prophet's followers are thought to have been dark-skinned peoples from Abyssinia. However, the standard explanation for racial differences continues to be the myth of the sons of Noah, which is hardly flattering to black people.[8]

The Kano Hausa ascription of positive values to lighter skin, for example, to the Arabs and Fulani, is probably a reflection of religious and socioeconomic values. For the past hundred and sixty years, Fulani and Arabs have been dominant in Kano society and have regarded themselves as being closer genealogically to the Middle Eastern sources of religion.

The ambivalence of Kano Hausa attitudes toward the Arabs is important in explaining the extraordinary spread of reformed Islamic brotherhoods in Kano. From 1935-1955, there was a complete replacement of Arab dominance in the elite structures of the brotherhoods by black West Africans, mainly Hausa, but including Kanuri, Wolof, Yoruba, and Fulani.

TABLE 3. BASES OF ETHNIC IDENTIFICATION IN KANO

Principle	Example of Ethnic Group	Explanation
Religion		
Pagan	Maguzawa	Non-Muslim Hausa
People-of-the-Book	Nasarawa	Christians
Muslim	Musulmi	Muslims
Place of Birth	(Anywhere)	Usually Location of Mother's family
Family Origins	Auyokawa	People who originally came from Auyo
Family or Clan	Sullubawa Dambazawa	Persons from the Families of Sulluman and Dambazau
"Land"	Arewa	Persons from Northern Nigeria
Linguistic	Hausawa	First-Language Speakers of Hausa, Yoruba, Arabic (respectively)
Urban	Kanawa	People of Kano
Skin Color	Turawa	Europeans (Light Skin)

The colonial period in Kano reinforced the idea of skin color as a criterion for differentiating "communities" of people. The British administrators preferred to be called *turawa*, after the light-skinned Arabs of Tripoli, rather than *nasara* (Christian). Interestingly, in French-controlled portions of Hausaland (for example, Zinder, Maradi), the preferred term for Europeans continues to be *nasara* rather than *turawa*. The increased utilization of skin-color symbolism in Kano to reinforce culturally distinct communities (Europeans vs. Kanawa) resulted later in the Kano conceptualization of certain African members of the colonial civil service as "black Europeans" (*bakaken Turawa*).

Summary: Hausa concepts of ethnic classification are arranged around the principles given in Table 3.

PLURALISTIC CONFRONTATION IN URBAN KANO

Two aspects of ethnic confrontation in Kano City will be mentioned in this essay: Hausa-Fulani relations, and Muslim-non-Muslim relations.

HAUSA-FULANI RELATIONS

In Kano City ethnic division of labor was essentially complementary rather than competitive. The dependence of the Fulani ruling class on Hausa merchants, traders, and craftsmen, and the wealth which circulated as a result of the Kano Market seemed to have created a deferential administrative attitude toward the Hausa economic classes. Perhaps as a result, the wealthy and specialized classes were allowed to continue their economic activities unimpeded while the emirate system drew its financial resources primarily from the rural districts. The Fulani administrators were not in economic competition with significant segments of the Hausa urban community.

The effect of external pressures on the Kano city-state may have contributed to the success of the pluralistic market system in nineteenth-century Kano. Early attacks by the Kanuri of Bornu, by the Kanuri of Damagaram, and by the non-Muslim Ningi from the south created a climate of common danger to Hausa and Fulani alike, yet did not result in political integration.

There was little direct involvement by the Hausa community in the factionalism of the Fulani political system. The most dramatic evidence of this neutrality occurred during the Kano Civil War (1893) when the two Fulani coalitions within the city engaged in killing and destruction, yet the Hausa communities remained disengaged from both sides.

Not until the 1920s and 1930s did the rural "settled" Fulani begin to migrate to the city. Economic competition was thus created for the first time between unskilled Hausa and Fulani workers.

Finally, despite the tendency for Fulani rulers to take Hausa wives or concubines, there was no general intermarriage between Hausa and Fulani sectors of the city until later in the colonial period. In short, until the 1930s the Hausa-Fulani urban relationship was one of live and let live, with strong economic division of labor, and almost no social or political interdependency.

MUSLIM–NON-MUSLIM RELATIONS

The Kano emirate state discouraged contact, other than commercial, between Muslims and non-Muslims. In 1912, non-Muslims were prohibited from living in the "old city" although prior to that time, a few European merchants had established dwellings near the market. During the colonial period, relationships which did exist were cordial. Non-Muslim "animists" were regarded as potential converts to Islam and the arts of religious persuasion could be best practiced within an atmosphere of good will. European Christians were regarded as "people of the book" and were, hence, acceptable for certain types of relationships. Likewise regarded were the few Maghrebian Jewish merchants who were usually trusted trading partners.

However, marriage restrictions between Muslims and non-Muslims in Kano were strictly enforced. Muslim men could marry non-Muslim women if the children were raised as Muslims. Non- Muslim men could not marry Muslim women under any circumstances. Serious legal problems were created if wives of non-Muslims were converted (as might occur if the woman's parents converted). However, in practice these problems occurred mainly in those rural areas with Maguzawa populations.

The effect of these regulations on inter-ethnic marriage is obvious. Southern migrant Christian men in Kano New City were legally prevented from any form of intermarriage with Northern Kano women and had therefore to bring their wives from the "home" region. Conversely, inter-ethnic marriage between Muslim ethnic groups was legally sanctioned and required only social acceptance to be realized.

In other ways, religious factors discouraged Muslim–non-Muslim marriages. The custom of "wife-seclusion" (*kulle*) in Kano was probably a deterrent to non-Muslim women considering marriage with northern Muslims. The inequality in inheritance for a non-Muslim wife was another deterrent.

ETHNIC INTEGRATION IN URBAN KANO

EXTERNAL FACTORS

In many respects the pressure of out-group ascription has been essential in fusing together the Hausa and Fulani urban communities. The three major out-groups have been Europeans, southern Nigerians, and Arabs. In point of time, the Arab confrontation preceded the confrontation with Europeans and/or southern Nigerians, and may be used to illustrate the general hypothesis.

Kano urban traders traditionally plied the trade routes to the north and east. Hausa migrant communities were well established in various parts of the Arab world. Within this context, the Arab ascription of *Tukrur* ethnicity to black persons from the western Sudan seems to have been instrumental in creating a sense of unity among the northern groups. The three major locations of Hausa migrant communities within Arab lands were North Africa, Saudi Arabia, and the Anglo-Egyptian Sudan.

The number of Hausa migrants in the urban centers of Mecca, Medina, and Jedda has probably never been large. Within the migrant communities of *Tukrur*, Hausa developed as a *lingua franca*. Yet by external standards, the Hausa, Fulani, and Kanuri ("Bornu") were lumped together, along with minorities such as the Nupe. According to Lethem:

The Takarir in the Hejaz are principally in Mecca, Medina, and Jeddah. If information given me in Jedda is reliable there are about 3,000 in Mecca and about 2,000 in Medina. In Jeddah, I estimated the number at about 1,000. In these communities, Hausa are generally most numerous, Bornu, however being also numerous in Mecca, but Fulani comparatively few . . . I visited the settlement at Jeddah . . . The inhabitants divide themselves as usual into three sections, Hausa, Bornu, and Fulani, each under a Sheikh. The Hausa Sheikh was in reality a Nupe—born in Mecca . . . He is, for a Takruri, well off and a man of the world and has travelled much—Java, Penang, Singapore in the east and El Obeid in the West . . . (Tomlinson and Letham 1927: 48)

A first-hand account of the Hausa communities at Mecca is recorded in the diary of a Hausa pilgrim from Katsina. Thus, according to Alhaji Sayidi:

At Mecca we stayed in the house of Inuwa, a native of Kano. He and Mallam Musa, a native of Musada, keep lodging houses for the use of Takarir. Alhaji Haroun, son of Mallam Inuwa, is the Mutowaf for Hausa speaking pilgrims. He is assisted by Usman, son of Alhaji Mohammad and his brother Abdu . . .

There are three men at Medina who act as Mutowaf for Hausa pilgrims: Alhaji Ahamat Sinuw, an Arab of Jalala; Alhaji Yahaya, a native of Kano; Ahamat Hindi, an Indian.

The Takarir settled in Mecca live in the quarter called Musfala. There is also a settlement outside the town called Jarwal which is frequented by Takarir visitors of the poorer class. The Takarir of Mecca seem to be in slightly better circumstances than their compatriots of Jeddah. Many of them make a livelihood as butchers and petty traders.

Of the Takarir from Nigeria, the majority come from Bornu but there are many Hausa and Fulani, Nupe, Yoruba . . . All speak Arabic, but use Hausa amongst themselves and have taught their children to speak Hausa . . . (Alhaji Sayidi Katsina 1929)

Notably, urban-location identifications in terms of places of origin were attributed to some of the key individuals mentioned above. With the increased contact between Kano and the Arab world, especially with the Kano-Khartoum air service beginning in 1935, the impact of Arab "out-group" ascriptions of ethnic identity in Kano increased in importance. Kano City traders or pilgrims who had traveled in the Arab world returned to Kano with their experiences of ethnic reclassification. By the late 1950s several thousand pilgrims a year were leaving Kano for Mecca, and returning with some notion of the "Arab" world reference system.

INTERNAL FACTORS

The end result of integration in Kano Old City has been to produce an urban culture of relative uniformity. Although this culture is predominantly "Hausa," it is different in many respects from any of the component contributory cultures. Thus, the Kano urban culture has clearly shifted from a pyramidal authority system to a hierarchical authority system in the past sixty years. This centralization process has been an important step in the integration of the diverse ethnic groups. The initial use of Hausa language as a commercial and religious language led to its widespread adoption as a first language throughout Kano Old City. Children were socialized to Hausa language and culture through the neighborhood koranic schools. The previously existing religious homogeneity allowed for inter-ethnic marriages to occur once conditions were ripe.

The preconditions for integration in urban Kano included the fact that economic pressures of the cash economy were creating a new class system and a rapid increase in rural migration to the city. In the former process, new class identities became competitors to the various communal identities. In the latter process, the rural migrants came to feel that the urban identities were more functional than their former rural identities. These patterns of integration may be summarized according to the three levels of integration theory: interaction flow, functional interdependency, and value congruence. (a) The interaction between Hausa and Fulani groups in Kano increased dramatically after 1920 with the growth of the groundnut industry in Kano. The increased transaction flow of goods, messages, and persons was a natural concomitant to this reorientation of the economy. (b) Functional interdependency is always implicit in a system of ethnic division of labor. However, the rapid increase in urbanization resulted in a modification of the ethnic division of labor, at least to the extent that it encouraged the development of an unskilled working class. According to the 1926 Kano City "assessment" the 11,431 taxpayers in Kano City could be divided into 45 occupations. Even by that time, the five occupations with the largest number of practitioners were those which could accommodate rural migration: capmakers (21.03 percent), mallams (11.50 percent), tailors (7.67 percent), petty traders (6.70 percent), and laborers (5.34 percent). This class of occupations drew on both Hausa and Fulani rural sources. Income tax receipts indicate that these occupations were the lowest paid in the Kano urban area, and even the highest paid of these (petty traders) earned only .06 percent of the average administrative-class income. The effect of this embryonic class development was to draw the Hausa merchant class and Fulani administrative class closer together. This combination of administrators and merchants became increasingly dependent upon each other for political and economic support. (c) Value congruence between the Hausa and Fulani communities was increased in two ways: through the development of trans-ethnic religious brotherhoods in Kano, beginning in the interwar period; through the assimilation of Fulani (and other) groups into Hausa culture, beginning, on a significant scale, in the postwar period.

The influence of religious elites on the integration process at all three levels seems to be of particular importance. Islamic mallams within each of the ethnic groups were among the first to establish communication and interaction networks between ethnic groups. The structural linkage between ethnic based Islamic denominations created an interdependency which eventually led to the emergence of genuinely supraethnic religious structures and organizations. The demonstrable effect of this religious integration on the political system cannot be overemphasized. Finally, the espousal of "reformed" Islamic values appropriate to urban conditions created a new standard for normative behavior in general.[9]

THE ADAPTATION OF COMMUNAL IDENTITIES IN KANO

The processes of integration have effected substantial changes in the importance of the various communal identities in Kano City. Two new reference systems have emerged: a combined "Hausa-Fulani" identity, and/or a "Kano City" identity. Technically, neither of these is a "new" group, since linguistic and urban-locational identities have been part of the conceptual lexicon in Kano. Yet, the increased relevance of these identities should be noted. Finally, religious identity increased in importance and in many respects became the most fundamental of the communal identities.

The prior existence of communal-identity categories which could accommodate changes in ethnic boundaries resulting from twentieth-century economic, political, and urban change was an important factor in the facilitation of integration itself. "Detribalization" did not occur, creating (supposedly) a modern-sector class without communal identities; nor is it necessary to assume that all ethnic identities were in conflict with "national" loyalties.

The existence of a continuum of communal identities has two consequences of interest to this essay: the issue of "from tribe to nation" is rendered obsolete if it is assumed that these identities are incompatible; instead the phenomenon of "situational ethnicity" becomes of paramount importance. The notion of situational ethnicity is premised on the observation that particular contexts may determine which of a person's communal identities or loyalties are appropriate at a point in time. (Paden 1967)

The concept of "ethnicity" in Kano history has included at least eight categories: religion, place of birth, family origins, family or clan, land, language, urban location, and race. The urban pluralism in Kano during the early historical periods resulted in certain types of horizontal integration. However, a sense of common origins (*jama'a*) and/or a place or origin (*asali*) were predominant in establishing named ethnic identity in this early period. The dramatic changes in the twentieth century have resulted in the dominance of urban (*Kanawa*), linguistic (*Hausa*), and religious (*Muslims*) categories. The interesting questions remain as to how these categories overlap or adapt themselves to particular circumstances.

NOTES

1. Figures are 1964 estimates by Greater Kano Planning Authority.

2. The Hausa have increasingly used the term "barnawa" to refer to people (Kanuri) from Bornu.

3. In Bornu such groups now consider themselves to be Kanuri although memory of subethnic distinctions is still part of the local culture (Ronald Cohen: personal communication).   •

4. Interview with Babban Mallamai (Imam of Madabo mosque) Alhaji Ibrahim, August 9, 1965, Hausa. If this claim is correct, this would have been the first Muslim group to settle in Kano.

5. According to Kano oral history, the Prophet had left instructions that someone should go west for purposes of conversion, and should take a handful of earth from Medina. At the spot where the local earth was similar to that of the Medina earth, a mosque should be built. According to legend, al-Maghili visited Zaria and Katsina, but not until he came to Kano City did he find comparable earth. The spot became known as "sharifai" because Al-Maghili is regarded as a descendant of the Prophet.

6. Al-Maghili left Kano to return to Medina, but died in Tahout (Niger Republic) where some of his belongings are still said to exist. The three sons who remained in Kano were Muhammad Hanatari, Gaman Dodo, and Sidi Feri Isa.

7. The "Sharifai" clan has always had a special position in Kano. In precolonial times, they were completely exempt from taxation, and were, in fact, given money from the public treasury. During the period of both the Fulani Jihad and the Kano Civil War, the Sharifai ward was neutral ground, and anyone who went into the Sharifai mosque was given sanctuary.

8. On December 15, 1964, the Hausa broadcasting service of Radio Cairo featured listener questions to the "religious experts" at Al-Azhar University. The issue of the Islamic explanation of race was raised by letter from Kano. The Islamic textual answer which was given, and which was widely accepted in Kano, was that the Prophet Noah (Annabi Nuhu) had three sons. One day he called them to him, but one of the sons was with his wife at the time and did not hear his father call. The Prophet Noah thought the son was disobedient and said "May God make you black." The son which later came out of his wife's womb was black . . . Upon inquiry by the researcher as to whether there was any sense of shame associated with this story, most responses were negative, because "it was the will of God."

9. For a fuller description of the influence of religion on integration, see the author's doctoral dissertation: "The Influence of Religious Elites on Political Culture and Community Integration in Kano, Nigeria," Department of Government, Harvard University, 1,531 pp. Field research for the dissertation was undertaken in 1964-1965 on a grant from the Foreign Area Fellowship Program.

REFERENCES

Anderson, C. W., F. R. von der Mehden, and C. Young. 1967. *Issues of political development.* Englewood Cliffs, Prentice-Hall.

Brooke, N. J. 1933. *Census of Nigeria.* 1931, London.

Cohen, R. 1967. *The Kanuri of Bornu.* New York, Holt Rinehart and Winston.

Department of Statistics. 1952. *Population census of the northern region of Nigeria.* Zaria, Gaskiya Corp.

Gellner, E. 1965. "Tribalism and social change in North Africa," in *French -speaking Africa.* W. H. Lewis (ed.). pp. 107-118. New York, Walker.

Hiskett, M. 1965. "The song of Bagauda: A Hausa king list and homily in verse." *Bulletin of the School of Oriental and African studies.*

Last, D. M., and M. A. Al-Hajj. 1965. "Attempts at defining a Muslim in nineteenth century Hausaland and Bornu." *Journal of the Historical Society of Nigeria.*

Letham, G. J. 1927. *History of Islamic propaganda in Nigeria.* London, Waterlow and Sons.

Meek, C. K. 1925. *The northern tribes of Nigeria.* London, Oxford University Press.

Nigerian Archives, Kaduna. 1954-1955. "Tribal population statistics."

Paden, J. N. 1967. "Situational ethnicity in urban Africa with special reference to the Hausa." Paper presented at African Studies Association meeting in New York, November, 1967.

Palmer, H. R. 1928. "Kano Chronicle." *Sudanese memoirs.* Lagos, Government Printer.

Richards, A. I. 1966. "Multi-tribalism in African urban areas." *Civilizations.*

Sayidi, Alhaji. 1929. *Nigerian archives.* Kaduna. no. 3645.

Shibutani, T., and J. M. Kwan. 1965. *Ethnic stratification.* New York, Macmillan.

Southall, A. W. 1961. *Social change in modern Africa.* London, Oxford University Press.

INDEX

Abel, A., 68
Abira, 73, 80, 85
Abrahams, R. G., 18, 20, 105, 111
Acephalous societies, 11, 15, 17,
    26ff, 118, 127f, 180f, 198
Adelman, A., 24
Almond, G. A., 6
Alur, 11, 16ff, 22, 59, 71-91, 183
Amba, 11, 29
Amhara, 22
Anderson, C. W., 30, 245
Angola, 37
Ankole, 75, 90, 124, 136
Anthropology and modernization
    theory, 1ff
Apter, D., 8
Apthorpe, R., 28, 29
Arabs, 23, 31, 59, 163, 249, 255f
Ashanti, 119, 131
Associations, 26, 63f
Azande, 85, 185f

Babur, 161
Baghirmi, 12, 157
Bajun, 31
Bale, 59, 72
    see also Lendu
Balovale, 38
Bambara, 122
Bangala, 246
Bangare, 194
Banton, M., 124
Bantu migrations, 13
Barth, H., 157, 158, 159, 160,
    172, 173
Beattie, J. H. M., 73
Bela, 7, 124
Bemba, 40, 49f, 97
Benin, 183
Berbers, 251
Berry, B. J. L., 25
Bhaca, 220
Bhele, 220
Binger, L. G., 130, 196

Bird, J., 220
Blood-brotherhood, 11
Bohannan, P., 181
Bomvana, 219ff
Bond friendship, 36, 41, 46
Bornu, 15, 118, 150-173, 268
Bösch, P., 112
Brenner, L., 157, 162, 170
Brooke, N. J., 257
Buna, 119
Bureaucracies, 2, 29
Busansi, 191f
Bushmen, 177, 180
Buxton, J. C., 17, 179
Bwile, 40

Callaway, G., 227
Cameroons, 167
Carter, G. M., 178, 237
Cash crops, 87, 242
Caste systems, 20, 124, 210, 214
Chad, 24
Chappelle, J., 172
Chiefship, 11, 17, 57, 76ff, 103f,
    221ff, 223ff, 230ff
Chikunda, 39, 43
Christianity, 2, 58, 235
Clans and clanship, 42ff, 177f, 224,
    260f
Clientage and clientship, 11, 22,
    41f, 159f, 193
Clignet, R., 25, 26
Codere, H., 214
Cohen, A., 145
Cohen, R., 31, 150, 151, 152, 157,
    159, 161, 164, 165, 166, 167, 168,
    169, 170, 172, 183, 255
Coleman, J. S., 6, 9
Colonialism and colonial rule, 8,
    36f, 57, 74f, 88, 117, 127, 151,
    164ff, 201f, 213f, 217ff
Colson, E., 15, 27, 53
Comorians, 31
Congo, 23, 59f, 68, 71-91, 246